The Welsh in Liverpool

To Laura Myfanwy Jones and her two sisters,
Margaret and Winifred A Jones, who became part of our family
when they moved from Bristol Road, Wavertree,
to Calderstones Road, Allerton, Liverpool

The Welsh in Liverpool

A REMARKABLE HISTORY

D BEN REES

First impression: 2021

© Copyright D Ben Rees and Y Lolfa Cyf., 2021

The publishers wish to acknowledge the support of
the Books Council of Wales

Cover photograph: Alamy
Cover design: Y Lolfa

ISBN
hardback: 978 1 80099 083 8
paperback: 978 1 912631 36 0

Published and printed in Wales
on paper from well-maintained forests by
Y Lolfa Cyf., Talybont, Ceredigion SY24 5HE
website www.ylolfa.com
e-mail ylolfa@ylolfa.com
tel 01970 832 304
fax 832 782

Contents

Foreword

On 19 July 2018, at a special meeting of Liverpool City Council, I was accepted as a Citizen of Honour and received the title at a ceremony in City Hall on 3 October that year. During the last fifty years I have prepared many lectures and addresses, both in Welsh and in English, on the history of Liverpool and especially on the Liverpool Welsh. To date, I have published some thirty studies (see Appendix 2 for a selected guide). But, despite that, I had not covered every aspect of that history in detail. I decided I should put on record the amazing story of thousands and thousands of Welsh people who flocked to Liverpool for work and a better standard of living, while contributing extensively to the life of the city. Through immigration, the Celts from Wales, Scotland, the Isle of Man, Cornwall and Ireland (both North and South), made Liverpool a unique place. There is no city quite like it in England, as so many Celts settled in the town during the nineteenth and twentieth centuries.

Historians of the city tended to emphasise the contribution of the Irish. To a large extent the Welsh were ignored, as their efforts were focused on chapel and family life. Only a few ventured into the hurly-burly of city politics, where the Irish were much more prominent. Some Welsh who succeeded as builders, ship owners, doctors and gifted preachers have attracted attention. But what of those who had a much more difficult life and struggled to hand down their language, the literature, their Nonconformism and culture to their children? That is why I am so pleased that this book is now published in English for the second and third generation Liverpool Welsh who, although proud of their roots, are monoglot English speakers.

Without the Liverpool Welsh there would have been no homeland in Patagonia, nor Christianity in north-eastern India. Sacred music and the Welsh press would be the poorer too, without the city's composers, poets, writers, journalists and publishers.

I have listened to the advice of Saunders Lewis who said one should write without footnotes, but I owe a debt of thanks for years of research in publications such as *Y Brython, Y Glannau, Y Bont, Yr Angor* and scores of books, magazines, Welsh memories and manuscripts. I have had priceless help in translating the book into English and preparing the manuscript from Angela Lansley, Tony Fyler, the Rev. Robert Parry, Dr Pat Williams and Eirian Jones and the editorial office of Y Lolfa.

I am fortunate to own so many pictures and have been able to draw on the resources of the John Thomas Collection, Cambrian Gallery; Everton and Liverpool football clubs; the photographs of the late E Emrys Jones, Old Colwyn; Philip Cope, Blaengarw; Dr John G Williams, Allerton; Ray Farley, Crosby, and others.

My thanks go to Peter Lupson, a learner now fluent in Welsh, for the background to Everton and Liverpool football clubs.

D Ben Rees
Allerton
Liverpool

Chapter 1

The Welsh in Liverpool up to the eighteenth century

There were Welsh people in and around Liverpool before there was any mention of the village of Liverpool. There is no mention of it in the Domesday Book, that detailed register of all the lands, parishes and inhabitants of England, drawn up at the behest of William the Conqueror in 1086. There is mention of other local places, like West Derby, but the little village of poverty-stricken fishermen on the banks of the River Mersey was not deemed sufficiently important to have a name.

The reign of King John

Everything changed with the succession of King John. In 1207 he gave a charter to the village ensuring privileges for its inhabitants. Overnight, its status changed from a village to a town. It is in King John's Charter that, for the first time in any document, we see the name Liverpool.

The Sheriff's accounts for 1212 document 'the cost of transporting soldiers, cattle and pigs' sent from the military court in Lancaster via Liverpool to Chester and from there to Deganwy and Conwy, where the English army was desperate for want of food as it tried to hunt down Llywelyn, Prince of Gwynedd.

Liverpool and Wales

Another Welshman came to Liverpool in 1283 – a clerk from Caernarfon. His task was to buy wood to build Caernarfon Castle and to supervise loading about 40 tons of it onto one of the small boats. Liverpool fairs were very popular, with people from Wales and Cheshire flocking to them. In his charter to the Prior of Birkenhead, Edward II orders him to build independently a suitable lodging and to buy and sell food and drink to the keen fairgoers who came from afar to Liverpool, crossing 'the said arm of the sea'.

Soldiers from Wales regularly came to Liverpool before setting sail for Ireland. For instance, in 1362, Edward III ensured that thirty archers from Newport, eighty from Glamorgan and forty from the Swansea area headed for Liverpool. Every one reached the port safely. We do not know how big the port was. By 1700 it had a population of 5,714, but we do not know how many Welsh people lived in its 1,142 households. Certainly, as early as the thirteenth and fourteenth centuries, there was an exchange of food and people between Liverpool and the north Wales ports, especially Conwy and Beaumaris.

The influential Dafydd ap Gruffydd

The first important and influential Welshman of whose identity we are certain is Dafydd ap Gruffydd. He is said to have been one of the followers of the Tudors, many of whom moved from Wales to London during the reign of Henry VII. For his loyalty he was rewarded with the task of keeping an eye on the citizens of Liverpool and ensuring they paid their tolls and taxes. It was not an easy job, but he received a generous enough wage of £14 a year. In addition, he managed to get his hands on the key position in the town. He was made mayor of the borough twice, the first time in 1503 after only eight years in Liverpool, and the second time in 1515. After his death the office and responsibility passed to his widow, Alis Gruffydd, and to Henry Ackers (or Accres), his son-in-law. His name is also seen in connection with a windmill in the developing hamlet of Wavertree, which eventually became a focal point for the Welsh.

During Dafydd ap Gruffydd's period in office, the town's name is spelt Lyrpul, reminding us of the way the word is written in Welsh today: *Lerpwl*. The naturalist and traveller John Leland spells it slightly differently in the period between 1533 and 1539, as Lyrpole. But one could argue that there is a Welsh influence on the word Lyrpul by comparing it with the Welsh *Lle'r Pwll* (The Place of the Pool), the focal point of the interesting old town. This is open to debate and clearly one must consider other names spelt likewise: Litherpul, Liverpoole, Liverpolle, Lyerpull, Litherpoole, Leverpoole. But, to the Welsh speaker, *Lerpwl* is the name, rather than *Llynlleifiad* (or *Llynn y Lleifie*) which was used in the eighteenth century. While the hymnwriter Peter Jones (known by his bardic name of Pedr Fardd) claimed responsibility for this creation, the claim of the Irish must also be acknowledged. They argue that the Irish name for Liverpool is *Learphol* which is pronounced as *Lerpwl*.

Welsh vagrants

A fascinating character among the early inhabitants was Welsh Alice, though we know only a little about her. Alice was a homeless beggarwoman, feeble-minded and illiterate, and she crossed the River Mersey in a boat from Eastham in 1582 along with some 'felowe with a broken arm'. The stay of Alice and her injured friend was a short one: on the orders of the mayor the couple were thrown out of the port.

Vagrants from Wales and the north of England were a major problem to the Liverpool authorities. They were attracted to the port in the hope of finding some work and a better life. According to records of the time, others came because of the 'excedinge number of ale howses and typling ale howses' in the seven streets which comprised the town. Women more attractive and better dressed than Welsh Alice came too, ready to keep company with the soldiers (on their way to Ireland for a wage of threepence per day) and sailors from Wales and Ireland who landed regularly with fish and other foodstuffs.

One of the Welshmen who disembarked at this time was called Davie the Fish. He could only marvel at the variety of goods loaded and unloaded from the boats and small sailing ships. This included grain, iron, barrels of herrings, French wine, cheese, coal and salt.

In 1600 a nameless pauper from Ruthin was accused of bigamy and ordered to take himself off post-haste to the Vale of Clwyd or somewhere else. Liverpool would not welcome him, as he was not ready to contribute to the wealth of the city. He escaped lightly compared to others. For example, there is a 1565 record of a thief nailed by his ear to a post and cruelly whipped, naked 'from the myddyll upward' until blood poured from his back and chest.

Davie the Fish, however, dreamed of making his fortune and by 1619 he was well on the way to doing so. In a meeting in the Common Hall of Liverpool, it was confirmed by the mayor, the bailiffs and the council that fifty barrels of fish, the Welshman's cargo, were to be portioned out for a reasonable price to chosen citizens of the town and that each person would pay £2 into the town funds.

At that time, in the reign of King James I, there were many Davieses in Liverpool, some doing well but many more failing and suffering hardship on the streets. One of these, called John Davies, was badly injured by an attacker in 1617. Four years later, another John Davies, who had a business as an iron and steel dealer, had to face punishment for fraud. We find that William Davies, of Flintshire, had been selling drink at 'divine service', and another William Davies in 1619 appeared before the town council accused of having raped a thirteen-year-old girl on his boat.

The eccentric Moses Hughes

The difficult and eccentric Moses Hughes came to Liverpool from Brynengan (a hamlet in Caernarfonshire where the hymnwriter Pedr Fardd was born a hundred or so years later). Hughes was a loud man who delighted in challenging the authorities, especially the mayor and elders of the town. He would stand on the corner of Castle Street, letting loose a torrent of invective against the 'Liverpool fools' as he liked to call them. In 1685 he was brought before the courts and fined £6. He promptly called on the mayor and councillors to meet him outside the town hall, mocking them again for having released him with such a small fine when he had £20 in his breast pocket. In addition, he erected a large mirror in Castle Street so that the officials could see their silly faces and blush at their failure to extract more money from him. He taunted them further in a long speech about their folly, saying they thought he was 'only a poor old Welshman', but that he was as good as they were and his assets and wealth as great as theirs.

Moses Hughes was regularly to be seen in the streets around the town hall, welcoming the Welsh-speaking Welsh arriving from Anglesey and

Caernarfonshire. He would have been very familiar with the cruel and unjust practice of sending his fellow countrymen and women from rural areas to work on cotton plantations in the USA in the days before the black slave trade became widespread.

Hughes knew as well as anyone that transportation and forced labour was the punishment for Welsh who appeared before the courts. According to official records these unfortunates were described as 'apprentices' or 'migrants'. Children, and especially 'unfit' men and women, were sent officially for 'a number of years' – but, in reality, for ever – to plantations in the West Indies or to Virginia, Carolina and Georgia in the United States. By the time they reached America in those perilous boats they were desperately weak.

In October 1698 we know five Welsh people were in Liverpool docks, preparing for the long journey. These were Humphrey Howell from Merionethshire; John Davies and Edward Parry from Denbighshire; John Wynn from Ruthin, and the only woman, Joyce Cooper from Caernarfonshire. They were not unusual. There are many other lists of men, women and children from all the counties of north Wales who were sent by boat from the port. They ranged in age from eight to thirty. We should not forget the enslavement of the Welsh.

Early Welsh sailors

By the seventeenth century Liverpool could be described as a port, and William Ellis could be counted among those early Welsh sailors. We know that he regularly set sail from the port during the reign of Queen Anne and was a soldier during the reign of George I. But his remarkable life as a sailor, soldier and cobbler apparently encouraged him to live a long and healthy life. When he died in 1780, his age was recorded as 131.

A marked increase in port traffic from Wales in the second half of the seventeenth century caused the merchants and burgesses to build the first dock, sometimes called the Old Dock or Steer's Dock, after the engineer who was responsible for its construction. It was opened with great ceremony on 31 August 1715. The adjacent stream was closed off, and it became marshland and was eventually built over to form Paradise Street and Whitechapel. It was closed as a wet dock in 1826.

Those fishing in the River Mersey, many Welshmen among them, knew the tricks of the tide and the unseen dangers better than anyone, and when a schooner appeared they would immediately rush to offer their services.

They were the forerunners of the ships' pilots. As Beaumaris port was so important, Liverpool Corporation decided, in 1724, to send thirty pounds of gunpowder and seven pounds of explosives to blow up the dangerous Penmon Rocks in the channel between Puffin Island and Anglesey.

Turnpike tolls

Two years after traveller and writer Daniel Defoe visited Liverpool for the third time in 1724, and expressed frank views on the state of the town's roads, the trustees of the Turnpike Trust first met to enact a law for 'repairing and enlarging the road from Liverpool to Prescott and other roads therein mentioned in the County Palatine of Lancaster'.

Widening the road between Limekiln Road (today's Lime Street) and Prescott, through Twigg Lane and Roby, was their first achievement. The width of the new turnpike was four-and-a-half yards; it was made of sand and strong local stone and raised in some places to avoid flooding. Parishioners of Liverpool and West Derby were forced to work cheaply, or for nothing, on the roads for three days a year. But payment at the tollbooths, introduced in 1726, was compulsory. The owner of a horse or mule carrying coal paid a halfpenny, and a penny for a second horse. A wagon with a load of coal cost sixpence; oxen or bullocks between the shafts fourpence; while a Berlin carriage or chariot paid sixpence. Twenty sheep cost the farmer or drover fivepence. Not surprisingly, the Welsh, like the English, complained daily about this system for over half a century and there was great rejoicing in 1871 when the gates disappeared and the days of the tolls came to an end.

The importance of Anglesey

By the 1820s there was daily traffic between the Anglesey ports and Liverpool, largely because of the famous Parys Mountain copperworks. These were glory days in its history, with a host of sailing ships bringing the valuable metal to

Liverpool and Runcorn, with most of it eventually being taken on wagons to St Helens.

This was an exceedingly busy period and ships came to Liverpool every week – and sometimes more frequently – from the ports of Holyhead, Amlwch, Dulas Bay near Penrhos Llugwy, Traeth Bychan near Moelfre, and Traeth Coch, as well as Beaumaris and later Menai Bridge. These ships carried not only copper but produce from Anglesey's farms – cargos of oats, barley, flour, potatoes, butter, chalk, paving stones and, later, the hard stone Sychnant marble from near Traeth Llugwy for building the first of the port's docks. Anglesey residents ventured onto the boats to enjoy the journey to the growing town, where Welsh could be heard on the streets and in the port.

Liverpool pilotage service

There were often tragedies at sea within sight of Liverpool. In 1764 eighteen ships sank between the bar and the docks with the loss of eighty Welsh sailors and barrels of expensive tobacco. Consequently, the Liverpool Pilotage Service was set up in 1766. Every pilot was expected to own a small one-mast boat weighing about thirty tons, with a gun which could be fired and a telescope. But it was soon realised that, when the Mersey was at its most dangerous, this was insufficient. In 1770 three of these little boats capsized in fierce storms and all three pilots were drowned. So, each pilot was compelled to buy a forty-ton cutter, big enough to carry up to seven pilots. Three years later there were around six thousand sailors out of a total population of 34,000. The American War of Independence affected trade at the port, leading to three thousand being unemployed. The shipowners decided to reduce the wages of those in work, resulting in serious riots in 1775 when ten sailors were killed.

John Hughes, trader and mayor

By the beginning of the eighteenth century the Welsh population was large enough to support ambitious men to take leadership roles in the life of the town. One of these was John Hughes, who in 1716 asked the council for the right to set up a pottery business. Hughes was a pioneer of the pottery industry.

He was permitted to make 'sugar moulds or potts or other kinds of muggs' for an annual fee of half a crown. Pottery reached its zenith at the Herculaneum Pottery in Toxteth. The sugar industry had become very important. One consequence of the plague of 1665, followed by Great Fire of London in 1666, was that a number of sugar merchants moved from there to Liverpool to pursue their trade. Liverpool benefited from London's misfortune, and as a result of this Liverpool adopted a large number of London names such as Islington and Kensington.

John Hughes had won his place on the town council by 1705 but, because of his careless nature and lack of personal discipline, he soon transgressed as a councillor. In 1707 he was warned that if he did not change his attitude and attend meetings more regularly he would lose his membership of the council. Twenty years later he became mayor after standing in a public election. This was not traditional practice, but because Hughes was so difficult to deal with, and because of bitter clashes between various parties on the council, it became the custom in 1727 and for a short time thereafter.

Liverpool elections were notable for their scenes of uproar and for the way in which candidates tried to buy votes by preparing lots of food and drink for those with the right to vote. The election took place over at least three days and sometimes the candidates would be wandering the streets for six days to attract support. The result was a waste of resources and the creation of a lot of ill feeling. Nobody could stand without being significantly wealthy, and John Hughes had to stand against a privileged man, Thomas Brereton, who would later represent Liverpool as an MP in Westminster. Hughes managed to seize the reins, but the year of his mayoralty was annoying for everyone. Often, as a ploy to prevent the council disagreeing with his policies, he would refuse to call meetings. He presided over one of the most tumultuous years in the history of Liverpool Corporation. Often people on the streets shouted 'Go home to Wales' or 'Good morning, wild Welshman' but no-one got the better of him. He gave as good as he got and threatened them mercilessly. Naturally the workers in his pottery were respectful towards him as he paid their wages, but a number of his co-councillors were tired of him in 1736 and he was removed from office.

Thanks to his many supporters among both the Welsh and the English, he was restored to office within four years after making a public apology for his failings.

The larger-than-life Councillor Owen Prichard

By now another Welshman had shown his mettle within the town council, namely Owen Prichard. He hailed from Anglesey and had made his fortune selling whisky, beer and strong drink. He knew everyone in Welsh life and in the world of trade. He was on good terms with the Morris brothers of Anglesey – Lewis, Richard, William and the youngest John, who moved to Liverpool and spent a lot of time in the town during 1738–39.

In his letters John, who lodged with a woman called Mrs Partis in a house called Scipio near the docks and paid 3*d.* to 6*d.* per week for his food and board, often spoke of William Hughes, his cousin, who kept a shop in the town. His last letter from Liverpool (or, as he called it, Nerpwl) is very sad as he has in his possession a 'black boy, about sixteen years old, for sale on behalf of a friend of his'. Clearly, none of the Welsh he associated with wanted to buy the boy and John would have been happy 'to sell him for £30, or even something over £25'. What happened to the slave boy? Did John Morris manage to sell him? We do not know.

Owen Prichard was elected Mayor of Liverpool for 1744–45. In 1745, Captain Robinson brought the news to Liverpool that Prince Charles, the Young Pretender, had landed in Scotland. When Prichard heard this, the information was immediately sent to the Home Secretary, and the mayor set about defending the town in case the prince marched on Liverpool on his way to London. The sum of £6,000 was set aside to cover the costs and the mayor and corporation succeeded in forming a battalion of 900 soldiers, known as the Liverpool Blues. Aware of this, the Jacobites bypassed Liverpool but the Liverpool Blues decided to go as far as Carlisle to fight against the Duke of Cumberland.

The mayor was ready to use his own money to promote trade and was prominent in supporting the Greenland whale fishery. The first ship to sail into Liverpool as part of this venture was the *Golden Lion* in 1750, and that journey, under Captain Metcalf, was a successful one. The alderman, together with thirty-seven other leading Liverpool citizens, bought a half a share in the *Golden Lion* on 18 December 1749. The majority had bought one share and the others a half, as did Owen Prichard. But it is quite possible that the prominent Welshman, like other traders, was also promoting slavery.

This is what the Welshman Gomer Williams, an early chronicler of the Liverpool slave trade, has to say:

> So catholic was the spirit of enterprise displayed by most of these gentlemen, that their commercial operations embraced not only whales but negroes, and for one whale's blubber melted by their agency, they might have counted thousands of human hearts either stilled forever, or crushed by lifelong slavery.

And so the hands of the renowned Welshman were not clean of the inhumane practices linked to slavery. It could be said that the whole town thrived on this sinful trade.

Prichard, though not a slave owner, was involved in the world of privateering. Many made their fortunes seizing ships laden with treasure on the high seas. The most famous privateer known in Liverpool, and for that matter throughout Britain, was Captain Fortunatus Wright. An idealistic captain with his dealings shrouded in secrecy, his uncommon bravery struck fear into the French fleet. In 1746, for example, he managed to overpower sixteen French ships worth £400,000 in the Levant and then eighteen in the Caribbean. Prichard's second wife was Wright's widow and the marriage is indicative of the circles in which he moved.

The short curacy of Goronwy Owen

Prichard was instrumental in securing a curacy at Walton Parish Church, a suburb of Liverpool, for the poet Goronwy Owen (1723–69). In his letters, the clergyman talks of him in Welsh as 'Aldraman Prisiart' and also mentions his desire to move from Donnington to a more Welsh area. He was concerned that his children failed to speak Welsh as he believed they should and that he was of little help to them. He became curate of St Mary's Church of Walton-on-the-Hill in April 1753. He was given an additional £13 to teach Classics, among other subjects, in the grammar school near the church.

His life in Liverpool, as everywhere else he lived, was troubled. He failed to attract the attention he deserved in Wales and spent his whole life as an exile.

He hated almost everything, his world and his circumstances. He compared the residents of Walton to Hottentots, a South African tribe he had never laid eyes on but deemed wild and uncivilised. He hated his work as a shepherd of souls and as a Classics teacher. He wrote innumerable letters, many during his short time in Liverpool, to the Morrises and others: literary letters clearly conveying his longing for Anglesey, his great poverty and his desire for books to read – Welsh classics, old manuscripts, grammars, Greek and Latin books. We know he enjoyed taking a walk to the port to speak Welsh with sailors from Anglesey, to enjoy the company of those from foreign countries and to discuss his excruciating longing for his birthplace.

He enjoyed strong drink, and Alderman Prichard would make sure his thirst was slaked. Goronwy hated the folk poets he heard around him in Liverpool as well as in Wales and whose work he knew: 'gutter poets', as he called them. His standards were high, and he restored the *cywydd* metrical form and used it with unusual mastery. (For a definition of this metrical form see the Glossary.) He idealised Anglesey and was remembered by successive generations of those who moved to Liverpool. Acknowledged as one of the giants of Welsh literature, he knew hardship, poverty and the affliction of losing his little daughter Elin.

At his home in Walton he composed an elegy in commemoration of her. The following stanza of the poem is familiar to the Liverpool Welsh, and translated by the Celtic scholar, Kenneth Hurlstone Jackson, reads:

> Too sad is the grief in my heart! Down my cheeks
> run salt streams.
> I have lost my Ellen of the hue of fair weather,
> my bright-braided merry daughter.

Owen's ideas about the function, form, structure, intention and the value of poetry strongly influenced Welsh literature. Within two years, he gave up teaching and preaching in Walton, taking a curacy in Northolt on the outskirts of London. It is said that he was disappointed in Northolt and then decided to emigrate to Williamsburg, Virginia, far from Anglesey and Liverpool.

We see from the letters of Goronwy Owen that another Welshman, Edward Owen, was curate of Crosby Church (another north Liverpool district which became a Welsh colony). He came from the Llangurig area of Montgomeryshire and, like Goronwy, was a scholarly man. But the poet did not think much of him as he was constantly saying that the days of the Welsh were numbered! Edward Owen moved to become the headmaster of Warrington Grammar School and rector of the town where there were pockets of ardent Welsh people.

We have Goronwy Owen to thank for references to many a Welshman who came to visit the growing town.

The revivalist John Thomas of Rhayader

One of the Welsh revivalists who visited Liverpool to promote his book was John Thomas from Rhayader in Radnorshire. He was educated in the Calvinistic Methodist College in Treveca, near Talgarth in Breconshire, under the Protestant reformer Howell Harris, and became an itinerant preacher during the Calvinistic Methodist Revival before accepting a call to the ministry in the Congregationalist chapel of Caebach in Rhayader in 1767.

We do not know which printer John Thomas used in Liverpool. But the details on the cover read: '*Traethawd ar Fywyd Ffydd* (A Treatise on a Life of Faith) by W A Romaine MA, translated by Ioan Thomas by permission of the author. Liverpool. Printed in Morfa Street 1767.'

It is dated Christmas Eve, 24 December 1767. He also includes two lines in Welsh which say, 'From my labours in Liverpool in an expensive place, far from my native hearth'. It seems that the hymnwriter and preacher therefore spent his Christmas in Liverpool in 1767, guiding his book through the press. It was a considerable task. To start with, he had to travel from Rhayader to Liverpool, most probably on foot, only to find there were errors committed by the compositor. He recognised that they had escaped notice, as he had left them 'in the hands of the English while I was away'. Then he set upon the critics, the 'fault-finders', this being the only approach of many reviewers in the early years. The saint from Rhayader accused them of nit-picking rather than trying to understand the spirit and thought processes of the author.

The Baptist evangelist David Jones

When the zealous Baptist evangelist David Jones (1708–79) settled in the heart of Liverpool with his wife and children after his pioneering work in the Wrexham area, he was absolutely delighted by his new surroundings. Almost every day he would go from his home to the streets of Liverpool to proclaim the good news, and most of the time he would be speaking in Welsh as there were many Welsh people to be found and ready to listen. When he died, the funeral was held in Low Hill Cemetery in Everton.

It was not only the Welsh who flocked together to Liverpool. These figures demonstrate the growth of the population during the eighteenth century:

Year	Number of houses	Inhabitants
1700	1,142	5,714
1720	2,367	1,838
1742	3,600	18,000
1760	5,156	25,787
1801	11,784	77,708

Calling for workers

The Industrial Revolution was taking place throughout the counties of the north of England and factories and mills were becoming part of the landscape. The goods produced there proved positive for the port of Liverpool, as they required raw materials, especially cotton; there was plenty of work for people used to hard graft.

There was a call for workers to build a canal from Liverpool to Leeds in 1770, an enterprise that was completed within four years and gave Liverpool a proper boost. Canals like Bridgewater, the Sankey, the Leeds-Liverpool, the Trent and Mersey, the Shropshire Union and the Weaver Navigation linked Liverpool with the Lancashire and Staffordshire coalfields, the salt-fields and cheese country of Cheshire, the Manchester area and the West Riding. Liverpool merchants did not miss an opportunity and were soon heavily involved in buying and selling cotton and woollens, ironmongery, hardware and pottery, as well as glass. All these products were traded by ambitious Welsh merchants in their stores and warehouses.

Building the docks, however, required labour. The first dock, The Old Dock, opened in 1715; the Salthouse Dock was opened in 1753 and the George's in 1771, enlarged in 1825 on the site which included the elegant offices known as the Royal Liver, the Cunard and the Dock Board. St George's Dock was known as 'the Welsh Basin' by locals, as it was there that all the Welsh ships would load and unload until it was closed in 1900.

On the northern edge of St George's Dock were the slate yards. As Liverpool grew there was an evident demand for slates. Welsh speakers were in charge of these slate yards, and ships from Port Dinorwic, Bangor, Caernarfon and Porthmadog could be seen unloading stone and slates each week. The ships now gave a different appearance to the River Mersey. In 1701 only 102 ships were seen on the river; by 1751 this had risen to 543 and in 1783 to 3,420.

We know that, in 1783, 446 ships belonged to the Port of Liverpool itself and, of this number, eighty-six were involved in the slave trade, with Welsh sailors aboard a number of them. This was a time of extensive migration from Wales. The Welsh came to seek an escape from poverty and the meagre wages paid to workers there.

The Welsh and the building of the docks

The great building developments on the Mersey were attractive and, according to published records, there were numbers of Welsh people working on the King's Dock, which was completed in 1788, and the Queen's Dock, completed in 1796. Those who had experience as quarrymen in Caernarfonshire and coalminers in north-east Wales were ready for the task. Welshmen also formed the majority of the quarrymen in St James Quarry, which later became the cemetery now beside the Anglican cathedral. In this cemetery can be found the graves of successful Welshmen such as David Roberts, a timber merchant who lived nearby in Hope Street. The distinguished businessman Robert Herbert Williams, better known in poetic circles as Corfanydd, who was born in Liverpool, testified that it was largely the Welsh who built the docks mentioned above. Ships from north Wales's ports were prominent on the river and in the docks. Many of them were taking emigrants to the New World.

William Gibson stays in the town

It was with the intention of emigrating to the USA that William Gibson from Conwy came to Liverpool in 1794 with his young son John, who became one of the most important sculptors of the nineteenth century. The family joined the English Baptist chapel in Byrom Street on 1 August but soon they found nearby the Pall Mall Welsh Calvinistic Methodist Chapel and enjoyed the excellent provision there for children and young people, particularly in the Sunday school. Instead of going to America, the family stayed in Liverpool and raised three outstanding sculptors within the Welsh community.

Another place where Welsh speakers were in the majority in the eighteenth century was in the cotton factory. This was a large factory built by Kirkman and Co in Vauxhall Road, between Midghall Street and Banastre Street. Liverpudlians called it 'the Welsh factory'. By the last quarter of the eighteenth century the Welsh had won respect and praise as hard and honest workers.

A number of them rose to the highest office. Robert Jerman from Anglesey was superintendent of Bootle Water Company, which was formed in the 1780s. Another of the same calibre was John Owens of Flintshire, who was appointed chief overseer of the Duke's Dock – a most important position; and William Morgan from the Vale of Clwyd was appointed his deputy. Robert Edwards, who became the superintendent of the Old Quay Company, was from Anglesey.

Their influence was such that many Liverpool-born English were annoyed at the appointments; indeed, we are told that there was no major work without a Welshman to oversee the project. These, and others like them, made a lasting impression as incomers who saw Liverpool as their town of refuge.

Chapter 2

Welcome to Liverpool

There is an air of romance about the beginnings of Welsh society in Liverpool, but it would be a mistake to give the impression that it was an irresistible town for those from north and mid Wales. Even by the end of the eighteenth century, it was still a small town. To the north it reached no further than the far end of Old Hall Street, and to the south to Pitt Street, where many of the early settlers lived. Eastwards, the port stretched to Whitechapel and Church Street. Open countryside surrounded the town as Windsor, Toxteth, Islington and Kensington had not yet been developed, nor had St Domingo, Everton, Kirkdale and Anfield.

The streets of Liverpool

The famous Castle Street, its castle long disappeared, was unpleasant and narrow — too narrow for two carriages to pass each other. Byrom Street, which today is near the Birkenhead Tunnel and leads to Walton, was another narrow street. Where St George's Hall now stands, stood the town hospital and, behind the hospital, where today we can enjoy St John's Gardens, was the asylum and the Sailors' Hospital. Later on, St John's Church was built, with its churchyard where many generations of Welsh people are buried.

Lime Street was not a railway station, just a row of primitive, poor dwellings. They stood in Bolton Street, opposite the main entrance of the now-famous station. Where the busy station stands now was the limekiln that gave the street its name. This area became a well-known meeting place for the Welsh in the nineteenth and twentieth centuries. Higher up there was open land with only the occasional house. For instance, there were just two houses in Edge Hill.

The area around Mount Pleasant contained merchants' houses and was the birthplace of the renowned William Roscoe, but it would have been considered out in the country. The shopkeepers and office workers in Castle Street, Dale Street, Water Street and Lord Street lived above their shops and offices.

The homes of the Welsh

The Welsh made their homes mainly around Old Hall Street and Tithebarn Street. Quite a few lived in James Street and Chapel Street in narrow and confined court housing; some lived as far out as Pitt Street. According to John Hughes Morris:

> They say you hear as much Welsh in those parts of the town as anywhere in Wales and the English often call the streets 'Welsh Court', 'Welsh Yard', 'Welsh Chapel Court' etc, instead of by their proper names.

By land and sea to Liverpool

Were it not for ships, it would have been hard to reach Liverpool. Before 1766 there was no link with the rest of England other than travelling on foot or on horseback to Warrington to catch the stagecoach. This ran twice a week and took three days to reach London. But after 1766 some deliverance came in the form of the new London Road, running out of Liverpool to Warrington. Nevertheless, for generations, until the railway was built, it remained difficult to reach the port by land. Here are the words of James Hughes (Iago Trichrug), who lived in the London area, a notable hymnwriter and expounder of the scriptures. In the year 1826 he was unable to come and preach in Liverpool because of the high cost of transport:

> Damn their prices! Four guineas to take someone like me there and I am not worth fourpence to anyone in the world! I'm afraid to venture out at this time of the year even though it costs only half the price. Who can put up with cold and sleeplessness all night on a fast-moving coach? I'd rather sacrifice two guineas than lose my health for ever.

Salvation came to those who wanted to come from north-west Wales through the shipbuilders, especially the Amlwch Nautical Company which, by 1786, was sailing ships weighing more than fifty tons, transporting copper to Liverpool and the Sankey Canal and carrying coal from the Lancashire coalfield back to Anglesey. A prominent Welshman called Michael Hughes was in charge of the St Helens Copperworks.

People from Anglesey also travelled on these ships and on a sloop called *Jane and Betty*, owned by Anglesey farmers, which sailed regularly between Bangor and Liverpool. Captain Richard Pierce and two assistants sailed the sloop for years and regularly lodged in Liverpool. One winter they paid a woman who was cooking for them £6-7-4. But the most interesting note was one he got when he was back in the port of Beaumaris. He was reminded that he had returned to Anglesey 'without a sweetheart and I am still in hopes to have your company when you will return to Liverpool again, now I am alone, the cat … [has] left the house, and the mice have room to play.'

The best way to reach Liverpool was by another slightly smaller sloop, the *Darling*, which sailed regularly for a long time between 1781 and 1893, usually from Holyhead to Liverpool via the Menai Straits. The alternative was to walk from Caernarfonshire or Denbighshire as far as Flint or Bagillt, and then cross the River Dee to Parkgate in a small boat. Then one would have to walk across the Wirral to Birkenhead and cross the Mersey in a sailing boat or rowing boat, all depending on the weather.

Some migrants coming from south and mid Wales and Montgomeryshire would come via Chester, as a coach ran at least three times a week to Eastham. The village was a centre for the Welsh throughout the nineteenth century and, indeed, from as early as the last quarter of the eighteenth century. It was the meeting point for coaches from Chester and those from Wales to Manchester. There people would change horses and stay overnight in lodgings, while others would take a ship to Liverpool. According to the first journal which appeared in the Welsh language, *Seren Gomer*:

There was as much Welsh heard among people in the lodging houses of Eastham and their friends on horseback as anywhere on the far side of Offa's Dyke. The number of Welsh names on the gravestones is evidence of this to anyone who walks through the cemetery.

Crossing the Mersey

But it was not at all easy to cross from Eastham to Liverpool as the river was so wide and the current strong. At its worst it could often take two hours or more to make the crossing and the price would be higher if the boat was not full. Among the people who regularly made the crossing were the three Calvinistic Methodist preachers from Bala – Thomas Charles, Simon Lloyd and Dafydd Cadwaladr. Thomas Charles almost lost his life when a storm arose suddenly while crossing to Liverpool.

We can trace the Welsh Calvinistic Methodist cause in the town back to a Welsh sermon preached by Owen Thomas Roland, a blacksmith from Penrhosllugwy on Anglesey, in the English Wesleyan chapel in Pitt Street in 1770. This was the chapel in which the renowned John Wesley preached on his frequent visits – often at six o'clock in the morning. There would be a high proportion of Welsh people at those meetings, and on Sundays before the first Welsh Calvinistic Methodist chapel in Pall Mall was built. Many had to flee from Wales because of persecution.

In the words of Welsh religious historian John Hughes Morris:

> They were mocked, they were persecuted, they were mercilessly oppressed in
> their own country; they were turned out of hearth and home; their livelihoods
> were taken from them so that they had no choice but to leave their country and
> try to find the freedom to worship God according to their own consciences among
> strangers and those speaking another language.

Owen Thomas Roland – a pioneer

Such was the case for Owen Thomas Roland, who was persecuted by the clergy on Anglesey and had no alternative but to make the long journey to Liverpool on foot. Although he was almost totally Welsh speaking, he was warmly welcomed at the English Wesleyan Methodist chapel in Pitt Street. Roland was encouraged to spread the gospel to many of the monoglot Welsh speakers by the banks of the Mersey, who came from a similar background to his. His stay in Liverpool was a short one and he will be remembered as a pioneer. After nine months he walked back to Anglesey to see if he would get a warmer welcome, but he did not forget his compatriots in exile.

William Llwyd of Flintshire

One of those who frequented the English Wesleyan chapel was William Llwyd, who with some of his friends decided to set up prayer meetings in his home in Pitt Street. According to the local directory his home was 'back of 92 Pitt Street', suggesting that it was the house of a poor worker. According to the temperance pioneer Corfanydd, his house was 'in the next court to the lower corner of the Wesleyan chapel'. Today, even the chapel has disappeared, but this was a gathering point for the Welsh who were thirsting for the gospel of Christ in their own tongue.

Llwyd, a native of Ysgeifiog in Flintshire, was supported by three other young men: Owen Owens from Llanrwst, and Evan Roberts and his brother from Denbigh. But Llwyd was the natural leader. When he left home in 1781, he found it hard to find regular work by the River Mersey. For some time he worked with shipwrights, but lost his job as he had not served an apprenticeship like the rest of the workforce. He tried to set up his own business selling hosiery house-to-house; this time from his home in 6 Liver Street, a narrow street off Park Lane. He later moved to 12 Union Street, and then to Milk Street, where he died on St David's Day 1810.

Llwyd managed to get three preachers from his home area to come regularly to Liverpool, namely Humphrey Owen from Y Berthen-Gron Chapel, Lixwm; William Davies from Y Golch, and Robert Price from Plas Winter in Halkyn, all zealous Calvinistic Methodists from the Holywell area. Before long, his home proved too small and people congregated in an unpleasant old warehouse belonging to Billy the Ragman, where the bodies of people drowned in the Mersey were laid out in their coffins.

More than a thousand people flocked to the funeral of William Llwyd when he was buried on 5 March 1810 in the churchyard at St Paul's Square, proof of the deep impression he had made. His wife Mari had been a great support to him – and in establishing a chapel for the Welsh.

Support from Thomas Charles

In 1785 Thomas Charles of Bala visited the dark and uncomfortable old warehouse where Llwyd held his meetings – described by William Davies of Holywell as being like a shed for gypsies. After his return to Merionethshire,

Charles set about promoting the cause of the poor and underprivileged exiles he had met in Liverpool.

He used his wide network to collect money towards building a chapel and supporting the Welsh to buy a piece of land in Pall Mall, and there, opposite the home of the artist George Stubbs, was built 'a perfectly plain building... eleven square yards... and, at the front, between it and the road, there was a piece of land or an open court, about the same size as the building'.

Pall Mall Chapel is opened

The first Welsh Calvinistic Methodist church in Liverpool was opened on Whit Sunday 1787, an anniversary which was very important in the town's history. On that date every year for 150 years, the Liverpool Assembly's three-day-long services of preaching were held in each chapel. Thomas Charles and his compatriots had been influential — as shown in the records of a session of the North Wales Association of Calvinistic Methodists at Rhosllanerchrugog Calvinistic Methodist Chapel on 2 April 1788. Both Thomas Charles and John Edwards (also from Bala) had, between them, collected £55 towards the Pall Mall Chapel from Anglesey and the counties of Caernarfon, Denbigh and Flint. In addition, Charles collected £5-17-6 in Merionethshire and Edward Watkin £6-2-6 in Montgomeryshire for the same cause. Richard Roberts of Melin-y-Coed, near Llanrwst, was repaid £70 (which he had lent towards the cost of the chapel), together with interest of £2-10-0. Additionally, Evan Davies, 'a capable and conscientious craftsman', was paid £21-10-0 for his work on the chapel's seats, doors and windows.

In the Bala session of the association on 18 June 1788, Humphrey Lloyd, who laid the foundations, was paid £5 which he had lent to Thomas Charles. We do not know the name of the blacksmith who worked on the chapel but he was eventually paid £3-14-10½ and must have been a very patient man. On the last day of the year, 31 December 1788, in the Dolgellau session of the same association, a payment of £11-7-10 was made to clear the debt owed by Pall Mall elders to the carpenter Evan Davies.

Thomas Charles's influence was evident and in the last session of the North Wales Association in 1789 in Ruthin, £1-4-4 was collected towards Pall Mall Chapel and £10 was paid to George Gittins, of Rhosllanerchrugog, 'in part for Liverpool Chapel'. Gittins was among the most generous Calvinists towards the poverty-stricken Welsh in Liverpool. Indeed, the North Wales Association, which met at Machynlleth on 8 April 1790, heard that another £40 was paid towards the chapel, and in the records of an association meeting held at Denbigh on 29 December 1791, there is reference to a Peter Williams of Y Berthen-Gron Chapel, Lixwm. That day the association repaid him £40 which he had lent towards the Pall Mall Chapel. He received interest of £2-0-0 for his generous gesture. The whole sum raised amounted to £303-6-6½, and one has to admire the success of Thomas Charles and his co-workers. The cost of the building, at £600, was twice that amount, but it is worth noting this was the only time the Liverpool Welsh depended so utterly on the people of north Wales for help in building their Nonconformist and Anglican meeting places.

We know the Liverpool Welsh gave a lot of their own time in helping the builders and thus saving a great deal of money. One night, four boys carried wood from the sawmill to Pall Mall. They had almost reached the chapel when they were accused of having stolen the wood and spent some hours under lock and key until they had managed to persuade the authorities of their honesty.

A focus for migration

Building the chapel gave a boost to migration from Wales. As Calvinistic Methodist leaders had travelled the length and breadth of Wales collecting money, the word spread to even the remotest parts of the Llŷn peninsula. Now they knew they would have a spiritual and social centre in the town. Soon it was necessary to enlarge the chapel, putting in two extra galleries, one to the right and the other to the left of the chancel.

Among the immigrants of 1789 was a young man from Eifionydd, Daniel Jones, the son of Methodist exhorter Robert Jones, of Rhos-lan, near Cricieth. He was only fifteen when he settled in Liverpool and soon became a stalwart at Pall Mall. Jones was welcomed to the chapel by William Llwyd, Thomas Edwards and Thomas Hughes, the last two being recent immigrants themselves. Thomas Edwards was a smith by trade from Llanelidan. Overnight he became a preacher, as did Thomas Hughes, a carpenter. They were both part of the immigration which took place in 1786–87 and thus had a role in the building of the chapel.

The chapel depended heavily on them, and Daniel Jones was a most useful acquisition as he was able to get his father to persuade preachers to come on a Sunday to Liverpool. Indeed, he went in person to the North Wales Association meeting held at Pwllheli in 1794 to try to tempt preachers to Liverpool.

Fear on the streets

By 1793 the town was in turmoil as Prime Minister William Pitt persuaded a deputation to visit London to discuss how to defend the port against the threat of a French invasion. A prison was opened in Great Howard Street and, within five months, French prisoners of war had reached their new home. By 1799 there were 4,009 in the prison and many in the Welsh community showed kindness to them. They supported their plays and entertainment and bought many of the toys the French had made in captivity.

Most of the Welsh arrivals soon faced hardship. The cost of essentials was exorbitant – tea cost fourteen shillings a pound, sugar was fifteen pence, and salt fivepence. But the greatest hardship was the press gangs.

Throughout the 1790s Welsh sailors lived in continual fear. Daniel Jones from Rhos-lan, near Cricieth, describes graphically an incident on a cold November night in 1793:

> Last Friday, some of the members had a narrow escape as they were coming out
> of the chapel meeting; they managed to escape to a house and close the door with
> the gang at their heels. Wales should thank God for the freedom to practise its faith
> without the fear of being forced to enlist in the army or on a man-of-war ship.

Naturally, preachers from Wales, having heard about the press gangs, were fearful of venturing to Liverpool. Daniel Jones gives us a glimpse of this, advising two preachers, John Roberts of Llanllyfni and John Edwards from Anglesey, to 'come by day before dark and take lodgings in Thomas Hughes's house near the chapel'.

He describes the suffering and pain experienced by many families:

Last night there was widespread terror throughout the town, dreadful press gangs, dragging scores of people to war, willing or unwilling. Women were weeping, mothers and sisters wailing. 'Oh my husband!' said one; 'Oh my son, my son,' said another. There is nothing but the sound of weeping from one end of the town to the other… I saw a gang dragging a man who, from his clothing, looked like a gentleman. The captain of one vessel from Belfast refused to respond to the cruelty of the gang in Strand Street. They shot him there and then and pierced him with a sword. There lies his body today, an example for all passers-by to see.

It is not surprising that sailors from Wales often jumped ship when they entered the Mersey to swim to the safety of New Brighton and Seacombe. There they always got a warm welcome from the famous innkeeper Mother Redcap, whose house was on Liscard Beach. She became widely known as a friend to sailors from Wales and everywhere else and, according to the Liverpool historian Ramsay Muir, she had 'subterranean hiding places for them'.

A hymn book for the Liverpool Welsh

Daniel Jones was occasionally able to forget about the press gangs as he bore the considerable responsibility of seeing a volume of Welsh-language hymns through the process of publication in Liverpool for his father, Robert. The work was printed at Nevills in Castle Street and the publication was called *Grawnsypiau Canaan* (Bunches of Canaan Grapes). The year 1795 was an important occasion, as most of the hymns had been composed by the eighteenth-century revivalist William Williams Pantycelyn.

Robert Jones offended Williams's admirers throughout Wales by editing some of these hymns, but the arrival of *Grawnsypiau Canaan* was enormously important. This was their hymn book for years and the hymnwriter's emphasis on India was one of the reasons for establishing a missionary movement among the Liverpool Welsh. Williams died in 1791, two years before William Carey left England for India. Williams wrote his hymns when there was opposition to missionary work. Carey was inspired by Williams's English hymn, 'O'er Those Gloomy Hills of Darkness'. Indeed, it is said that it became the national anthem of the missionary movement across Britain. It was a very popular collection and 4,000 copies were sold within a short time.

Shocking news from Fishguard

With all the rumours about France being able to entice the fleets of the Netherlands and Spain to join in the overthrow of the British fleet, the danger of invasion was very great, as was proved on 22 February 1797 when news reached Liverpool that the French army had reached the outskirts of Fishguard. The word spread through Liverpool like wildfire, creating unprecedented panic. Liverpool was the target: privateers lived there, warships were built there, and it was a town which concealed pirates and slaves. Half the town's population rushed off towards Ormskirk. Daniel Jones saw one vehicle after another, laden with belongings, lining up through Old Hall Street, Prescot Road, Mount Pleasant and Brownlow Hill, with mothers and children in tears. Every road out of the town looked as if a great fair were taking place. There was a call for volunteers, and within four days there were more than a thousand men ready to defend the town. None were more energetically involved than the Welsh townspeople. They were now no longer incomers but Liverpool residents. To Daniel Jones, his compatriots felt 'indignant that our enemy would set foot on Welsh soil and they felt bound to defend the honour of their country'.

Despite the alarm, their fears were unfounded as the women of Fishguard managed to frighten the French off, but it showed how easy it was at that time to create panic across the whole town.

The Anglican Church prepares for the Welsh

The Welsh incomers were extremely fortunate in the extent of the provision made for them by the Anglican Church. In that Church in Liverpool were two cultured Welshmen. The first was the Rev. Lewis Pugh, curate of St Ann's Church and living in 16 Christian Street, Everton Road. The other was the Rev. John Davies, curate of St Paul's Church and living at 28 St Paul's Square. In November 1693, the Bishop of Chester decreed that Welsh-language services should be held in St Paul's Church and that Lewis Pugh should lead services in St Nicholas Church on Sunday evenings. St Paul's Church was packed to the rafters for the Welsh services. It had a choir and a supporting band, and the sound of the bassoon, the newly-invented clarinet, as well as the flute could be heard. The precentor was the Anglesey-born Edward

Jones, a carpenter by trade and an accomplished bassoonist. He was the first of a host of precentors who served the town's chapels for generations.

Lewis Pugh is described as a fervent Welshman and proud of the inhabitants in the Welsh town around him. It is said that Liverpool Corporation paid him £60 a year as a 'representative' and 'Welsh reader' among the Liverpool Welsh. He received an additional payment for ministering at weddings and funerals. And from 1793 to 1813, he was the most prominent Anglican priest among the Welsh. It was not possible to marry legally in Pall Mall and the vows had to be taken in an episcopal church.

Tragedy struck on Sunday morning, 11 February 1810, in St Nicholas Church. Twenty-two worshippers were killed and many more injured when, a few minutes before the beginning of the service, the stone holding the clock tower moved and the whole construction fell through the roof into the centre of the church. Lewis Pugh was on the point of entering the church when one of the teachers of Moorfield School turned to him and said, 'For God's sake, Mr Pugh, turn back!' He took heed and his life was spared. The teacher who warned him lost her life, as did seventeen of the children in her care.

Extending the chapel

On 31 March 1797 we find Daniel Jones writing to his father and to Thomas Charles about the yearning of the Welsh who belonged to Pall Mall Chapel to enlarge it for the incoming migrants in the near future.

> We see the need to extend the chapel; the society has increased to 120 or more, with a larger congregation on a Sunday afternoon than the chapel can comfortably hold and, as so many thousands of our fellow Welsh are in the town, we are sure that, if there were room, many more would come than do now. So it was decided in the aforementioned meeting to send to you and Mr Charles... to you and those appointed trustees. Are you willing?

The trustees took some time to debate the suggestion but, by 1799, they were ready to approve the idea. The chapel was extended for the second time and the work was completed by October the following year. William Llwyd was thrilled to see his vision come to fruition: to set firm foundations under the Welsh community on the threshold of a century which would see the Welsh flocking to Liverpool.

He never thought the Welsh would achieve so much in the town which was growing before his very eyes. This would create a Welsh middle class for the first time ever, a class which would belong to two worlds, the cosmopolitan world of Liverpool, and the Welsh world with its emphasis on faith, language, values and culture. Their story is as much part of the history of the Welsh nation as it is part of the history of Liverpool.

Chapter 3

More Welsh incomers

At the end of the eighteenth century, the Welsh had only one centre in Liverpool and that was Pall Mall Chapel. After the morning service, the Pall Mall congregation would walk all the way to St James Church, in Hill Street, to take the Eucharist.

The Welsh Baptists

By 1795 there were a few Welsh Baptists living in Liverpool, but they were not prepared to support the Welsh Calvinistic Methodist chapel in Pall Mall. They preferred to go to an English Baptist chapel than support a Welsh chapel of another denomination. Three pioneers of the Welsh Baptists were the flourishing draper William Williams and his wife, and the energetic Hugh Evans from Nefyn. But the Welsh Baptists tended to be rather quarrelsome and found it hard to live with each other because of their conflicting doctrinal beliefs.

The Rev. Evan Evans (1773–1827) of Cefn Mawr, near Rhosllanerchrugog in Denbighshire, was their saviour. He was not prepared to let them persist in their fractious ways. One of the literary greats of Liverpool described him as 'brave as a lion and he would preach until the sweat ran from him: from his ears, his hair and his chest'. It was said his habit of shouting too much while preaching in Cefn Mawr, Liverpool, and London led to his premature death. He once admitted the fault but added, 'sometimes you have to shout'. He incorporated the branch of the Liverpool Welsh Baptists into a branch of his chapel in Cefn Mawr and all was well from 1805 to 1810.

At the same time, we should not forget the contribution of that fine Welshman, the Rev. John Blayney. He was always on the move, preaching everywhere, although clearly at times tending to be over-enthusiastic. Blayney and Evan Evans paved the way for the important theologian, the Rev. J P Davies. His stay in Liverpool was short, but the fact that he came at all tells an important story.

The rise of the Welsh Calvinistic Methodists

Liverpool was becoming an important religious centre and the Calvinistic Methodists, as well as other denominations, began to ordain laymen into the ministry. At this time there were three Welsh Calvinistic Methodist clergy available for the whole of north and central Wales and the exiles in Liverpool – Thomas Charles and Simon Lloyd, both from Bala, and William Lloyd from Caernarfon. Daniel Jones depended on his father, who in turn sought the advice of the outstanding cleric, Thomas Charles, on the subject of ordination, and in 1811 the Calvinistic Methodist movement became a new denomination, to the great delight of leaders in the town.

Dic Aberdaron and the Gibson brothers

The Liverpool Welsh had good friends, not only in Wales but among prominent civic leaders who showed them exceptional kindness. One of those was William Rathbone II who died on 11 February 1809. But the most important of all was William Roscoe, who used his talents to oppose slavery and campaign for progressive causes.

He also cared for eccentric Welshmen like Richard Robert Jones (1780–1843). Dic Aberdaron hailed from the Llŷn peninsula and became famous throughout north Wales for his ability to learn languages. He was a wanderer and, from a distance, was described as like an apparition with his beard, long hair and dishevelled clothing, pushing a sort of barrow where he kept his papers, dictionaries, grammar books and his untidy scribblings. He came to Liverpool in 1804. He never stayed anywhere for long, but Liverpool was the place in which he remained longest and there he had the patronage of William Roscoe, who prepared a house for him so that he had no need to sleep rough as he normally did.

On 27 February 1834, some of Dic's books were stolen and also two of his harps. Then, two days later on St David's Day, he was attacked in St John

Street near Dale Street. Again, on 6 April, as he went to buy a halfpenny worth of buttermilk for his dinner, one James O'Hara attacked him without any provocation. His left shoulder bone was fractured as well as three of his left ribs. At the time he was preparing a book on how to learn Hebrew and fortunately Alderman John C Williams, originally from Denbigh, arranged for all his books to be taken to his home for safe keeping.

The most important man to receive patronage from William Roscoe was undoubtedly the sculptor John Gibson (1790–1866) who was born in the Conwy area but moved to Liverpool at the age of four, as his parents wanted to emigrate to the United States. When his mother saw the condition of the sailing ships they had second thoughts, and decided to make their home in Liverpool where they became an important part of Welsh society. John and his brother Solomon (1796–1866) were educated in Pall Mall Chapel under the tutelage of the hymnwriter and poet Pedr Fardd (Peter Jones, 1776–1845). He, like Daniel Jones from Eifionydd in Caernarfonshire, was one of the immigrants of 1795. Peter Jones managed to combine his work as a tailor with teaching in the Sunday school and in the Welsh-language school which was established in Pall Mall. He became one of the foremost Calvinistic Welsh-language hymnwriters and his hymns are still popular today.

It was their links with William Roscoe that changed the worlds of both John and Solomon Gibson. John's earliest work can be seen in Sefton Anglican Parish Church on the outskirts of Liverpool where a statue to Henry Blundell was erected in 1813. Roscoe invited him to come every week to his mansion in Springwood to see carvings and books he had brought from Italy. It was also he who advised him to go to Italy to be trained. Gibson reached Rome on 20 October 1817 and was trained by two of the foremost sculptors in the world, Canova and Thorvaldsen. He did not return to Liverpool until 1844 when he received a commission from Queen Victoria and carved a statue of her. He was also commissioned to sculpt statues of William Huskisson in 1840 and 1847. His statue of George Stephenson, the railway pioneer, was erected in St George's Hall in 1851. Before leaving Liverpool he made a bust of William Roscoe.

Solomon's sculptural works are also important – *Cupid and Psyche* and *Venus Lamenting the Death of Adonis* were shown in the Liverpool Academy in 1812. In 1844 he bequeathed to future generations a monument to the lexicographer John Davies of Mallwyd, near Dinas Mawddwy. He became a classical scholar and was extremely knowledgeable about early Welsh literature. He benefited significantly from his brother's generosity and received the sum of £100 every year from him. He died in Paris on 29 January 1866, two days after the death of his brother John.

The third brother, Benjamin Gibson (1811–51), moved to Rome to be an assistant to his eldest brother in 1837. He died on 13 August 1851 and above his grave, in the Protestant cemetery in Lucca, there is a monument by his brother John. Ben Gibson's work can be seen in a memorial erected in 1829 to Matthew Gregson, one of the prominent citizens of Liverpool.

Betsi Cadwaladr, the famous nurse

The Bala preacher David Cadwaladr (1752–1834) and his wife Judith had nine children, the best-known of whom was Elisabeth or Betsi. In 1803, at the age of fourteen and without informing the rest of the family, she decided to leave home, walking from Bala to Chester and then taking a boat to Liverpool. She arrived at five o'clock in the morning and wandered from one street to the next when she realised that a man was following her. She turned off into a dirty, mud-filled court. There was not a sound to be heard, every door was locked and there was not a living creature on the streets. She saw a door open and a woman threw water from a bowl into the gully. Remarkably, the woman called her by name, having recognised her because of her father's visits to the Pall Mall Chapel. Her son was a sailor and his mother had risen early to get him ready for his voyage. She welcomed Betsi Cadwaladr into her home, prepared food for her and then made her rest. The following day, the kind woman took her to her cousin's home in Brisbane Street. There, they discovered that her cousin, a sailor, was away in the Caribbean, but his wife was at home and found her a place to stay.

Betsi recalled seeing a thief breaking into a house in Church Street. In Welsh she shouted, 'Stop thief! Stop thief!' The thief turned down into a gully called St Peter's Alley with Betsi hot on his heels. Within seconds she managed to throw her arms around him, bring him to the ground and jump on his back. By now two watchmen had arrived – this was before the town had set up a police force. She told them the whole story and the thief was taken off to the French prison, as it was known.

In Liverpool, Betsi Pen Rhiw, as she was called at home, had to change her name to Elizabeth Davis as the English-speaking residents of Liverpool had problems in pronouncing Cadwaladr. She found work as a maid with Sir George Drinkwater, a prominent citizen in the town, and later met the successful politician George Canning during a parliamentary election. She frequented Pall Mall Chapel where she heard the itinerant preachers, especially the outstanding John Elias (1774–1841). He came regularly from Anglesey to Liverpool, and leaders like Thomas Hughes admired him greatly. Hughes was not only a preacher. He built chapels in Manchester and north Wales. His daughter Mary married the Rev. Richard Williams (1802–42), a native of Llanbrynmair in Montgomeryshire, and another prominent figure among the Liverpool Welsh.

Captain of faith

Another noteworthy character was a ship's captain, Owen William Morgan. He made Liverpool his headquarters, although he also had a home on Anglesey. Once, after waiting six weeks for favourable weather, the wind rose on a Sunday. As the captain believed the Sabbath should be kept holy, he refused to sail. The same happened on the next Sunday but he stuck to his principles. He watched as most of the other captains set off, leaving him alone with his ship and crew. Despite the difficulties, and cost what it may, he was not one to compromise his beliefs. When he finally had the chance to leave Liverpool he soon discovered that the other ships had only made it as far as Hoylake and Llandudno and Captain Morgan soon caught them up.

His influence, together with that of William Llwyd, was crucial in promoting Pall Mall Chapel.

The Welsh Independents in Cavendish Street

Sadly, the Welsh who flocked to Liverpool could not put aside their religious denominational differences. They wanted to meet, as they did in the old country, as Welsh Independents, Baptists and Calvinistic Methodists. This may seem folly to us today but respecting their background was at the root of their beliefs, as was also the case in Welsh communities in the United States and Patagonia. Because the Welsh Calvinistic Methodists were strong on Anglesey and in Arfon and Merionethshire, most of the immigrants supported the Calvinistic Methodist chapels in Liverpool. But, in 1800, a number of families came from the Llanbrynmair area of Montgomeryshire, where Yr Hen Gapel (the Old Chapel) which belonged to the Welsh Independents, was very influential.

They originally planned to emigrate to the United States but, after a few days at sea, they soon realised the boat was letting in water. There was nothing for it but to turn back. It was a bitter experience and those who remained lost all their confidence about venturing across the Atlantic in search of a better life. A good number were monoglot Welsh speakers brought up in the Welsh Independent tradition and it was important for them to stay together. A message was sent to their Calvinistic minister, the Rev. John Roberts (1767–1834), who exerted considerable influence and his support was important.

In 1802 the Welsh Independents decided that they wanted a spiritual home and managed to acquire a small house in Cavendish Street. Although there were only fifteen members originally, that was the beginning of the denomination in Liverpool. They had sufficient faith to call the Rev. John Jones from Ceirchiog (County Oak) in the heart of the Anglesey countryside to come and minister to them. He was full of passion, a great communicator and his powerful ministry bore fruit. Within nine months there were so many worshippers in Cavendish Street on a Sunday that there was not enough room. They bought a chapel which was for sale in Edmund Street, a poor area with many Roman Catholics living in the hovels round about, and the minister stayed with them until 1813 when he was called to Talgarth in Breconshire. There he continued his ministry until his death in 1845.

Flock without a shepherd

After his departure, the flock was without a shepherd for four years. But they were lucky that the principal of one of the denomination's academies in Wrexham, the very able Calvinistic theologian George Lewis (1703–1822), thought the world of the Liverpool's Welsh Independents. He had seriously considered emigrating to the United States when he was a minister in Llanuwchllyn; however in 1815 he received two invitations, one from Edmund Street Chapel, Liverpool, and the other from the Independents' chapel at Llanfyllin. Accepting the call to Liverpool would mean moving the academy to Liverpool – something which was not acceptable to the London Congregational Board – but on the other hand it was perfectly prepared for him and the academy to move to Llanfyllin. This is what was said of the support the Welsh Independents of Liverpool enjoyed in Wales:

> Liverpool Independents had ardent supporters in Wales, none more so than a family from Caernarfon, a father and two sons. The father was John Griffith (1752–1818), who ministered for twenty-two years in Caernarfon. But he supported his son John Griffith the younger (1799–1872) to travel regularly to preach, especially when he was ministering in Manchester and later in Buckley. The youngest son, William Griffith (1801–81), travelled regularly from Holyhead, where he lived all his life, to preach to the Independents in the city. Indeed, he received an invitation to Liverpool but preferred to stay in Holyhead where he lived out his life of goodness.

There are others who also came, most often because their children were living in Liverpool. That is the main reason that we come across the name of the Rev. John Hughes, the minister of Dinas Mawddwy in Merionethshire. His son William Hughes lived in Basnett Street.

Building Tabernacle Chapel

By 1817 the Independents were able to set about building a fine new chapel called Tabernacle in Great Crosshall Street and succeeded in attracting one of the followers of the Rev. John Roberts, namely the Rev. John Breese, as minister. He was originally from Llanbrynmair and many of the congregation knew all about him, his family and his background. He was a good choice as he came from the same theological standpoint as John Roberts, that is moderate Calvinism. When Roberts published the volume *Galwad Difrifol* (A Serious Calling) in 1820, he invited six of his theological followers to contribute to it and John Breese was one of those. Breese worked amazingly hard and would walk regularly from Liverpool to Manchester and back – a distance of sixty-five miles – so that he could keep an eye on the Welsh Independents in that city too. When he moved in 1835 from the Tabernacle to the chapel in Heol Awst in Carmarthen, he was suffering from exhaustion and his health continued to be poor until his death in 1843.

Among those early Independents there were some memorable characters like the precentor Sion (John) Jones. He and Sion Edwards, the tailor, were great friends. Thomas Lloyd was a man who ploughed his own furrow but because he was so hard-working, he received support from many of the other leaders. His deputy was James Dowding. Richard Jones was another unique character. With David Thomas, he was responsible for heating the early chapels. At this time there were five coal yards at the far end of Old Hall Street and all sold coal in one-ton sacks apart from Mr Clark, who was prepared to sell by the hundredweight. Richard Jones was the man responsible for filling and weighing the sacks. He spent every day from Monday morning to Saturday evening at the task and, at the end of his week, would travel to Edmund Street to kindle the fire for the weekly meetings.

In addition he, Dafydd Thomas and Thomas Llwyd would spend a good hour every Sunday morning before the service, as well as an hour in the afternoon before Sunday school, knocking on doors to remind people of the arrangements for them and their children – first in Cavendish Street, then in Edmund Street and later still in Great Crosshall Street.

The families who refused on a Sunday would get another invitation during the week to come to what was called 'the ABC meeting' where they learned Welsh. The main reason for failing to turn up on a Sunday was often the lack of respectable clothing, but during the week the majority would take advantage of the resources available to help them read and write. A high proportion of Liverpool Welsh could read neither Welsh nor English, and it became a great crusade among the chapels and churches to teach them the rudiments of both languages.

'Williams Y Wern', silver trumpet of the Independents

After the ministry of John Breese, the Welsh Independents managed to persuade one of the most notable preachers of the day to come to the Old Tabernacle, namely William Williams of Y Wern, near the mining village of

Rhosllanerchrugog. He had known poverty in his childhood as severe as many of his countrymen in the Liverpool slums. This dated back to his early years in a smallholding called Cwmhyswyn Ganol, Llanfachreth, Merionethshire. Inspired by hearing the gospel in a service at Beddycoediw Farmhouse, he was supported to go to Wrexham Academy and was ordained in two nearby chapels, Y Wern and Harwd. There, apart from three years in Liverpool, he remained until his death in March 1840.

The Liverpool Welsh loved the great preacher, his face sparkling with pride, amusement and mischief. He did not have the oratorical skills of John Elias, another who was often to be seen on the streets of Liverpool at this time, but with his deep, quiet voice, he was able to speak clearly and in a colourful way to his congregation. As the historian, the Rev. Dr R Tudur Jones, noted:

> No raving, no thumping the pulpit, no breast-beating. Just speaking extremely strongly and directly to the hearts and minds of men.

The Revival of 1839

Williams Y Wern left Liverpool at an exciting time as the Welsh Independents experienced a period of fervent religious revival. This was in 1839 and the medium was Benjamin William Chidlaw who had emigrated with his family from Bala to America in 1822 and had come back to visit his beloved Merionethshire. He lit the flame in Liverpool among his fellow Welshmen and it spread instantly to the quarry village of Deiniolen, then to Llanuwchllyn and from there to south Wales. He gave new confidence to the Welsh Independents of Liverpool. The combination of Williams and the 1839 Revival paved the way for more great preachers to settle in the port, not just for three years but often for three decades or more.

The charm of Thomas Charles and his greatest disciple

One of the most important figures in the campaign to educate the Welsh in writing and reading was Thomas Charles of Bala. He was primarily responsible for establishing the Welsh Sunday schools movement for both adults and children. It was he who, in May 1806, on his return from a meeting of the working committee of the London Missionary Society, emphasised the need for a day school in Pall Mall. The main purpose for his visit was to open a second Calvinistic Methodist chapel in Bedford Street. He preached three times on that occasion, once in Welsh and twice in English.

His chief disciple was Peter Jones, better remembered now as Pedr Fardd. Welsh people were now making their homes in streets far from the area around Pall Mall, Old Hall Street and Edmund Street – the Welsh town as it had been known. Now they were to be found in New Bird Street and New Ormond Street, and so the Calvinistic Methodists rented a meeting room in Jamaica Street, albeit against the advice of the Pall Mall leaders. Jamaica Street in 1803 was right on the edge of town and beyond it were fields and a few houses and farms. But, on 26 May 1806, Thomas Charles was delighted to be opening the second chapel in Bedford Street and, in a letter to his friend Mrs Astle, he says: 'In Liverpool, the congregation is huge. Thousands come each time. There's a great increase among the Welsh.'

The following year Charles's day school opened, with Peter Jones at the helm teaching Welsh, English and history, which he continued to do for twenty-three years.

A Welsh charity school

In Russell Street there was a Welsh charity school. It was opened on St David's Day 1804, to the considerable rejoicing of scores of poor Welsh families, and was one of the early 'ragged schools', caring for children who were without warm, clean clothing. The children were provided with food and clothes and were mainly taught the alphabet to help them learn to read. Apprenticeships were to be had as well and the school was supported by voluntary contributions. The charity's patron was King George III himself.

In 1823 another house was bought next to the Welsh Anglican Church of St David so that a school for girls could be established. The schools were under the care of trustees including a treasurer and a secretary. By 1823 and 1824 there were 314 boys and ninety-one girls in their care. The average cost for educating one child for a whole year was twelve shillings. The first teacher of the boys was the Welshman Thomas Roberts. He was a good disciplinarian, able to keep the children contented under his tutelage. The first headmistress was Isabella Hill, also able to keep order, sensitive and well versed in her Welsh. This advert for the school appeared in the *Liverpool Courier* on 6 January 1808:

> All parents who wish to obtain admittance for their children into the above institution must attend the school in Russell Street on Tuesday at twelve o'clock when applications for admission will be received.

The school proved a great blessing to that section of the Welsh community living in poverty and hunger, and it is not surprising that the Irish copied the Welsh and established a similar school in the same street, which is today to be found behind the car park near the Adelphi Hotel. The Russell Street school depended heavily on two individuals, Owen Williams and Owen Jones, both of whom regularly visited the children, counselled them and supported them and the staff. Every St David's Day, each child was expected to recite a piece of scripture to them both.

We do not know anything about Owen Jones but Owen Williams and his son and grandson were extremely important to Liverpool. The son was the politician Owen Hugh Williams, who was widely admired. He refused the chance to be lord mayor of the city because he felt that his real work was to care for those who had elected him, not to spend valuable time in unending gatherings. The grandson was the lawyer and ship merchant Owen Harrison Williams.

Early Welsh societies

The Liverpool Welsh had a good number of societies in the early years of the nineteenth century. A number were established to care for the Welsh in sickness and poverty and to celebrate Welsh culture and especially, of course, St David's Day. The societies which received the support of the Welsh Anglicans in Liverpool were the Cambrian Druid and the Loyal and Honourable Society of Ancient Britons, first established in London in 1715. Every year, on St David's Day, these Welsh societies would join in a procession through the streets of Liverpool – as they did in London – carrying the Red Dragon flag. Everyone was sure to have a leek in his cap or on his lapel. The *Liverpool Advertiser* for 27 February 1804 noted:

This anniversary will be celebrated at Mr Lilliman's, the Liverpool Arms Hotel, on Thursday 1 March, where the Ancient Britons will be happy to meet their friends and the well-wishers to the Institution at 10 a.m. to accompany them to St Paul's Church, where a sermon will be preached on the occasion by the Rev. Lewis Pughe MA. Dinner on the table at four o'clock.

The Welsh would celebrate throughout the day and, interestingly, their inspiration came from the Anglicans rather than the Nonconformists. We have seen how important Lewis Pugh was to the Welsh community and also noted the contribution of St Paul's Anglican Church. Lilliman's Hotel, too, was an important meeting place and frequently attended by members of the Ancient Society of Britons.

Liverpool's first Welsh Anglican church

The Prince of Wales, later George IV, visited Liverpool in 1806 and gave fifty guineas to the Welsh Anglican community towards a fund to build St David's Church. But it took the Welsh Anglicans at least twenty years to bring the plan to fruition. There was considerable discussion about where the new church should be located. Should it be built in Russell Street, where there was already provision for poor Welsh children, or at the same location as the Scottish Presbyterian church in Oldham Street, within a stone's throw of Renshaw Street, one of the main streets of the town?

In January 1825 Liverpool Corporation donated a wedge of land, 1,161 square yards in size, on Brownlow Hill and donated £60 a year towards the cost of maintaining a ministry there. The foundation stone was laid in September 1826 and there is a description of the ceremony which took place on 15 September with the Bishop of Chester, the mayor, the town leaders and prominent Liverpool Welsh present. Through the efforts of politicians Robert Peel and Lord Kenyon, the local committee had received a further grant of £500 from the king. A special trowel was used for the event and was inscribed with the words:

This trowel was used by the Rt Rev. Charles James Bloomfield DD, Lord Bishop of Chester, at the laying of the foundation stone of the Welsh Church of St David, Liverpool, and presented to his Lordship by the Trustees of the Church,

15 September 1826. 'He loveth our nation and hath built a synagogue.' (Luke: Chapter 7, verse 5)

Dr Bloomfield was not the only English person to support the Welsh. The Rev. David Hewitt was English by birth but mastered Welsh in nine months and became a leader in Welsh society. He is the first Welsh learner we know about among the Liverpool Welsh, though many were to follow his example over the years.

Rose Place Chapel

Around that time the Calvinistic Methodists decided to establish a branch under the mother church of Pall Mall in the Baptist chapel in Great Crosshall Street. A suitable place was sought to the north of Conus Street on the corner of Rose Place. Robert Jones of Rhoslan disapproved. He wrote to his second son Samuel to say so:

> I am of the opinion that two chapels in Liverpool would be better than three, one big one in the most convenient place and Bedford as a chapel of ease.

But it made no impression on people like Thomas Hughes, as he was determined to have another chapel. It was he who planned it and he worked on it every moment he could:

> He could be seen there at his carpenter's bench, in his shirtsleeves, from six o'clock in the morning until six in the evening and preaching more often than not three times on the Sabbath.

He carved the pulpit with his own hands: this being the most important item in the plain chapel which held 700 people. Thomas Hughes won the day and nobody was prouder to see the chapel open on Good Friday, 24 March 1826. The preachers were Henry Rees of Shrewsbury and James Hughes (Iago Trichrug) from London. The chapel's cellar became a very useful and important place, especially when another school was opened for the Welsh under the care of Owen Brown, a Welshman getting on in years but an excellent teacher. He was very successful, and when the cellar became too small for all the children who flocked there, they set about collecting money to buy another big house in Prince Edward Street for the Welsh school.

The impact of the Wesleyan Welsh Methodists

We must remember that the Welsh Wesleyans were also an important part of the Liverpool story and we know how those Methodists supported the Welsh in Pitt Street during that time.

Their mission dates from about 1791, and the man who lit the flame was Evan Roberts. He, along with William Lewis and Richard Davies, hired a small room in Midghall Street in Vauxhall for their meetings. In 1803 the Methodist Church decided to send a Welsh preacher by the name of John Bryan to nurture the cause in Midghall Street and to attract more to attend the fellowship. When he arrived there were sixty members at the most but, within three weeks, he succeeded in winning another forty Welsh converts. Within a year, the sixty had increased to 200 and this gave them the confidence to buy Maguire Street Chapel. There the Welsh Wesleyan Methodists stayed until 1813, when they secured the Unitarians' old chapel at Benn's Gardens. There had been a chapel there from 1727 and it was re-opened with much rejoicing as the Welsh chapel on 22 November 1813. The Welsh Methodists bore witness there until August 1860.

Religion and radicalism

By the end of the 1820s the Welsh were looking after their successful enterprises, their language, their culture, education for their children and for the children of the disadvantaged in their midst; they were establishing societies and extending invitations to ministers to share their zeal and learning with them. To some, like Robert Jones of Rhoslan, the structure the chapels provided kept the Welsh out of trouble. For him, and other political leaders of the time, the advice was simple: Behave yourself and keep away from any form of radicalism. It is not easy to translate into English the unique style of Robert Jones:

> ... with the Sunday Schools' teaching and reading the Word ... they are educating and training young people and others in the real principles of the faith as well as

the duties relating to God and man, and thus and with the seal of the Lord upon them, our nation was saved from the destructive plague of godlessness and revolt against the government. Oh Wales, hold on to what you have so that nobody takes away your crown.

Chapter 4

Missionary vision of the faithful immigrants

Preachers of every denomination who came to Liverpool had a profound effect on the Welsh there, and in the 1830s and '40s two movements began to exert a large influence – the temperance movement and the missionary movement.

The temperance movement

Liverpool had more than enough venues for hard drinking and the Welsh were among those tempted daily into the world of the tavern. However, there is no mention of chapels preparing *cwrw'r achos* (beer for the cause) for visiting preachers to enjoy with their Sunday dinner as they often did in Wales.

The Temperance Society was formed in 1832 with the aim of emphasising the virtues of abstinence. Beer could be drunk but whisky and gin should be avoided. Many, like Robert Herbert Williams (Corfanydd) of Basnett Street, felt the message should be much more forceful. His Society for Total Abstinence was the first of its sort to be formed, not just among the Liverpool Welsh but in Wales generally. At the end of one of his meetings he managed to collect five names in the Pall Mall vestry. Of those, we must note that of Owen Edwards of Williamson Square – one of the visionaries of the Welsh settlement in Patagonia. By the time of the society's first anniversary in March 1836, 122 Welsh people had signed the pledge.

But, at that anniversary, there was a debate as to whether to follow the path of temperance or total abstinence. John Hughes, the first to sign up, argued forcefully for abstinence, while the Rev. Richard Williams rose to say that he and his wife Mari (the daughter of Calvinistic minister Thomas Hughes) would take a glass of beer with their supper each evening at 17 Standish Street. In his innocence he asked of the chairman: 'What should we do about that?' and the response, within seconds, was, 'Put it aside at once, Mr Williams!' And thus began the Temperance Revival in the Liverpool Welsh community which, within a short time, spread to every part of Wales.

By 1837 there were seven temperance societies at Liverpool churches and two across the River Mersey among the Welsh of Seacombe and Birkenhead. By 1839 membership of the Rose Place Calvinistic Methodist Temperance Society was 900, that of Pall Mall Chapel 803, Bedford Street Chapel 630 and Oil Street Chapel 155. There was not the same fervour across the Mersey, with only thirty signing the pledge in Birkenhead and fifty-four in Seacombe. Throughout the century, up until the middle of the twentieth century, there were strong leaders at the helm of the movement, none more effective than the talented Welsh Independent minister, Dr John Thomas of Liverpool – historian, politician, author, editor and first-class preacher.

Women, too, played a vital role. The Abstinence Society of the Sisters of Rose Place was a first among the Liverpool Welsh, but also the first of scores of similar movements in every denomination. And we should remember, too, that it was the Liverpool Welsh churches under the leadership of John Roberts of Hope Street, later MP for Flint Boroughs and also an elder at Princes Road Calvinistic Methodist Church, which brought about the campaign in 1879 for the closure of public houses in Wales on Sundays. This became a reality in the Sunday Closing (Wales) Act of Public Houses in 1881.

The next generation carry the banner

By 1830 the second generation of Liverpool Welsh had inherited the convictions, organisation, language and culture of their parents and there are two excellent examples of this. First is John Roberts (known in Welsh circles as Minimus), the second son of Richard Roberts, a ship's chandler in the town.

After leaving school he followed his father into the same trade, but his main interest was the Bedford Street Welsh Calvinistic Methodist Church where, as a young man of only nineteen, he was elected an elder. There was a group of similarly enthusiastic young men who met at least weekly for fellowship. One of them, David Roberts of Llanrwst, became one of the most prominent wood merchants in the town in the Victorian era and fell in love with John Roberts's sister.

Another was Josiah Hughes, born on 4 March 1804, son of the strict teetotaller John Hughes and his wife Martha, of Mansfield Street, Islington. Josiah was fired by missionary vision and, after ordination in the Congregationalist English Church in Great George Street on 18 February 1830, he became the first Welshman of the town to offer himself as a missionary. However, the London Missionary Society opposed his chosen destination of India, but he won the blessing of the Rev. John Elias of Anglesey and of the Liverpool Welsh Calvinists. His journey was arduous, with the ship letting in water all the way from Liverpool to Madras. It took him seven months to reach Malacca, where he performed good works until his sudden death in the community from cholera on 25 November 1840.

A break with the London Missionary Society

In Malacca, Josiah Hughes became friendly with Jacob Tomlin and, by 1836, they had both broken their links with the London Missionary Society. Tomlin and his family left Malacca in 1836 and, on their way back to Liverpool, made a detour to visit the Khasi Hills in north-eastern India. He was there for nine months and his impressions were published later in *Missionary Journals and Letters* (1844). When he arrived back in Liverpool, the London Missionary Society continued to resist the attempts of two other Welshmen who wanted to go as missionaries to India.

One of them, Thomas Jones (1810–49), had been brought up in Liverpool and was now among the early students of Bala Theological College. The London Missionary Society decided he should consider South Africa as his field of work. He agreed, but then changed his mind. India was his first choice and he had supporters in Liverpool, some remembering both him and his family. Having failed to convince the Society, he returned to Liverpool on 28 January 1840 and went to see his long-time friend John Roberts (Minimus). He put him in touch with John Hughes (Josiah's father) of Mansfield Street, and a public meeting was arranged in the vestry of Rose Place Chapel for

Friday evening, 31 January 1840, under the direction of the well-loved preacher Henry Rees.

At this historic meeting, Henry Rees had no option but to propose the creation of a missionary society for the Calvinistic Methodists of Wales.

Pioneers of the Liverpool Foreign Missionary Society

Richard Williams (1802–42) was minister of Rose Place, Mulberry Street, and a zealous man – a cousin to radical reformer Samuel Roberts of Llanbrynmair and one who warrants a place as one of the founders of the Welsh Calvinistic Methodist Foreign Missionary Society (now known as the Foreign Mission of the Presbyterian Church of Wales). He was the first chair of its executive committee, and the treasurer was David Lewis (1808–76), a notable banker in the town. A native of Carmarthenshire, he came to Liverpool as a young man and stayed in the town all his life, becoming a very influential figure. In 1834, when he was only twenty-six, he was chosen to be an elder at Rose Place. He was especially effective at organising fundraising appeals and did this regularly. More often than not, he would finish his skilful appeal with the call, in English, for 'a long pull together'. He was an officer of the society from its inception in 1840 until his retirement in 1873. He and his wife also brought up two of the most powerful Welsh Presbyterian ministers of the Victorian era, the Rev. Dr W Dickens Lewis and the Rev. Thomas Phillips Lewis.

Another pioneer, mentioned earlier, was David Roberts (1805–86) a native of Llanrwst, one of the most famous elders in nineteenth-century Liverpool. He and his son, John Roberts MP, and the rest of his family were fervent about mission work and he was the treasurer of the fund for helping infirm Welsh missionaries, widows and orphans in north-east India.

Among the vice-presidents of the missionary society we find the name of David Davies, Mount Gardens, as his door was always open to welcome young men from Wales visiting Liverpool. Some of these, such as Owen Thomas of Bangor (who later became a minister in Liverpool) and John Parry of the Manchester Welsh, were studying at Edinburgh, and when they needed assistance they called on the generous elder David Davies and his daughter, Miss Anne Jane Davies, later of Bedford Street, who did a huge amount of work for poor Welsh people and for the mission in India.

The builder Owen Elias of Anglesey was among the pioneers but, due to his success as a builder, he is mentioned in another chapter. Another missionary pioneer was John Lloyd, who came to Liverpool in 1800 and, within a few years, the widower entered his second marriage to the widow of John Caius, who kept the chapel-house in Pall Mall. He came to be known as John Lloyd Chapel-House and his home was a meeting place for most of the ministers who came to Pall Mall Chapel in Liverpool over the weekend.

There were two William Joneses among those who supported the missionary endeavours. One was known as William Jones the Machine because of his occupation, which was looking after weighing machines. He was elected an elder in Bedford Street Chapel in 1827. When John Elias of Anglesey visited the town, he was asked for his advice on his friend – they both came from Eifionydd originally. He replied: 'He is very zealous: he needs something to do. Make him an elder!' He suffered a lot of ill health in the latter part of his life and, to his great disappointment, had to move from Liverpool to his daughter's home in Tavistock, Devon, where he died on 20 August 1846.

The other was William Jones of Berry Street, a very valuable officer at Bedford Street Chapel and the only one elected in 1839. Originally from the village of Treuddyn, near Mold, he was a pharmacist and very different from the flamboyant William Jones the Machine. He was always quiet and rather a placid Christian. He died in 1885.

In the same chapel in 1843, another of the pioneers was elected elder, John Jones of Thackeray Street. He came from a well-known family. His father was the great-grandson of Joseph Jones of Seiniad, Ruthin, one of the first Calvinistic Methodist preachers in north Wales and one of the supporters of Howell Harris at the time of the schism with his co-reformer, Daniel Rowland of Llangeitho, between 1750 and 1763. The great-grandson Joseph Jones had been an elder in two churches before his time in Liverpool – in Mold and in Llyn y Pandy – and he was an elder in Bedford Street until his death in 1836. His son by his first wife was John Jones of Thackeray Street, and he was father to one of the leaders of public life in Liverpool for decades, Alderman Joseph Harrison Jones. A school in the Paddington area of Liverpool was named after the alderman but its buildings have disappeared now and there is no physical record of the huge contribution he made to civic life.

There was no-one more passionate than John Hughes of Mansfield Street. He was from Abergele and came to Liverpool at the end of the eighteenth century. By 1813 he was among the elders at Pall Mall Chapel and, when another chapel was set up in Rose Place, he moved there as leader. According to the Rev. Dr Owen Thomas, he had more natural theological ability than most of his contemporaries, and when he spoke in any meeting his address and observations were equal to those of the most prominent ministers, such as Henry Rees and John Hughes. He brought up two sons who devoted their lives – one as a missionary and the other as an evangelist. He died on 26 January 1843 and was buried in the churchyard at Low Hill, his friend Henry Rees officiating.

In the same street as John Hughes – Mansfield Street – there lived another Welshman inspired by the missionary vision. He was Robert Pierce, who was born in Liverpool in 1807 and was a friend and contemporary of Josiah Hughes. Pierce's priority was Rose Place Chapel and later the foreign missions. His wife was sister to Rice Price, another of the Rose Place Chapel elders. Pierce had better educational opportunities in Liverpool than the rest of his contemporaries and became a very successful merchant. He made a fortune, retired to a fine house called Tŷ Agored on the outskirts of Mold, and died an untimely death in 1856 aged only forty-nine.

There were five other generous and supportive pioneers worthy of mention: Edward Price Hughes (Mill Street), talkative and full of good humour; Benjamin Williams (Whitechapel), whose hero among the ministers was the Rev. John Hughes of The Mount off Hope Street; Thomas Morris (Lord Street), a native of Cardiganshire; Owen Griffiths, about whom unfortunately we know only his name, and Matthew Jones, the most important of the five.

It is he who should be remembered for setting up Hygeia Street Sunday school, from which later sprang the Lombard Street Calvinistic Methodist Chapel (later Newsham Park Welsh Calvinistic Methodist Chapel). He was appointed by the Liverpool Presbytery as supervisor of its mission stations in Widnes, Wigan, St Helens, Earlestown and Southport, which he often visited and provided the pulpits with ordained preachers or lay preachers or young ministerial students on Sundays. He supported a host of young men in Liverpool to consider the Christian ministry as a vocation and career, and eight of these disciples responded positively. Among the Liverpool Welsh they were known as the disciples of Matthew Jones, the coal merchant from the streets of Islington.

Preparing for the mission

After incorporating the Foreign Missionary Society, the next step was to choose a mission field and they began a correspondence with the Rev. Dr John Wilson, an Anglican missionary who, for a while, corresponded with John Hughes (father of Josiah Hughes). Dr Wilson exhorted the mission to work in northern Gujarat.

The young missionary Thomas Jones wanted to spread the word in the area around Allahabad, in the northern territories, in particular in the North-Western Provinces. But the deciding factor, based on the experience of Jacob Tomlin, who had been there himself and now lived in Wavertree, Liverpool, was the climate in the hills. Another factor was that John Roberts (Minimus) and his father were on very good terms with the shipping company, Messrs J B Yates of King Street. This was a well-known company in the port of Liverpool and they were owners of ships such as *The Jamaica*. She was due to sail to Calcutta in November 1840 and they were prepared to give Thomas Jones and his bride Anne a passage for £50 less than the going rate, according to the historian J Hughes Morris. The outcome of extensive debate in Liverpool and at the North Wales Associations in Pwllheli (9 and 10 September 1840) and Dolgellau (21 and 22 October 1840) was that, despite the opposition of the pulpit giant John Elias, dubbed by his detractors 'the Pope of Anglesey', the arguments of the Rev. Richard Williams and Minimus prevailed.

Still working in the world of ships, Minimus volunteered to be the unpaid secretary for the Liverpool Welsh Calvinistic Methodist Missionary Society on its formation. He was totally wedded to the work and nothing was too much for him. His home was always open to put up missionaries before they left the port of Liverpool for India, or when they returned home on leave. Roberts and his family were immensely kind.

But towards 1860 the relationship between him and his colleagues in Liverpool soured. He moved to live outside Mold but continued the work for the missionary society until 1866 when he finally broke his link, to the great distress of his brother-in-law David Roberts of Hope Street and Abergele. He moved to Edinburgh, where he became the secretary of The Lord's Day Observance Society for the whole of Scotland. He died in Edinburgh on 6 January 1880 and hundreds turned out as his body was taken from his home to the railway station on his journey back to Liverpool. On the Friday morning there was a service in Princes Road Chapel, and he was buried in St James's Cemetery with a memorable tribute from the lips of Dr Owen Thomas. His hymns, such as *Bywha dy waith, O! Arglwydd Mawr* (Revive your Work, O Great Lord), are still sung, and his vital contribution to the vision was recognised in Liverpool on Wednesday evening, 14 November 1840, when a packed Rose Place Chapel gathered to wish the young missionaries *bon voyage*.

Farewell to two brave missionaries

A new hymn by Pedr Fardd was sung at that service for Thomas Jones and his wife Anne as they left for India. The words express the missionary zeal of the time, a zeal which took root among the Liverpool Welsh who did everything in their power to wish the first two missionaries well – and indeed every other one who sailed from the port for the next 130 years. Crowds gathered on 25 November 1840 to see *The Jamaica* under Captain John Johnson leaving for Calcutta. The couple had a long, disagreeable and stormy voyage and Anne was sick almost every day for the five months. Thomas Jones performed wonders in Cherrapunji and the hills, put the faith on a firm footing, opened schools and managed to get David Davies, of Seel Street, Liverpool; John Roberts (Minimus) and the Rev. William Hughes of Wrexham, a minister who came regularly to Liverpool, to meet all the building costs.

Daniel Jones follows Thomas Jones to north-east India

Another missionary who, like Thomas Jones, fell victim to the harsh conditions was Daniel Jones (1813–46), the son of the hymnwriter and teacher Edward Jones (1761–1836) of the small farmstead of Maesyplwm, in the Vale of

Clwyd. Before sailing from Liverpool, he went to see his old home, and found it in ruins. That was the experience of many an exile both in Liverpool and elsewhere – he was one of thirteen children who left the village of Prion in the Vale of Clwyd.

On 10 September 1845 he travelled with his wife Anne (née Evans) from Wrexham to Liverpool to attend a meeting called at Bedford Street Chapel to wish them well. The ship, *Cordelia*, under the captaincy of Enos Hughes, a Welshman from Birkenhead, failed to sail until 13 September and the following week at sea was a rough one. They saw the hills of Khasi on 21 February 1846, five months after leaving Bedford Street.

Daniel Jones soon contracted jungle fever and died on 2 December 1846, aged thirty-three. At the same time, his wife gave birth to a daughter who died soon after and the body of the little one was placed in the same coffin as that of her father.

Reasons for risking your life

There was great grief in Liverpool when John Roberts (Minimus) heard the news at the beginning of 1847, but no-one from the executive committee thought for a moment that they should refrain from sending more young people there. It is worth asking what drove the pioneers and the missionaries to face such sacrifice. There are a number of reasons.

We cannot forget how important India was in the life of the Liverpool Welsh. This was the jewel of the British Empire and Thomas Jones preferred to go to India than to South Africa. Indeed, it was on the issue of the mission field that he decided to break his link with the London Missionary Society. William Williams of Pantycelyn was very fond of writing in his hymns about India, and considered going there as a medical missionary in the 1730s – and his missionary hymns were very influential.

Every one of the Welsh missionaries came from religious homes with chapelgoing parents, many of them in positions of leadership. Some were children of the manse and Dr R Arthur Hughes (1910–96), son of a minister born and brought up in Liverpool, admitted that he 'wanted to repay the Christian faith for what he had experienced in his home life'. This motivated others too.

Then there was the chapel, the minister and leaders. The warmth, fervour and numerous activities of the chapels spurred young people on. Religious experiences, in particular the religious revivals of 1859, 1882 and 1904–05, reinforced young men and women in their conviction to accept the huge challenge.

The importance of the Liverpool Welsh in the missionary movement was extremely important. Many a significant missionary was raised in the Liverpool chapels and we can take two examples to demonstrate this. Edward Hugh Williams (1865–1962) was a missionary in India for fifty-five years. He was born at 25 Premier Street, Everton, on 2 September 1865, the son of Owen Williams (1834–1908) and Elinor (1834–1907), both originally from Anglesey. He was raised in the new Calvinistic Methodist chapel in Fitzclarence Street, Everton, and educated at St Saviour's School until he was thirteen, when he went to work in the office of the Welshman John Thomas, a stockbroker in Sweeting Street. He later worked in the office of Dodd and Oulton, and from there went to his uncles' company, Thomas Brothers of Hornby Street, before finding work in the Sun Foundry with Messrs Smith in Dale Street. He was moved to the company's headquarters in Glasgow and became involved in the work of the United Presbyterian Church in Renfield Street. There he heard the Rev. James Gray of Rajputana, India, appealing for a missionary. Within a month he told the chapel minister of his desire to serve the Universal Church in India. He moved back to Liverpool in February 1885 to his uncle Henry Williams's office at 10 Conyers Street, Kirkdale, and started going to Latin and Greek evening classes at Mount Pleasant. He was accepted into Bala Theological College in 1891 and was ordained a minister before leaving for India. He sailed from Liverpool on 23 September 1893 on the *City of Corinth* and reached Calcutta on 24 October. By the beginning of November, he was installed in Shelta mission station.

He worked with great energy and without fear among the Mikir tribe. He was a country doctor in the real sense of the term and, as one of his co-missionaries, Gwilym Angell Jones, said of him: 'Many of the babies of Khasi and Jaintia slid smoothly into this old world through his ministry and his black bag.' He returned from India in 1947 and went to live in Ravenhill, an area on the outskirts of Swansea.

Another example is the Rev. Dr Hugh Gordon Roberts (1885–1961) who, according to the Welsh scholar R M Jones, was 'one of Wales's greatest sons'. His father, David Roberts, was an elder in the Welsh Presbyterian Church in Catharine Street, Liverpool, and came from a large family of doctors associated with an area known as Mynydd y Gof not far from Holyhead on Anglesey. Gordon Roberts was privately educated, and after leaving Liverpool College became an accountant. In 1905 he heard the revivalist Evan Roberts preaching in Liverpool. This was the hour of decision. He set his sights on missionary work, and urged on by his father went to follow a medical course at Liverpool University. He graduated in 1912 and was appointed surgeon at the Women's Hospital. His fiancée Katie (née Jones) was a member of the same chapel in Catharine Street Presbyterian Church of Wales and they were married in 1913 before leaving for the Khasi Hills. He campaigned to build a Welsh Mission Hospital which was opened in 1922. He put £2,000 of his own money towards building the hospital and another £2,000 from his salary as a surgeon during the First World War towards buying resources for it. Dr Roberts was the superintendent, chief physician and surgeon and the hospital became an object of admiration in Shillong and among the social and political leaders in Assam territory. It is little wonder that, in 1946, he was given a doctorate with honours by the University of Wales in recognition of his huge contribution towards meeting the medical needs of those living in the Khasi Hills. He retired in 1953 after seeing another hospital built under his oversight in Jowai. His successor was another surgeon associated with Liverpool, Dr R Arthur Hughes, rightly called the 'Schweitzer of Assam'.

Finally, we should mention the effects of missionary visits and the urging of missionary secretaries. Visits by missionaries were keenly anticipated when they came back on furlough and there were always meetings to hear about their work. At the General Assembly of the Welsh Presbyterian Church in Aberystwyth in 1866, the Rev. Josiah Thomas (1830–1905) was appointed successor to Minimus. He moved from Bangor to Liverpool, and the missionary society, which had until then been fairly unexceptional, became a very strong and useful witness within Welsh Nonconformity. Josiah Thomas was moving to a town where his brothers, Dr Owen Thomas, Dr John Thomas and the temperance campaigner William Thomas, were exceptionally hard-working. Josiah Thomas remained in the office for thirty-four years and was followed, in 1900, by the Rev. Robert John Williams (1857–1933) who was there for another thirty-one years. He, too, did great work as secretary and took great pride in the missionaries' work.

Women form the mission's backbone

The greater part of the support and organisation for the missionary vision depended on Liverpool Welsh Calvinistic Methodists. A builder called James Hughes, a member of Bedford Street Church responsible for several grand houses in Devonshire Road and Princes Road, built a little street off Mann Street near the riverside and called it Khasi (Khassia) Place in memory of the first mission. The street has disappeared now.

But the outstanding contribution came from the sisters of the various chapels. By 1881, through the zeal of two women steeped in its history and workings, there was formed the Women's Missionary Committee of the Merseyside Presbyterian Chapels. The women were ably led by Mary Roberts of 63 Hope Street, the daughter of builder and timber merchant David Roberts, as well as Annie Davies, daughter of David Davies of Seel Street and later Mount Gardens. The committee's task was to inspire women and children with missionary work and, before long, fourteen missionary sisters' societies were set up in Liverpool and its district. There would be regular executive committees, with an opportunity to read the letters sent by missionary wives or visitors to the mission field in north-east India, or Assam as it was also called. The committee carried out worthy and important work, collecting the unbelievable sum of £11,579-17-10 in its first thirty years. By the first decade of the twentieth century, the Liverpool sisters had collected an eighth of the amount collected by the whole denomination. Not surprisingly, the Rev. R J Williams noted that the women of the Liverpool Welsh Calvinistic Methodist chapels set the standard for the rest of the denomination. He was absolutely right.

Another focus of their benevolence was Dr Gordon Roberts's venture in planning a hospital. In 1920 he addressed the sisters on the need to raise money for the hospital planned for Shillong and its district. There was a special effort and, in 1920, £965-15-9 was collected, and £1,104-10-10 the following year.

Yet another example was the formation of a movement called the Linen League with the aim of supporting medical work. Each sister who belonged to the league was expected to contribute a shilling per year to the cause.

By the end of the nineteenth century, the missionary vision was a bright one. Annie Williams (1874–97), a young Liverpool Welsh woman, sailed from the port on 10 October 1896 to look after the girls' department of the Collegiate School in Shillong. She was trained at Edge Hill College, then actually located in Edge Hill and not, as today, in Ormskirk. She had an unusually dangerous voyage. She was lucky to reach Calcutta alive, and having reached Shillong had to face one of the most harrowing experiences – the great earthquake of 1897, when the Welsh mission in Assam lost all its buildings in the hills. The missionaries were in dire straits but, within a short time, Annie Williams had won the affection and loyalty of them and her fellow teachers. But her time was short. While comforting three small children with cholera, she contracted it herself. She died on 21 August 1897 after only ten months in Shillong, and her parents David and Anne Williams, members of Anfield Road Welsh Calvinistic Methodist Chapel, received the sad news from the lips of Josiah Thomas.

As John Hughes Morris (another of the Liverpool Welsh) said:

> With her death, the mission lost one of the purest characters and one of the missionaries best suited to the work that was ever in their service.

Her sacrifice inspired Liverpool to increase its support for the needs of India.

Chapter 5

The Liverpool Welsh
and poverty

Some of us who have chronicled the history of the Liverpool Welsh tend to give the impression that the Welsh succeeded beyond all expectations. While that is true for a good number who were builders and merchants in the town, it is not true of a large swathe of them.

The role of the workhouse

From 1834 the law required every large parish to provide a workhouse. Many decided to combine resources and build one as a joint venture. A workhouse, which doubled as a hospital, was built where Liverpool's Metropolitan Cathedral stands today. To save money all sorts of people, as well as the poor, were sent there – including the elderly and some disabled people. It was the responsibility of the parish where the person was born to provide support, but it was not easy to obtain.

One example was a widow called Mary Lewis, from a Welsh background and the mother of six children. Officers in Liverpool wrote to the town officials of Beaumaris several times asking for help as she wanted to set up a business keeping lodgers and sewing. A character reference in support from a cultured man called Thomas Jones, known by the bardic name Gwynedd, was enclosed. He said he knew her well, adding that she was 'a very striving, industrious, steady, persevering woman and a very worthy object of your notice and sympathetic assistance'. But the appeal fell on deaf ears. By 1835 she had been turned out of her home in Liverpool and sent back to Beaumaris.

No help in time of need

Another example is that of Sarah Williams, also living in the town centre but originally from Beaumaris. She asked Beaumaris for 'a few pounds' to help her in her time of need. Her husband was unable to work because he was sick and blind. In 1832 she sent a letter saying: 'We experience the extremes of nakedness and destruction – having scarcely the necessities of life.'

She added this warning:

> … if the requested cannot be complied with, there is no use in my husband returning to Beaumaris to preach – besides, my four children and myself must follow him and you will be good enough to provide some residence for us – for here it will be impossible for us to make a living without assistance.

She was asking for temporary help and one can see how hard it was to get any assistance.

The Irish arrive in their thousands

During the 1840s Liverpool saw huge Irish migration to the town because of the failure of the potato harvest, and thousands upon thousands left their homes for Liverpool and the USA. They were not necessarily welcomed – Edward Rushton, stipendiary magistrate, described them as belonging to three classes, 'paupers, travellers or thieves'.

According to the 1841 census there were 49,639 Irish in Liverpool, about 17.3 per cent of the population, including both Protestants and Catholics. The Irish Catholics depended heavily on the Catholic churches and, in the 1850s, a young Liverpool-born priest, Fr James Nugent, returned from Wigan. He had a vision, and with others set out to educate, seek work for, comfort and safeguard the Irish community. As he was a teetotaller by conviction, he built bridges with the teetotal Welsh and co-operated with Anglican, Unitarian and Nonconformist leaders and with other leading Welshmen for the rest of the century.

During the same period the Welsh also flocked to Liverpool and its surrounding towns in their thousands. Welsh communities were formed in Birkenhead, Wallasey, Southport, Prescott, Newton-le-Willows, Warrington, Widnes and Runcorn.

Conflict between the Welsh and Irish

The pressures of poverty and hunger came to a head in 1855 when many Irish and some poor Welsh people revolted in what became known as the Bread Riots, when there was no bread to be had in the shops. Henry Rees was greatly perturbed by the economic situation and the clashes between Irish and Welsh, and sent a letter to the theologian Dr Lewis Edwards on 19 February 1855:

> People are wandering about in search of food, breaking into shops and taking flour by force.

Sympathy for the poor

During the ministry of Rev. William Williams 'Y Wern' at Tabernacle Welsh Independent Chapel between 1837 and 1840, a society was set up under the auspices of the Sunday school to care for young people who were sick and poor. Similar societies were also set up by Bethel Welsh Independent Chapel in Park Road, Dingle, under the minister Thomas Pierce, and by the 1860s it was clear that the Welsh chapel leaders wanted everyone who could speak the language, rich as well as poor, to be identified in some way or other with the Welsh Christian community.

The great majority of the poor disregarded religion, and in the ministers' addresses for the annual chapel reports they listed the main reasons: (1) Marked indifference towards the services and other provision; (2) Lack of 'respectable' clothing due to poverty; (3) A preference for the fellowship of the taverns; (4) A long lapse in religious activity; and (5) Lack of respect for the Sabbath.

Chapel leaders realised that there was no hope of attracting these poor Welsh to attend services in the big, grand chapels where middle-class Welsh were in the majority. These Welsh, in their best clothes, did not want to sit next to Welsh folk in their smelly rags.

Building mission rooms and chapels

It was realised that a way of resolving the issue could be to build mission rooms run by the successful chapels. That is how the mission room came into being in Burlington Street, and the Welsh Urban Mission was set up in 1870. One of the leaders in this enterprise was the serious-minded Rev. Owen Thomas who moved from London to Liverpool in 1866 and, in 1870, undertook the ministry of one of the most influential of the Welsh churches – the Welsh Presbyterian Church in Princes Road, Toxteth, one of the most beautiful buildings in the whole town.

The Town Mission Committee

The first missionary appointed by the Urban Welsh Mission was Hugh Roberts of Cranmer Street, working in the Pall Mall–Cranmer Street area which, by the 1870s, was quite a poor area. In 1872 another missionary, John Owen of Bethesda, was chosen to assist him and to keep an eye on the Welsh poor in the southern part of the town. In the same year a home for Welsh women in straitened financial circumstances was opened in 127 Duke Street under the care of Mrs Anne Ellis – a way of keeping an eye on young Welsh women in the dock area, which was known as a centre for prostitution.

One of the sisters who worked hard among the Welsh poor in Liverpool was Mary Pugh (1815–98), the daughter of Llanidloes musician James Mills and his wife. Mary's brother David Henry Mills made a name for himself as a soloist and conductor in Liverpool, and he was always on hand to help his sister when she arranged concerts for the very poor. In 1843 she married the wealthy stockbroker Eliezer Pugh and the couple worked industriously in the mission room in Kent Square and among young Welsh girls who came to Liverpool.

Welsh prostitutes and their customers

In the 1850s the two local papers, the *Liverpool Mercury* and the *Liverpool Courier*, made frequent mention of Welsh prostitutes. On 31 October 1851, one John Jones, a sailor, found himself in a house in Banastre Street where he lost ten shillings. It was reported that he was:

> … a simple, innocent-looking Welshman… [who] then related his unvarnished tale in broken English. He had arrived in town on Wednesday by one of the Welsh steamers, and in the evening had been at the Railway Hotel in Tithebarn Street.

He was afraid that the guesthouse would be too expensive and went out to look for somewhere cheaper, and that is how he came across the prostitute known as Maria Roberts. She and her master, Michael Cunningham, saw their chance of extracting some easy money and, having got him into her bed, she put her hand into his trousers and found ten shillings. It is likely that John Jones was playing the respectable and appealing Welshman to further his case. Maria Roberts was jailed for two months.

Four years later, a respectable Welshman called Thomas Jenkins lost £1-10 in Preston Street after going there at the invitation of a prostitute called Maria Dismond. Jenkins was studying for the Anglican priesthood at St Aidan's College, Birkenhead. During the case he admitted having lost money in the same house some months previously and, to the surprise of the judge, the court heard that this was the fifth time he had accused prostitutes of stealing money from him. Maria Dismond was spared jail and it was decided that the prosecutor and barrister would write to the principal of the college, Dr Baylee, giving him an account of the behaviour of the student priest in the Preston Street area.

Mary's mission among the poor

Mary Pugh set up a home at 114 Myrtle Street for young women who were tempted through their poverty to go into prostitution, and worked hard as a missionary in Myrtle Street and Kent Square. Both Mary and Eliezer Pugh also gave financial support to the Burlington Street Mission Hall which was opened in February 1874. In its first year, twenty-five poor Welsh adults became members but there were about eighty who came along to listen to sermons on a Sunday. At least eighty-five adults attended the Sunday school and forty-five children were taught about the evils of alcoholic drink, primarily on a week night in the Band of Hope.

On Easter Tuesday 1874, a tea was held at the Burlington Mission Hall and over 200 poor Welsh folk came together to enjoy the feast. It was noticeable that a good proportion were lapsed chapel members.

Dr Owen Thomas and his helpers

Another Welsh mission hall, largely operated by members of Princes Road Chapel, was opened in 1874 at 246 Beaufort Street under the leadership of the Rev. Dr Owen Thomas and his helper John Owen. This John Owen was small of stature, a missionary 'to his fingertips', self-possessed and full of confidence. During the incumbency of Ceinwenydd Owen, the mission hall was moved from Beaufort Street to Yates Street. Persuading enough Welsh folk from a grim environment to come to Yates Street and keeping them within the fold was a demanding task for the urban missionary.

It was noted at a meeting of the Liverpool Presbytery of the Calvinistic Methodist Church that 'many went from cellar to cellar and attic to attic to pray with the people'. One of these was Owen Thomas. He was exceptionally supportive towards the Liverpool Welsh poor and it was he who set up a clothing society at Princes Road Chapel, Liverpool, whose aim was:

> … to give a measure of help towards clothing the poor who belong to the church
> and congregation, especially with those clothes that are most needed to keep them
> warm during the cold winter months. It does this through supporting provision and
> care among the poor themselves; through contributing a small sum in addition to that
> that they make in their weekly payments. And this report (written on 31 October
> 1878) together with the Elders' Report shows that the great mass of the poor
> appreciate the society and try hard to do their part in order to gain these advantages.

W H Parry on 'the sins of the age'

In 1868, W H Parry, who lived in 46 Wesley Street, published a 53-page booklet entitled *Y Cymry yn Lerpwl: Eu Manteision a'u Hanfanteision* (The Welsh in Liverpool: Their Advantages and Disadvantages) and arranged for it to be printed by T Hughes, of 53 Netherfield Road North. Parry feared that many of the Welsh poor whom he knew were being drawn into the taverns that were open from six o'clock in the morning (many even from four o'clock) until midnight. He was an uncompromising Puritan who thought one should read the Old Testament's Book of Proverbs daily:

> We have often heard about men raised from poverty and obscurity to high and
> honourable office, some of whom ascribe their success to their detailed study of the

Book of Proverbs in their youth and to their conscious striving to conform to its instructions.

W H Parry was accurate in referring to the opportunity Liverpool residents had for drinking. The missionary Ceinwenydd Owen cited the example of the wife of a craftsman telling him about the thirst of her husband. He spent £71 on alcohol for himself in the year 1877. Owen describes this Welshman coming home from the tavern on a Sunday evening:

> But before half an hour had passed, the table and chairs would be smashed to smithereens, his wife dragged around the house by her hair and the children's heads banged against the wall. The expense and extravagance wrought poverty on the family.

Owen spoke of the state of the Welsh living in all those damp cellars, many of them around Sefton and Princes Park. He refers in one of his reports and articles to a young girl from Anglesey married to a cruel, drunken Irishman and how she suffered at his hands. Then he mentions another suffering Welsh family: a man, woman and five children in a cold cellar with only one chair in the room and a table – all that was left after the husband had smashed the rest in his drunken episodes. Often on a Friday night, they had only sixpence to get food by Sunday for the following week. The rent of the cellar was two shillings per week. The family's only hope was the generosity of Princes Road Chapel through the Yates Street mission hall. He was thankful for the number of Welsh girls who were ready to act as teachers, all of them serving as maids and nannies in the homes of the wealthy capitalists who lived in the fine houses near Sefton Park. Some came from further afield – from Mossley Hill and Aigburth, and in all weathers. Language teaching was also a problem. As W H Parry says:

> The Welsh parents in this town are also disadvantaged when it comes to bringing up their children to be Welsh speaking, as we believe they should be obliged to do.

But, as he says, the children who heard Welsh only in Sunday school found it boring:

Many of them follow their parents in Welsh worship on the Sabbath but receive little blessing or enjoyment from the service.

Despite this, according to Owen, the young women in Yates Street managed to teach many of those poor children Welsh.

A clothing club called the Dorcas Club, under the care of some hard-working sisters, belonged to the mission room. In 1879 there were seventy-four club members and the weekly payments totalled £19-17-5. The sisters themselves contributed £8-14-0 and the rest came from the coffers of the mission room. Owen speaks proudly of the comfortably-off young girls and women turning out in the cold, icy and snowy weather of 1878 to visit poor Welsh people in great need of food, clothing, money and heating in the Toxteth Park cellars and garrets.

The support of Dr Hugh Owen Thomas

Another who did great work among the Liverpool poor was the well-known doctor, Hugh Owen Thomas, of Nelson Street. His biographer David Le Vay says of him:

> An idol of the poor, he was known to every working man of Liverpool, then
> a drunken and dissolute city. One of the most criminal towns. He traversed its
> roughest quarters. Cheered by both Catholics and Protestants.

The poet R M Davies (Erfyl) pays him a well-deserved tribute in his Welsh *englyn*:

> A man of enormous promise – well earned
> Is Hugh Owen Thomas,
> The city's prestigious colossus –
> Assuming the role of a novice.

And he did serve both rich and poor.

Dr Robert Gee and his ministry to the poor

Another Welsh doctor who devoted his time and talent to help the poor of many nations was Dr Robert Gee (1819–91), the brother of the publisher and radical Thomas Gee of Denbigh. Robert Gee came to Liverpool in 1846 as a medical practitioner. He was only twenty-seven and soon attracted attention in the town for his enthusiasm and medical skills. For forty-three years he was the official physician to the Liverpool Vestry, and found it hard to get experienced nurses to care for the poor in Brownlow Hill Workhouse Hospital. He thought the world of the matron, Agnes Jones, who transformed the workhouse hospital in her short life. Dr Gee was also responsible for another hospital in Everton. Unlike Dr Hugh Owen Thomas, he was a very religious man and, like his brother, was heavily involved in the Liberal Party. He was elected an elder at Mulberry Street and Chatham Street Welsh Calvinistic Methodist Chapel. Without fail, at the end of the Sunday evening service, he would give an address in English on the sermon he had heard in Welsh.

Mission schools – 'islands of hope'

Clearly, the mission halls and rooms were islands of hope to the children of the poor. One of these schoolhouses which has been forgotten in the volumes on the history of the Liverpool Welsh was the Portland Street mission hall. It arranged, as so many others did, an annual tea party as well as a Christmas party. Then, in the summer, it organised trips to the countryside around Liverpool, which meant so much to these impoverished Welsh children from the Kirkdale area. In *Y Genedl Gymreig* (The Welsh Nation) in 1887, it says of the Portland schoolroom:

> There was the pleasure of seeing scores of the poor children of this mission hall enjoying themselves through the doings chiefly of the gentlewomen Misses Parry, the daughters of the Rev. John Parry, York Terrace.

Miss A Davies of Bedford Street bought a house in Kent Square for £250 at her own expense, and converted it into a mission hall, with Thomas Morgan as its leader. He was a native of the Corwen area, and when he first came to Liverpool he found work with the Corporation cleaning the streets. He attended Chatham Street Welsh Methodist Chapel, where he and his minister, the Rev. Henry Rees, were often two matchless speakers in the prayer meeting. The successful businessman Eliezer Pugh, an elder at the chapel, recognised his natural spirituality and his zealous missionary skills among the poor. He employed him to fulfil this task, paying him thirty shillings per week for his ministry in the Kent Square-Duke Street area. When he died on 30 November 1875, a rich woman who had witnessed his ministry exclaimed: 'Oh for the faith of Thomas Morgan!'

But it was not easy to maintain discipline among the children who came to the various meetings of the mission halls. In the words of the historian of the Liverpool Presbytery, John Hughes Morris:

> It has to be said that the children who came to the meetings were particularly undisciplined; sometimes they fought with each other, while others put the lights out suddenly, or again brought with them gunpowder and fireworks which they set off in the middle of the service! But the dedicated workers did not lose heart and in time they saw some of those boys and girls who came from the lowest courts in the town rise to respectable and useful positions, in the world of commerce, education and civil society, ascribing their success to the love and education they received in Kent Square Mission Hall.

A meeting at St George's Hall, just before Christmas, is described by a Welsh reporter:

> It was a sight to remember: seeing the ragged little creatures going to the wash-place, the old rags cast aside and the children dressed in new clothes (new to them) and delighted.

We should note, too, the contribution of Thomas Lloyd Jones, a Welshman from Felin-fach in Cardiganshire, who was in charge of the Mill Street mission run by the Unitarian Church, which was, for many years, a powerhouse for the poor of Toxteth Park and Dingle.

Baths and wash-houses

Since the days of Kitty Wilkinson in the 1840s, there had been public baths. The first was opened in 1842 in Upper Frederick Street and a large number of public baths and wash-houses were built in the next two decades. This provision was very important for the women to be able to wash the family's clothes and for the poor to have free baths. Another valuable resource was the Tontine Club, so that the poor could have sick pay and receive some money for funeral costs. Many of these clubs would depend on the chapels – for instance, the Cambrian Club met in the schoolhouse of Beaconsfield Street chapel.

The great problem for the Welsh poor was finding work. There was employment to be had at Liverpool docks but the process was completely random. Labourers were paid by the day and, for the most part, by mid-century, at a rate of threepence per hour in coupons rather than in hard cash. A general labourer would be able to earn a pound a week, and in the 1840s the numbers seeking work were swollen by the thousands and thousands of Irish who arrived in the town. A pound a week was not enough to sustain a family. It is no wonder that the lowest strata of Welsh society spent years in the workhouse and poorhouse – and so it was throughout the century.

Chapter 6

Men of medicine

Ill health was an ever-present companion in the homes of the Liverpool Welsh in the eighteenth and nineteenth centuries. Life expectancy in the Liverpool slums in 1845 was only thirty-five years, and the majority eked out their lives on a poor diet of flummery, oat bread and salt meat. Thousands lost their lives in the cholera epidemics of 1832 and 1849, as well as from typhoid fever and consumption. Smallpox was particularly cruel as it could cause blindness, infertility and scarring of the skin. Serious accidents happened regularly at the docks and in the building industry. Liverpool's great need was for medics who could bring them some comfort from their pain-ridden lives.

The pioneer Evan Thomas

Within a few months of Evan Thomas (1804–84) arriving on the shores of the Mersey from Anglesey, he had made his presence felt. His original plan was to sail to the USA, where two of his sisters had settled in Wisconsin. But when he reached Liverpool he found that he did not have sufficient money to buy a ticket. He found work in a foundry in Vauxhall where he witnessed frequent accidents.

Like his grandfather Evan Thomas (1744–1814), of Llanfair-yng-Nghornwy, and his father Richard Evans (1772–1851), of Llanfaethlu, his talent for care brought comfort to the injured. After lodging with a woman called Mali Bach in Fazakerley Street, he set up a surgery at 72 Great Crosshall Street where he treated all ranks of people. We know that one of the relatives of the Duke of Westminster went to him for treatment. Evan Thomas was not aware who this man was, as his dress was sufficiently ordinary for him to charge only £1-20 for the treatment. Within a few days he received a note of thanks from him, informing him of his identity and enclosing an extra £3. There was talk of appointing him to a nearby hospital but the registered doctors opposed it – he had no degree or even a diploma.

Around 1833, Evan Thomas married Jane Ellis Owen, Bodedern, Anglesey, and they had five sons – all of whom became doctors – and two daughters.

The eldest son, Hugh Owen Thomas

The eldest son, Hugh Owen Thomas, was born on 23 August 1834 in Ty'n Llan, Bodedern, while his mother was visiting her parents, as she wanted him to be born in Wales. He was a weak child, so he lived with her parents until he was thirteen. Owen Roberts, his primary school teacher, steeped him in English literature, especially Wordsworth's poetry, and persuaded him to move to a private college in New Brighton to study science. In addition, he was educated in medicine by his mother's relative, Dr Owen Roberts of St Asaph. Before leaving the village of Rhoscolyn, he had an unfortunate accident. One of his friends threw a stone which struck him in the eye, causing a turned-out eyelid condition called ectropion. For the rest of his life he wore a cap with the peak pulled down over the injury.

He was very close to his mother, who died when he was fourteen, and his father was determined that he and the rest of the boys would receive a university education to avoid the criticism he experienced – and the many legal cases he had to fight.

The case against Evan Thomas

Probably the case which attracted most attention was held on 8 February 1834 before Edward James and other judges in the Liverpool Court of Passage. A butcher called Crowley went to see a doctor by the name of Thorburn after experiencing an agonising pain in his right leg. When there was no improvement he visited Evan Thomas who bound his leg and cleaned it with cold water. However, his leg soon became paralysed and had to be amputated. In his defence, Thomas spoke of the sixty, or as many as eighty, patients per day who came to his surgery without complaint. He testified:

I asked him who had ordered the leeches to be put on his leg and he said he had put them on himself. I told him he had not done very right. I examined it very particularly and found nothing wrong there. I also examined his leg and found it ruptured in the sinews. I made the best examination I could and then put a wet bandage on, from the toe up to the knee. I did it moderately tight. I used no splint. I ordered hot bran poultice to be applied on Saturday, because the foot was rather cold. I never had any difficulty before.

The jury delivered a verdict in his favour, but a number of Liverpool doctors were determined to get the upper hand and would secretly bribe patients who were critical of him. Thomas was prosecuted on nine occasions, including once for manslaughter, but, because of public support, the sympathy of the press and his own sincerity, he was found not guilty each time.

An accusation of manslaughter came in 1857 after a cooper died when a wound on his hand led to blood poisoning. Thomas's eldest son Hugh was called to give witness, as he had seen his father treating the patient and his testimony was helpful. Thomas was acquitted once more, and his barrister was highly critical of the doctors who were harassing him. A huge crowd of Liverpool citizens, including a significant number of his Welsh supporters, assembled outside the court and a brass band played popular songs.

Like father, like sons

The five brothers went to Edinburgh University and from there to University College London: indeed, at one point, all five were there together. The eldest son Hugh went on to Paris, returning to Liverpool in 1858 and joining his father and brother Richard Evan Thomas (1836–75) in the surgery at 72 Great Crosshall Street.

Reluctantly, Hugh Owen Thomas left his father's practice after two years. Both were hugely popular, but they often disagreed about treatment. Their relationship was further complicated by his father's remarriage.

After his death Evan Thomas was buried with his first wife on Merseyside. He had a unique funeral: the hearse passed Great Crosshall Street and then went on to Wallasey Cemetery where a Welsh choir sang hymns. There was quite a dispute when the vicar of Wallasey objected that the choir members were Welsh Independents and not Anglicans, but a compromise was found and his funeral wish was fulfilled.

Dr Hugh Owen Thomas, a giant of British medicine

When he left his father, Dr H O Thomas moved to 11 Nelson Street. There he set up a workshop and employed assistants to work in metal and leather and two people to make plasters. He turned another house that he had bought in Hardy Street into an eight-bed private hospital.

His wife, Elizabeth Jones from Rhyl, whom he met at Chatham Street Welsh Calvinistic Chapel, was wise, supportive and very different from her gruff, impatient husband. At the beginning of the cholera epidemic in Liverpool, soon after qualifying as a doctor, Hugh started to believe that cigarette smoke would protect him when he was treating cholera victims. It appeared to work for him, and he became a complete chain smoker.

Although small and as thin as a rake, he worked hard from morning until midnight. The only holidays he took were to see his mother's grave and to visit family on Anglesey. When most of the household were sleeping, he would begin on his academic studies. He always boasted that he would die in the traces and so it turned out. He started work at 5 a.m., calling on patients in their homes. A carriage decorated with red flags was built for these visits by staff in his Nelson Street workshop. He adopted the colours of Liverpool and Wales and everyone knew who was approaching when they saw his bright red carriage pulled at speed by two spirited horses. After dark, the carriage could be seen with a torch on each corner, flashing like an ambulance.

He would arrive back at Nelson Street by 8 a.m. to have a simple breakfast of tea and fruit with his wife and colleagues. Bananas he loved, but they were not easily obtainable, and he would get them from Spanish seamen who came for treatment. Between 9 a.m. and 2 p.m. he would see, on average, thirty to forty patients. If a splint were needed, the workshop would make one within an hour. Lunch would be on the table at midday, as then he would go to his hospital in Hardy Street to perform operations. Then, between 6 p.m. and 7 p.m., he would examine yet more patients in Nelson Street before going out in his red carriage to complete his day's visits. He would be back by 9.30 p.m. to do further research and draft articles and books and sometimes to devise more technology to help his patients. He struck a bargain with William Dobb the printer, who lived in a little shop in Gill Street, and he published medical articles for private circulation, as well as the books that he prepared. Probably, of his thirteen volumes, the first, in 1875, *Diseases of the Hip, Knee and Ankle Joints, with their Deformities: Treated by a New and Efficient Method* was the best seller. On average he saw eighty patients per day. Indeed, an American doctor who spent a day at Nelson Street said that he had seen 146 patients that day and a further sixteen in their homes.

His Sunday morning clinic would be for those impoverished people who could not afford to pay even a penny. While his wife Elizabeth would walk about a mile to the ten o'clock morning service at Chatham Street Chapel, he would be treating the wounds and injuries of the Liverpool poor. Hundreds of poor people came on a Sunday morning. Very often he would ensure that a disabled person be taken on a trolley by his staff to the consulting room, and would often give cash to the wife when her husband was poor or out of work and suffering after an accident.

He looked forward to Sunday night as a chance to relax with his wife and others from the Welsh chapel or the neighbourhood. Mostly, he listened to Verdi and played a silver flute he had fashioned himself. He liked it when they had all gone and he had a chance to read, especially left-wing, anti-Establishment literature. Thomas was not just an orthopaedic surgeon. He would treat cancer of the breast, cancer of the tongue, ovarian cancer, and the specialists in the Liverpool hospitals knew of his skill in treating intestinal blockages.

He held very strong convictions about medicine. He continually emphasised the need for plenty of fresh air for those suffering with tuberculosis. Bowel and intestinal surgery should not be performed in his opinion unless the patient had been given enough opium to sedate him or her. He was highly regarded for his treatment of kidney stones. It was his excellent work in Liverpool which inspired three of the most famous orthopaedic surgeons in the world to model themselves on him, namely Sir Robert Jones, Sir Herbert Barker and Professor Rushton Parker of Liverpool University.

But the splint which he invented was one of his greatest contributions. He was not at all a favourite in the medical world – any more than his father – but for a different reason. Many medics opposed him, despite his superb qualifications, because of his self-certainty and unwillingness to engage in debate. He rarely travelled to medical meetings. In the 1870s he received an invitation from the British Medical Association to demonstrate how he treated TB in the joints. He said they should bring the conference to Liverpool. It was held in 1883 with a session on the practices in Nelson Street. The brilliant doctor presented thirty patients with TB of the hip, each of them cured by splinting.

Dr Thomas died suddenly on 6 January 1891 at the early age of fifty-six. He and another doctor, Dr Robinson, had been called to Runcorn on a very cold day to perform surgery. Coming home on the train, he began to sneeze and cough. The cold turned into pneumonia. His friend Dr Carter and his clever colleague Robert Jones were called to see him but, despite their care, obsessive smoking and hard work had taken their toll. Death overcame the genius. He was buried in Toxteth Cemetery on a stormy day. Thousands of mourners turned out, hundreds of dockers among them. Sailors, his large circle of friends from the Welsh communities, business people, civic leaders, city and hospital doctors, women and children of all ages were present. His funeral was deemed to be one of the biggest ever seen, not just in Liverpool but in the whole of Victorian Britain.

The service in the Nonconformist chapel in Toxteth was taken by the Welsh Baptist minister, the Rev. Dr Abel J Parry of Cefn Mawr, Denbighshire, who had spent many of his formative years in Liverpool. He said of him:

> Although, to the sadness of some of those of us who had the privilege to know him, he did not remotely see eye-to-eye with those of us who held to the Christian faith, none of us could fault his Christian life. When we look at the contentment of his life, the honesty of his friendship and his goodwill, our friend was one of the most Christ-like people I ever knew.

He was regarded as one of the brightest stars of Liverpool life and among the most famous surgeons in Britain. He is commemorated in the Liverpool Medical Institution on Mount Pleasant, and on his unusual tombstone in Toxteth Cemetery.

Continuing the good work

Hugh Owen Thomas's pioneering work was continued by his wife's nephew, Robert Jones (1857–1933), whom they had adopted after his journalist father died in 1875, as they had no children of their own. Jones was admitted to Liverpool Medical School, a red-cheeked lad with fair hair and always an unusual cap on his head. He became a fellow of the Royal College of Physicians at twenty-one and trained at Dublin University; he then returned to help at Nelson Street and to learn his craft. Dr H O Thomas appointed him doctor to the health clubs, which played an important part in the Sunday morning clinic.

Robert Jones was appointed surgeon in Stanley Hospital in 1880 and, five years later, thanks to his uncle, opened his own practice at 22 Great George Square, very close to Nelson Street. He was given further responsibilities in 1888 with the beginning of the building of the Manchester Ship Canal. Twenty thousand men worked on this project and were living in tents and huts. Jones was the consultant surgeon and dealt with the huge task of treating frequent accidents and diseases. He was helped by fourteen other doctors and he was director of three hospitals that were built in Eastham, Latchfield and Barton. He always ensured that a plentiful supply of Thomas's splints was available in each.

In 1889 he was appointed surgeon at the Southern Hospital in Liverpool where he accomplished his finest work. He and a Dr Holland were the first to use X-rays there. He heard of the technique's success in Germany and travelled there, buying the apparatus which was to transform British medicine. Like his mentor, he always worked hard. About 700 people came every fortnight to his clinic in Nelson Street to be treated free of charge. At the Southern Hospital he came into contact with Agnes Hunt, an amazing medical woman from Shropshire who brought him a number of disabled children from Oswestry for treatment. He realised the main problem was lack of vitamins and healthy food, and suggested building the Royal Liverpool Children's Hospital in Heswall. Then, with Agnes Hunt, he was responsible for the establishment of Gobowen Orthopaedic Hospital after beginning on the work in the small hamlet of Baschurch.

With the advent of the First World War, Robert Jones was required by

David Lloyd George to organise treatment for the thousands of soldiers. In February 1915, the Military Orthopaedic Hospital was built at Alder Hey in the West Derby area of Liverpool with 200 beds. Jones did tremendous work with his team of surgeons at Alder Hey and, within a short time, he was appointed a brigadier, superintending several hospitals and a total of 23,000 wounded soldiers.

He was invited to superintend the British hospitals in France, where the situation was transformed completely. Before he took over an average of 8,000 soldiers with fractured femurs would die. Jones had thousands of Thomas's splints sent to France with startling effect. The number of soldiers dying was reduced from eighty per cent to twenty per cent. The French had refused the Thomas splint in 1870 but by 1915 attitudes had changed. Robert Jones became popular with US medics and a good number of the most able came to support him in the orthopaedic centres.

He received a number of honours, including a knighthood, and was fortunate in the support of his wife, Susie Evans, a Liverpool Welsh woman who was the daughter of William Evans, an influential city councillor in the Anfield area. They were married in 1887. He was knighted in 1919 and raised to the peerage in 1926; he had degrees from seven universities, including Yale and Harvard in the United States. Sir Robert had a Liverpool home in the Sefton Park area, but he spent his last years in a handsome mansion called Bodynfoel, situated in the peaceful parish of Llansantffraid-ym-Mechain in north Montgomeryshire, sharing his home with his daughter and his son-in-law Sir Frederick Watson. He died in Montgomeryshire on 14 January 1933 and his remains were placed in the Anglican Cathedral in Liverpool.

In the view of Lord Moynihan, Dr William Mayo, Dr Goronwy Thomas, Dr Robert Owen and others, Sir Robert Jones was the greatest orthopaedic surgeon anywhere in the world at any time.

Chapter 7

Welsh publishing in Liverpool

Despite being in England, Liverpool played a prominent role in Welsh publishing thanks to the entrepreneurs, men of letters and poets who settled there in the nineteenth century. It was at Nevetts printing company in Castle Street that the early hymn book *Grawnsypiau Canaan* was produced.

John Jones arrives in Castle Street

John Jones was born on 29 May 1790 in Llansantffraid, Conwy Valley, but moved to Liverpool when he was eleven and was apprenticed for seven years in the printing house of Messrs Joseph Nevetts and Co. at 9 Castle Street. He rose to become the manager and, by 1816, when the fourth impression of *Grawnsypiau Canaan* appeared, it was labelled 'Printed by John Jones of Nevetts Printing House'. By then he was a partner in the company, and so when its founder Joseph Nevetts died in 1832, the company was taken over by the Welsh-speaking Welshman.

By this time the publisher was prominent within the Welsh community, friends with the hymnwriter Pedr Fardd and on good terms with some of the most eminent preachers of the period, such as John Elias from Anglesey. Indeed, he was best man at the second marriage of Elias to Lady Ann Bulkeley in the Welsh Church of St David in Russell Street in 1831. Like many other Welsh publishers, he was himself fond of writing. He and John Roberts (Minimus) prepared the first biography of John Elias, published in 1850. But despite all his hard work in Pall Mall Chapel, he failed to escape the strictures of Calvinism.

In November 1830 there was a by-election in Liverpool. The conflict between the political parties was intensified by bribery, and one of those who sold their vote for £30 was John Jones. This gave Samuel Jones, the second son of Robert Jones of Rhoslan, the opportunity to expose him and culminated in his expulsion from Pall Mall Chapel, whereupon he immediately joined the congregation of the Welsh Independents at the Tabernacle in Great Crosshall Street. He soon became a leader there and was among the founders of the other Independent chapel in the city, situated in Brownlow Hill and called Salem (later situated in Grove Street).

Then, in 1843, one of the most talented Welshmen of the century, the Rev. William Rees (1802–82, known by his bardic name of Gwilym Hiraethog) moved to Liverpool, and out of the collaboration between Jones and Rees sprang one of the most important papers of the day. It was called *Yr Amserau* (The Times) and was launched in 1843 with Jones as publisher and Gwilym Hiraethog as editor. Jones had published periodicals previously. He published the magazine *Y Cymro* (The Welshman) in 1822 in joint editorship with Pedr Fardd – but it was short-lived, as was the next magazine, *Y Brud a Sylwydd* (The Chronicle and Observer) which was started in 1828 by the lawyer Joseph Davies who worked in Liverpool but originally came from Builth Wells. It ran to eight editions between January and August 1828, and from the third edition onwards contained English as well as some Welsh articles. Davies, the editor, was one of William Owen Pughe's followers and, according to the Welsh scholar Sir Thomas Parry, the value of the magazine lay in the new Welsh words coined for the needs of the time. It was printed in Carmarthen and published in Liverpool.

Then, in 1835, Jones published a monthly periodical entitled *Y Pregethwr* (The Preacher), containing the sermons of the Liverpool Welsh preachers, under its editors Minimus and the Rev. Richard Williams. In 1836 he set up the periodical *Y Dirwestydd* (The Abstainer), reminding readers that it was among the Liverpool Welsh that the temperance movement had begun. Clearly, Jones was a man who seized every opportunity to launch new ventures, and after long discussions Rees and Jones decided to publish a Welsh newspaper. Jones both wrote articles and sub-edited the publication. The first edition of *Yr Amserau* came off the press in August 1843. The Liverpool Welsh were slow to respond, and Jones almost gave up the venture within six months. But Gwilym Hiraethog conceived the idea of contributing a series of letters under the pseudonym 'Rhen Ffarmwr (The Old Farmer). It was an instant success.

New printers for *Yr Amserau*

By 1845 Jones had given up his printing business and the work passed to M J Whitty and William Ellis. In the July edition Jones noted that it would still be advantageous to print in Castle Street, as his sons remained employed there. Whitty and Ellis continued to print and publish *Yr Amserau* until June 1849, when it passed into the ownership of John Lloyd (who had been a publisher in Mold).

John Jones had a daughter who was just as capable as her father in the world of publishing. Mary Ann opened a business as a printer and bookseller in Copperas Hill and School Lane in 1844 and then, by 1847, at 18 Tithebarn Street. It is her imprint which is on the biography of John Elias by her father and Minimus. She married Thomas Lloyd (a native of Aberystwyth who came to Liverpool in 1845 when he was twenty-three) and he joined her in the business. He was elected an elder at Rose Place Calvinistic Methodist Church in 1857 and remained so until his death in 1899, the chapel having moved years before to Fitzclarence Street in Everton.

Yr Amserau suffered for its opposition to the Crimean War in the 1850s. Initially it was published fortnightly at a cost of threepence-halfpenny, but by 1848 it was gaining strength and appeared weekly. In 1852 John Roberts (Ieuan Gwyllt) became deputy editor and then editor. The Welsh were bitterly divided over the issue of the Crimean War and Roberts had very little expertise in foreign affairs or, indeed, in current affairs. He was a hymn–tune composer of distinction, and while in Liverpool he became a lay preacher and eventually, when he moved to Glamorganshire in 1859, an ordained minister of religion. The price of *Yr Amserau* was again reduced to a penny but it continued to struggle and was eventually sold to Thomas Gee of Denbigh in 1859 and merged with *Baner Cymru* (The Welsh Standard) which was already published by Gee. The amalgamated weekly became known as *Baner ac Amserau Cymru*.

John Lloyd had been publishing *Cronicl yr Oes* (Chronicle of the Age) in

Mold before coming to Liverpool, and with the abolition of tax on newspapers he was determined to start a penny paper called *Y Cronicl*, to be edited by one of the most talented men of the Victorian era, Lewis William Lewis (Llew Llwyfo, 1831–1901). The outcome was that the new venture nearly killed off *Yr Amserau*. Lloyd panicked and immediately discontinued *Y Cronicl*, believing that readers would return to their first love.

Lloyd published another periodical called *Y Gwerinwr* (The Ordinary Man), a monthly paper to improve the reading habits of the Welsh working class on Merseyside. His inspired choice as editor was one of the most talented Independent ministers in Liverpool, namely Dr John Thomas. There were eighteen editions published from April 1855 to September 1856.

The Rhufoniawc Press

Another early publisher in Liverpool was Robert Lloyd Morris who came from Denbighshire and was known by his bardic name, Rhufoniawc. He served his apprenticeship in Holywell and Denbigh with the publishing entrepreneur Thomas Gee. By 1833 Morris had his own printing business in Mason Street–Villiars Street, Edge Hill, then in Tithebarn Street in 1836 and by August 1840 he had moved to Dale Street. Richard and Joseph Williams had published *Hymnau a Psalmau* (Hymns and Psalms) for the Calvinistic Methodists in 1840 and in 1842, while the fourth edition of the Welsh translation of Elisha Cole's book, *A Practical Treatise on the Sovereignty of God*, was another of their publications.

The importance of Morris to publishing in the town was that in 1840 he became owner and editor of the periodical *Y Gwladgarwr* (The Patriot) which, from its inception in 1833, was published in Chester. *Y Gwladgarwr* was in difficulties when Morris took over and he made a good attempt at improving it. But, despite his efforts, it came to an abrupt end with the June 1841 edition. He was a keen supporter of the eisteddfod movement and secretary of the Liverpool Cymreigyddion and it was he who organised the famous eisteddfod in 1840 in which Eben Fardd (Ebenezer Thomas) won the chair, with the local poet Pedr Fardd coming second. The two winning *awdlau* (odes) were published by Morris in 1841.

Periodicals associated with Patagonia

We should also refer to those periodicals which grew out of the vision to establish a Welsh homeland in Patagonia. The first was *Y Ddraig Goch* (The Red Dragon), a fortnightly newspaper focusing on the Welsh settlement which was published from 5 July until 4 November 1862 under the editorship of one of the pioneers, Lewis Jones. He was both the publisher and printer and, at that time, was living in the city centre at 44 Hanover Street. It sold for a penny.

The following year a periodical of the same name emerged from Liverpool. There is no editor's name on the six issues published (5 September to 14 November) and printed by Lee and Nightingale, 7 Lower Street. Then in 1867 there came yet another *Y Ddraig Goch*, this time edited by Thomas Cadivor Wood of Chester, the secretary of the Society for Emigration and printed by Isaac Foulkes of Liverpool. He had a great interest in the colony in Patagonia and published a magazine with a strange title that translates as 'Your Aunt Gwen, Entertaining, Wise and Good'. It came out in 1865 and the editors claimed that they were 'a committee of talented literateurs'. But they were not sufficiently talented to keep Aunt Gwen going for more than one edition in June 1865 – and that was the sad story of most such periodicals, even in the golden age of the Welsh in Liverpool.

A selection of short-lived Welsh magazines and journals:

- *Yr Annibynwyr* (The Independents) 1856–61: a publication for the most radical religious group in Liverpool. Dr John Thomas, a fiery orator, was the chief promoter and editor until 1861.
- *Y Llenor* (Litterateur) 1860–61: The main promoters were again all ministers, namely Dr Hugh Jones, Josiah Thomas and Dr G Parry of Chester. It was a twopenny monthly periodical.
- *Cronicl yr Ysgol Sabbothol* (The Sunday School Chronicle) 1878–80: Produced by the Rev. John Evans of Garston and the Rev. John Jones.
- *Y Meddwl* (The Thought) 1879: Five editions of this philosophical bi-monthly were published by the Cambrian Company, Liverpool.
- *Yr Ymwelydd Cyfeillgar* (The Friendly Visitor) 1880–81: Set up and edited by a Baptist minister, the Rev. L Lewis, it cost a penny.

- *Yr Ysgol* (The School or possibly The Ladder) 1880–81: A monthly magazine, published by the editors of *Cronicl yr Ysgol Sabbothol*.
- *Y Cennad Hedd* (The Messenger of Peace) 1881–85: a twopenny monthly magazine published and edited by the Welsh Independent minister at Grove Street Chapel, the Rev. William Nicholson.
- *Newyddion Da* (Good News) 1881: A quarterly magazine, costing a penny, with the aim of promoting the foreign missions of the Welsh Calvinistic Methodist denomination and edited by the Rev. Josiah Thomas. It was restarted in 1892 under the editorship of the Rev. Griffith Ellis, Bootle.
- *Y Wyntyll* (The Winnowing Machine) 1890: A bi-monthly, twopenny paper primarily for the influential church of Princes Road, edited by F Rees Jones and the solicitor Elwyn D Symond and printed by Foulkes and Evans.
- *Y Mis* (The Month) 1892: A twopenny monthly paper published and edited by the Rev. John Hughes of Fitzclarence Street and printed by W W Lloyd in Low Hill, Kensington.
- *Y Tyst Cymreig* (The Welsh Witness): Established by Gwilym Hiraethog, Noah Stephen and John Thomas as a weekly paper for the Independents. This paper is still in existence.
- *Y Dydd* (The Day): Published by Samuel Roberts in 1868 and merged with *Y Tyst* in 1871 as *Y Tyst a'r Dydd*. John Thomas was the editor from 1872 until his death in 1892 but the weekly *Tyst*, which is still in existence, was printed in Merthyr and edited in Liverpool. Today it is published in Swansea.
- *Y Dinesydd* (The Citizen) 1888–89: A weekly penny paper published by W Wallis Lloyd of Low Hill, Liverpool, it was edited by the Rev. Edmund Griffiths who was part-time in charge of the Welsh Calvinistic Methodist chapel of Carmel in Ashton-in-Makerfield, but a leading member of Chatham Street Chapel in Liverpool.

The importance of Isaac Foulkes

The man who put Liverpool on the map in the Welsh world of printing and publishing was Isaac Foulkes (Llyfrbryf, 1834–1904). He was apprenticed to Isaac Clarke, a well-known printer in Ruthin, but failed to complete his apprenticeship. Instead, at the age of eighteen, drawn by the appeal of Liverpool, he walked from Ruthin to Eastham and crossed the River Mersey, landing in Liverpool on Christmas Eve 1854. He managed to find work at *Yr Amserau* printing house in St Anne's Street and later worked with David Marples, a Liverpool printer who published a great deal of Welsh material.

In 1862 Foulkes set up his own printing company in King Street, where he lived with his wife Hannah (from Llanrhydd, Denbighshire). Before that, Welsh publications targeted the leaders and members of the Nonconformist chapels and were mainly aimed at Sunday school classes, preaching and temperance meetings. His vision was to expand the scope of Welsh literature, paying attention to the classics which were being forgotten.

He set about publishing the work of John Jones (Talhaearn, 1810–69), a colourful poet who had written an *awdl* (ode) to commemorate Prince Albert which sold very well. He also published a book of allegories and a short biography of Christmas Evans (1766–1838), one of the foremost characters of Welsh Nonconformism. Between 1862 and 1864 there appeared *Cymru* (Wales), a three-part collection of stories, traditions, legends and parables all composed and written by the publisher himself. In 1864–65 he published a useful book called *Adroddiadur* (A Book of Recitations), containing verses that could easily be recited at eisteddfodau and cultural meetings. He had invited Joseph David Jones (1827–70), the head teacher of a private grammar school in Ruthin, to collaborate with him in compiling it. He worked jointly with Gwilym Hiraethog to publish *Aberth Moliant* (The Sacrifice of Praise) and, after the death of Gwilym's brother Henry, published the winning elegaic *awdl* in his memory at the *Gordifigion Eisteddfod* (The Ordovice Eisteddfod), a Welsh society that flourished in Liverpool and Birkenhead. The eisteddfod, held on a huge scale in 1869, was largely organised by Richard Foulkes Edwards, known in bardic circles as Robin Ddu o Wynedd (Black Robin of Gwynedd). In 1870 the pair published the literary, satirical work of the poet Thomas Edwards (Twm o'r Nant) under the title *Cybydd-dod ac Oferedd* (Avarice and Vanity).

Foulkes's next venture was a definitive and substantial volume: *Bywgraffiadau o Gymry Enwog* (A Biographical Handbook of Famous Welshmen). The handbook continues to be a volume of considerable value today and Foulkes is the author of a significant proportion of the book. Then, in 1872 and 1873, the literary work of William Rees was published in a notable volume, *Rhyddweithiau Hiraethog* (Free Measures of Hiraethog), and he also set about publishing the poetry of the medieval poet Dafydd ap Gwilym under the editorship of the Rev. Robert Ellis (Cynddelw). He wrote two novels himself, *Rheinallt ap Gruffydd* (1874) and *Y Ddau Efell neu Llanllonydd* (The Twins or Llanllonydd, 1875) and then, in 1877, a volume called *Yr Ysgol Sabbothol* (The Sunday School) for the Sunday school movement. At this point he began to publish the work of his great hero, Gwilym Hiraethog, who had retired to Chester. Three volumes were published: *Helyntion Bywyd Hen Deiliwr* (Troubles in the Life of an Old Tailor), then *Llythyrau 'Rhen Ffarmwr* (The Letters of the Old Farmer) in 1878 and *Cyfrinach yr Aelwyd* (The Secret of the Hearth).

Foulkes realised that Welsh publishing required a definitive library based on poets of distinction. Consequently he published the poetry of Robert Williams (Robert ap Gwilym Ddu), the poet from Eifionydd, in 1887, and the following year the complete works of Goronwy Owen, *Holl Waith Goronwy Owen*, which made a huge impression and was one of the main reasons for Owen's popularity among the Liverpool Welsh.

By 1881 Foulkes was living at 18 Queensland Street and his eighteen-year-old son Arthur had begun his apprenticeship in the publishing house. There were four daughters younger than Arthur: Fanny, thirteen; Elizabeth, eleven; Emma, six; and Enid, three. Isaac himself was described in the census return as a master printer and he employed three men and two boys. Throughout the 1880s this small but important press was extremely busy and improving from year to year. The volume *Y Mabinogion Cymreig* (The Welsh Mabinogion), which appeared in 1880, was particularly significant, as was *Hanes Llenyddiaeth Cymraeg* (The History of Welsh Literature) by Robert John Prys (Gweirydd ap Rhys) which was published for the National Eisteddfod in 1885. In 1887 an attractive book of the work of Philip Yorke of Erddig, *The Royal Tribes of Wales*, edited by Richard William, was published.

In 1888 the manuscripts of the versatile stonemason from the Vale of Glamorgan, Edward Williams (Iolo Morganwg) – a hero in Foulkes's eyes – were published with an English translation and notes by his son Taliesin

Williams. By the 1890s Foulkes was one of the most important Welsh publishers, as he combined so many roles in one person: author, man of letters, editor, biographer, discerning businessman and shrewd publisher. Established in an office in Don Chambers, Paradise Street, in central Liverpool, he now saw the chance to provide a weekly paper for the Liverpool Welsh, the largest Welsh-speaking community inside or outside Wales.

Y Cymro

According to the talented journalist E Morgan Humphries, who married a Liverpool Welsh woman, the success of *Y Cymro* rested solely on the expertise of its editor and publisher Isaac Foulkes. In *Y Wasg Gymreig* (The Welsh Press), he says of him:

> His lively interest in all things Welsh, his knowledge of antiquity and literature, familiarity with everyday Welsh life and acquaintance with many of the foremost men of the day, together with his talent for expressing himself trenchantly and clearly, made their mark on the paper through and through.

It was this that made *Y Cymro* an attractive weekly paper. O Caerwyn Roberts, one of those who came to work in the office in 1890, said that Foulkes was not an easy man to work with at times. He could be tedious, angry and irascible. His weekly column could be cutting and critical, causing distress to those who came under his microscope. But it showed Welsh journalism at its best and began a tradition.

During the 1890s he gathered around himself a number of talented individuals. One of these was Lewis William Lewis (Llew Llwyfo), an experienced journalist and one who was extremely fond of his beer and wine. During his time at Paradise Street he wrote two novels which were originally published weekly in *Y Cymro*. One was called *Y Wledd a'r Wyrth* (The Feast and the Miracle) and the other *Cyfrinach Cwm Erfin* (The Secret of Cwm Erfin). One of the compositors in the printing house at the time was John Herbert Jones who, in the world of Welsh newspapers, became known as *Je Aitsch Y Brython* (J H the Briton). In 1906 he became the first editor of a new weekly paper that appeared as competitor to *Y Cymro*. Another multitalented man was T Gwynn Jones who served his apprenticeship with Foulkes from

1893 to 1895. He spoke well of his boss, since it was he who persuaded him to translate the poetry of Dafydd ap Gwilym, as well as allowing him the freedom to associate with and get to know a swathe of fervent socialists in the city.

Foulkes had excellent links outside the office and was very supportive towards Ellis Pierce of Dolwyddelan (Elis o'r Nant, 1841–1912). From 1874 onwards, Elis o'r Nant made a living as a door-to-door salesman of Welsh-language books in north Wales but came to Liverpool regularly. Another regular caller was Sir Evan Vincent Evans (1851–1934), prominent in the National Eisteddfod and among the London Welsh. Evans wrote regularly for the *Manchester Guardian* and had a weekly column in *Baner ac Amserau Cymru* and Foulkes persuaded him to write for *Y Cymro* on Welsh matters within Parliament.

But perhaps his greatest scoop was to persuade his friend the novelist Daniel Owen, from Mold, to write the novel *Enoc Huws*. It first saw the light of day in the pages of *Y Cymro* from 1890 to 1891. After that, his novel *Gwen Tomos* appeared in *Y Cymro* in 1893 and 1894. He had the business sense to realise that the novels in *Y Cymro* would increase its circulation – and he was quite right. But he was much angered when the tailor Daniel Owen sold the copyright of his novels to another publisher, Hughes and Son of Wrexham, for a better price than Foulkes had offered.

Under his bardic name of Llyfrbryf, Foulkes produced polished work, such as his biography of Daniel Owen which appeared in a handsome volume in 1903 and a second impression was issued the following year. Another literary figure with whom he had a close relationship was the poet John Ceiriog Hughes. He published his poetry and an appreciation by the poet-preacher Elfed together in 1899, entitled *Athrylith John Ceiriog Hughes* (The Genius of John Ceiriog Hughes). Llyfrbryf set about writing a biography of Hughes which was published in 1887. The first impression sold out quickly and a second was issued in 1902.

He supported other Liverpool authors, particularly the Rev. J O Williams (Pedrog, 1853–1932), Eleazar Roberts (1825–1912), the Rev. Peter Williams (Pedr Hir, 1847–1922), the Rev. Griffith Ellis of Bootle and the Rev. W O Jones of Chatham Street.

His wife Hannah died in 1900, but in 1904 he married again to Sinah from Hafod Elwy farmhouse on the Hiraethog mountain in Denbighshire. The publisher died soon after on 2 November 1904 and left £808-6-4 to his second wife in his will. The printing house passed to his son, but he had neither the resources nor the interest of his father. Arthur Foulkes managed to keep *Y Cymro* going for another five years but depended heavily on Hugh Evans, who was very much in the same tradition as Llyfrbryf.

The contribution of the Brython Press

Another important name in the world of publishing is that of Hugh Evans, the founder of *Gwasg y Brython* (The Brython Press). Evans, a native of Llangwm in Denbighshire, bought his first printing press in 1896 and it was set up in the bedroom of a shop opened at 444 Stanley Road selling writing paper, stationery and daily papers. The whole place was destroyed by an enemy bomb during the Second World War. His son, E Meirion Evans, who was apprenticed to Isaac Foulkes, was the first to work with his father and there was great rejoicing when the first Welsh book was published and printed in 1901 under the title *Teulu'r Bwthyn* (The Cottage Family). T A Davies started as manager with Hugh Evans in 1901 and remained in that position for forty-five years.

In 1906 Hugh Evans started a weekly paper called *Y Brython* (The Briton), and under the one and only John Herbert Jones (JH) it grew into a national paper. JH was appointed editor in 1906 and remained in that post until January 1932. He followed Llyfrbryf's example, using unusual colloquial words in his writings and with a style of his own. Many of his most articulate articles were collected and published by the press.

Hugh Evans died on 30 June 1934 and was succeeded by his sons E Meirion Evans and Howell Evans and grandchildren M Bronwen Evans and Alun H Evans.

The Brython Press developed a long association with the National Eisteddfod of Wales. For many years it was responsible for publishing the list of competition subjects, the week's programme and the book of compositions and adjudications. It also published the programmes of small local eisteddfodau and books in which other publishers (such as Hughes and Son of Wrexham and Gomer Press of Llandysul) saw no significant profit. At least 200 one- or three-act plays were published by the press. Certainly, the greatest service was the publication of *Y Beirniad* (The Critic) from 1912 to 1920 under the editorship of Sir John Morris-Jones.

The press also made an important contribution in providing reading matter in Welsh for children of all ages, giving a platform for the detective novels of the journalist R J Rowlands (Meuryn) and the Methodist minister George Breeze; novels by the temperance organiser Alwyn Thomas and books for teenagers by John Pierce, Joseph Jenkins and Gwyneth Wiliam.

The press was responsible for publishing many of the classics of Welsh literature during the twentieth century. One of these would be from the pen of the founder, Hugh Evans – it was called *Cwm Eithin* (Gorse Glen). It was the Brython Press, too, that published the poetry of the Anglican priest, the Rev. Euros Bowen; the Liverpool-born J Glyn Davies; the poems of the twice appointed Archdruid of the National Eisteddfod, Sir Albert Evans Jones, in *Cerddi Cynan* (The Poems of Cynan) which went into five impressions between 1959 and 1972, and all the books by the Rev. E Tegla Davies, not to mention another best seller, Sir Ifor Williams's explanation of place-names in *Enwau Lleoedd*.

There were around sixty people employed in the offices and the printing works, the majority Welsh speakers living in Bootle and Liverpool. The standard of his work was high, and this was evident when Modern Welsh Publications decided to co-publish *Y Tywysog Bach* (The Little Prince), the translation by Llinos Iorwerth Dafis of a French children's classic. The press suffered a huge loss in 1940 when its printing house in Stanley Road was destroyed during the Blitz on Liverpool, but within a year it was producing books and pamphlets from South Castle Street. The bookshop in Commerce Court was destroyed in 1941 but was re-opened in Hackins Hey two years later and the print department was moved to Edge Hill. The offices and printing house on Stanley Road were rebuilt and re-opened in 1948, remaining there until the closure of the press in 1977.

Filling the gap

With the disappearance of the Brython Press, there was a big gap in Welsh publishing in Liverpool but, since 1968, The Modern Welsh Publications Press has been publishing in a suburb of Liverpool. This was set up in Abercynon in 1963 by the present author. Its aim is quite similar – an attempt to break new ground with colourful children's books and the occasional volume on the fortunes of the Liverpool Welsh.

More Welsh-language magazines from Liverpool

During the reign of the Welsh weekly newspaper *Y Brython* there were other magazines published in Liverpool, noted briefly here:

- *Yr Ymwelydd Misol* (The Monthly Visitor): Appeared between 1903–09, edited and published by the Rev. O J Owen, minister of the Welsh Presbyterian Church in Rock Ferry.

- *Llais Rhyddid* (The Voice of Freedom): A periodical born when a new denomination called the Welsh Free Church was formed, following a scandal over the behaviour of the Rev. W O Jones, the minister of Chatham Street. This periodical lasted from 1902–26 under the editorship of the Rev. W O Jones and W A Lewis.

- *Y Banerydd* (The Standard Bearer) 1910–57: A Methodist Wesleyan Church periodical, edited for years by the Rev. Wesley Felix.

- *Ysbryd yr Oes* (The Spirit of the Age): A magazine which appeared between 1903–07 from the office of *Y Cymro* in Paradise Street.

- *Y Llusern* (The Lantern): This was edited by the Rev. Richard Humphreys, the minister of Chatham Street Chapel from 1903–07, another short-lived magazine.

- *Yr Esperanto Cymreig* (Welsh Esperanto): The man behind this was Gwilym Griffiths who lived in Cressington, a prosperous suburb of Liverpool and who worked for almost fifty years with the Cheshire Lines railway. In 1909 he published 10,000 copies of the magazine and it was sold throughout Wales and England and even in Paris to Bretons who were studying at the Sorbonne and other colleges.

- *Y Cenhadwr* (The Messenger): Missionary magazine of the Welsh Presbyterian Church from 1922 to 1974. The magazine was published continuously for sixty-two years, its aim being to tell the story of the men and women involved in missionary work. It had a very capable editor for twenty-eight years in the Rev. J Hughes Morris. Others edited it for shorter periods, namely the Revs D R Jones, David Edwards, Llewelyn Jones, Ednyfed W Thomas, R Leslie Jones and R Emrys Evans, all working as officers from the mission office at 16 Falkner Street, Liverpool.

- *Y Gadwyn* (The Chain): A monthly publication for the Welsh Independents from 1945 under the editorship of the Rev. J D Williams Richards and, later, the Rev. R J Mon Hughes. With his death in 2007, *Y Gadwyn* came to an end.

- *Y Glannau* (The Shores): This monthly magazine was launched in 1944 as the voice of the Mersey region branches of *Urdd Gobaith Cymru* (Welsh League of Youth), and edited by the Rev. Llewelyn Jones, the minister of Douglas Road Chapel in Anfield, and also for a while the editor of *Y Cenhadwr*. There were, at that time in the region, half a dozen thriving Urdd Gobaith Cymu branches, and the Urdd committee – largely through the efforts of O E Roberts, T Meilyr Owens and Edwin Jones – was largely responsible for the newsletter. Llewelyn Jones succeeded in attracting many prominent Welsh people to write for *Y Glannau*: some native to Liverpool like the historian John Edward Lloyd, Idris Foster, Professor of Celtic Studies at Liverpool University, and others such as Iorwerth Peate and W Ambrose Bebb, well-known nationalists within Wales. For the final seven years *Y Glannau* was edited by the Rev. R Emrys Evans of Birkenhead and the last edition was published in December 1958.

- *Y Bont* (The Bridge): In March 1959 a new Merseyside magazine was published. The editorial board included the editor, the Rev. R Maurice Williams, the minister of Waterloo and Southport Chapel; O E Roberts, a two-time National Eisteddfod prose medal winner, and Gwilym Meredydd Jones, another prose medal winner. The last edition, number 238, appeared in December 1978, three months short of its twentieth anniversary.

- *Yr Angor* (The Anchor): Successor to *Y Bont*, the first edition, under the editorship of D Ben Rees, appeared in June 1979 and was typeset initially at Dolydd near Penygroes by Mei Publications; then in County Press, Bala, and later by Aeron Jones of Llanuwchllyn. Its success has been due to its hard-working officers, the long-serving editor of forty-two years, the generosity of church and town societies and the backing of Modern Welsh Publications. Financial help was received through the Welsh Language Board and later from the Welsh Assembly. In 1993 the catchment area for circulation was extended to include the Welsh community of Manchester, Altrincham and Warrington. Ninety per cent of the articles and news come from Welsh exiles living in its catchment area.

Chapter 8

Liverpool Welsh chapels in the Victorian era

By the time Queen Victoria came to the throne in 1837, Liverpool Welsh chapels of every Nonconformist denomination had been established throughout the town and the temperance movement had a strong hold.

The importance of the chapel to the Liverpool Welsh

Welsh people who came to Liverpool were attracted by the chapel as it was a familiar institution from home. Their significance cannot be overestimated. It was they who owned the chapels, there that they found the companionship of fellow countrymen and they also knew that, if they were in difficulty, they had a place to which they could turn for compassion, advice and financial support. Chapels were organised to meet all their needs: physical, spiritual, emotional and cultural.

The Calvinistic Methodist Whit Weekend preaching festival

Because of the vast increase in the number of chapel members, the Welsh Calvinistic Methodists also started to hold an annual Whit Weekend Assembly in Bedford Street Chapel and it became an institution of the utmost importance. Eleazar Roberts recalled such an event in Bedford Street:

> New clothes and grand bonnets would be brought out on Whit Sunday to such an
> extent that some of the older members became vexed by it, warning against pride.
> I remember one old member called JC in a prayer meeting to pray zealously for the
> Lord's blessing on the meeting and for the sisters to be awakened to wish more for
> the outpouring of the Holy Spirit than for fine clothes, and he was so carried away

that he turned away from addressing the presiding elder to urge the sisters: 'Dear little women! Don't think so much about your new bonnets and coloured ribbons: pray for the Holy Spirit!' … Every cabby in Liverpool knew of the big Welsh meeting on Whit Monday.

By 1853 Bedford Street Chapel was too small and the *cymanfa bregethu* (preaching festival) was moved to Hegler's Circus and later to Sun Hall, Kensington, which could hold 5,000 people.

The English cause

By the middle of the 1840s Calvinistic Methodist leaders were concerned that a large number of young people were unable to follow the sermon in Welsh. It was also felt that they should cater for incomers from Welsh counties where English was the predominant language. Welsh people from Monmouthshire, Glamorganshire, Pembrokeshire and Radnorshire were moving to the town and the Rev. John Hughes, who came from Coedpoeth to minister in the town in 1838, was very keen on English-language religious and educational projects. He took great interest in the community in Scarisbrick, Windsor Street, Garston and Gill Moss in West Derby between 1845 and 1857. A day school was opened in Scarisbrick and a good number of future young Calvinistic Methodist students were nurtured there.

One of these, who was in charge of the English-speaking chapel of the Welsh Calvinistic Methodists in Windsor Street, was the extremely able scholar Thomas Charles Edwards. It was he who managed to persuade Welsh builders to raise a schoolhouse and chapel in Everton, mainly for Welsh people who could not speak the language.

Sacred singing under William Evans

The chapels placed much emphasis on *canu mawl* (songs of praise), especially after the publication of the hymnbook *Grawnsypiau Canaan* in 1795. One of the first singing leaders within the Welsh chapels was a plasterer called William Evans (1758–1822) of Agnew Court, James Street. Robert Herbert Williams (Corfanydd) said of him:

> William Evans knew nothing about notes, but he knew very well how to sing
> Pantycelyn's verses until he made the congregation forget themselves completely

in happiness and rejoicing. Early singing among the Welsh was more like chanting, especially among the Calvinistic Methodists and I heard no-one better at this style of singing than William Evans.

The special talents of John Ambrose Lloyd

In 1830 a young man of fifteen called John Ambrose Lloyd came from Mold to live with his brother Isaac Lloyd, intending to get experience teaching in a private school and then be able to apply for a larger school. But after his brother was appointed editor of the newspaper *Blackburn Standard*, John was chosen to be one of the teachers at the Mechanics' Institute and stayed there for ten years.

The talented young man was not alone in Liverpool; his cousin Emrys (later the Rev. William Ambrose, 1813–73) was a member of Tabernacle Welsh Independent Chapel in Crosshall Street. He came, with his cousin, to the literary society for the first time on 21 September 1835. He was a son of Enoch Lloyd, a prominent Baptist minister, and since Baptists do not practise infant baptism, he was baptised as a member of Tabernacle on 1 November 1835, at the age of twenty.

In 1831, he had already composed an excellent hymn tune called 'Wyddgrug' (Mold) in honour of his native town, specifically to accompany a hymn by the drover Dafydd Jones from Caeo, and so *Wele Cawsom y Meseia* (Behold We Have Received The Messiah) became very popular in Tabernacle and other Liverpool chapels.

He joined the Liverpool Philharmonic Society which had been established on 10 January 1840 and made friends with talented musicians such as the celebrated organist William Thomas Best, and another young musician, George Hurst. By now, a host of young Welsh people were coming to his home every week for singing practice, and out of this grew the Liverpool Welsh Choral Society under his leadership.

He gave up his teaching post, hoping that he would be chosen as full-time secretary of the Mechanics' Institute. But he did not get the post despite being secretary to other highly regarded organisations such as the Society of Builders and the company which published *Yr Amserau*. He went into business as a lithographer but it was not a success and, to the great loss of the Liverpool chapels, he moved to a hamlet called Bwlch Bach near Conwy in 1851 as a travelling salesman for Francis Firth's Trading Company (later Woodall and Jones). He lived in Chester (1852–64) and Rhyl (1864–74) and was one of the master composers for choral singing in the Welsh chapels of those towns.

On the boat home from a voyage to Syria and Egypt he fell ill and was taken to the house of his brother-in-law, Captain J C Jones at 11 Lodge Lane, Liverpool, where he died on Saturday, 14 November 1874.

His work was consolidated by his great friend John Roberts, known as Ieuan Gwyllt, during the period 1852–58 and particularly through the incredible work of Eleazar Roberts and John Edwards of Princes Road, teaching young members of the chapels the tonic sol-fa system.

Eleazar Roberts

It was Eleazar Roberts who spread the tonic sol-fa system not only through the Liverpool chapels of every denomination but throughout every sizeable community in north and mid Wales.

He attended Rose Place British School – the school closed when it was realised that it could not continue to be bilingual as the majority of children were English, but it came under the oversight of five Liverpool Welsh chapels and stands as an unusual example in the history of Welsh Calvinistic Methodism. He left when he was thirteen and was apprenticed as a clerk in a magistrates' court. He spent forty years in the magistrates' quarters in Liverpool and became chief secretary to Judge Stamford Raffles. But his greatest delight was chapel life, Sunday school, sacred music and contributing articles to the Welsh-language newspapers. He became an exponent of the tonic sol-fa method and published *Hymns and Tunes for Children* and *Lessons for the Welsh Musician*.

A 'Welsh cathedral' in Toxteth

It was in the Victorian era that the most attractive chapels the Welsh ever had were built – and according to the monthly Calvinistic Methodist periodical *Y Drysorfa* (The Treasury) in 1872, Princes Road was one of the most splendid. It was in the shape of a cross, 100 feet long and eighty feet wide. There was seating on the ground floor for 800 while the three galleries, one at the far end and two each side of the pulpit, held about 350. It is no wonder the building was called the cathedral church of the Liverpool Welsh. It cost £19,633-8-5 and by the time the Rev. Owen Thomas began his ministry there in 1871, £10,122-18-5 had been paid. The following table shows its growth during his ministry:

The Church				Sunday School		Collections		
Year	Communicants	On trial	Children	Total	Total number	Average attendance	The Ministry	Others	Total
1871	769	29	248	1,046	646	–	476	8,314	8,790
1876	956	20	290	1,266	707	–	646	2,597	3,243
1881	994	17	280	1,291	804	433	647	1,939	2,586
1886	962	10	280	1,252	641	377	595	1,059	1,654
1891	870	7	240	1,117	583	335	565	1,252	1,817

The minister, however, worried about his congregation's grasp of the language, as he made painfully clear at the monthly meeting of the Presbytery in Liverpool on Wednesday, 4 July 1883:

> It is a matter of concern that a large number of the young people in our congregations come to the services each Sunday, yet are unable to understand the sermon or the gospel in the Welsh language. At the same time, because of the family and community links, they do not want to break their link with the Welsh churches. The important question therefore is: What can be done to engage with this class?

Owen Thomas's successor, from 1895 to 1906, was John Williams of the village of Brynsiencyn, Anglesey. He saw the importance of the working classes who came to serve in the houses of the wealthy and middle-class families in Toxteth. He seized the opportunity and arranged that Princes Road Church would prepare a tea for them every Sunday afternoon. And that was the beginning of a tradition that spread to north Liverpool and Southport.

Chatham Street Chapel

In 1860, and within a mile of Princes Road, Chatham Street Chapel was built with seating for a congregation of 1,200. For the next eight years the minister there was the Rev. Henry Rees — considered to be one of the finest preachers of his time, and the first president of his denomination's General Assembly held at Swansea in 1864.

Bethel Independent Chapel

One might best describe Bethel Independent Chapel, Park Road, Dingle, as a hive of activity and there was constant concern among the deacons for the temporal needs of members. In April 1889 it came to the notice of the deacons that brother Lewis Jones was receiving only half a crown from the parish but paying three shillings a week for his lodging. It was decided to give him three shillings a week, so he had nothing to worry about on his rent.

Sometimes the chapel would pay funeral costs. When William Stephens of 123 Upper Hill Street, Toxteth, died on 9 April 1874, the funeral was arranged in Park Road Chapel and he was laid to rest in Smithdown Road Cemetery. Soon the deacons realised that the family could not pay for the funeral. Then the chapel bought his grave for £15, hired a hearse and carriages and prepared a funeral tea for his family and friends at Princes Road schoolroom. His wages were paid to his widow until the end of June.

The deacons of Bethel kept a beady eye on members in matters of faith, loyalty and their Christian way of life. The debate about the Old Constitution and the New Constitution within the Welsh Independent denomination was tiresome, to say the least, and on 1 September 1879 the matter was brought to the attention of a 200-strong congregation at Bethel. Three prominent Welsh Independent ministers — Michael D Jones, who was the main instigator for the Patagonia venture, Dr Pan Jones of Mostyn, a radical-cum-socialist, and David Rees of Llanelli were bitterly denounced by the minister of Bethel, the Rev. D M Jenkins.

On another occasion the case of Mrs Dilys Griffiths of Grove Street was discussed after she had been seen drunk on a Saturday evening in the Abercromby Square area. In deathly silence it was decided that the minister, deacons and congregation expel her from fellowship. Many of these who were disciplined in the light of their Calvinism – that is, their theological moral beliefs – were allowed back as members after a period of a few months. The system worked well. Members who were in dire straits financially would be helped as well as those who could be heavily fined, like Dilys Griffiths, by the secular authorities for their transgressions

Chapter 9

Patagonia and the Liverpool Welsh

The Welsh visionaries

In Liverpool the idea of the *Wladfa Iwtopaidd Gymreig* (Welsh Utopian colony) took root early on. Robert Owen (1771–1858) was a Welsh socialist and industrialist from Newtown who realised his vision in New Harmony, Indiana. Owen came to Liverpool occasionally and delighted in linking up with some of the town's reformers. But despite his greatness and the example he set as a humane and kind industrialist, his settlement was not as successful as he had hoped.

But the wish of the Welsh to establish a *Wladfa Gymreig* (Welsh Homeland) did not disappear, and the Church of Jesus Christ of Latter-Day Saints, known colloquially as the Mormons, attracted Welsh-speaking visionaries. Its resolute leader, Captain Dan Jones (1810–61) from Halkyn in Flintshire, knew a lot about Liverpool and convinced 249 Welsh people – the first of many cohorts – to venture to Utah. Another was Thomas Benbow Phillips (1829–1915) from Cardiganshire, who persuaded forty-one Manchester and Liverpool Welsh to sail to Brazil. A second ship *Irene* sailed from Liverpool in August 1851 and the *Madonna* in November 1851 carried yet more to South America. By Christmas 1851 there were eighty Welsh in his colony, the vast majority from Nant-y-glo and Brynmawr in Monmouthshire, Tregaron (the founder's home area) in Cardiganshire, and from Montgomeryshire, Denbighshire and Anglesey.

Another equally energetic figure was Samuel Roberts (SR, 1800–85) of Llanbrynmair. He persuaded his friends and followers who suffered from avaricious landowners to emigrate with him from Liverpool to Brynyffynnon in East Tennesseee on 6 May 1857. His brother Gruffydd Rhisiart Roberts had gone the previous year to pave the way. But SR failed dismally, because the overseers of the land duped him and the American Civil War (1861–65) broke out. His views on peace, war and slavery found no friends among his fellow Welsh ministers and newspaper proprietors there. He escaped back to Wales within nine years, glad to be alive. He was welcomed with open arms by a sizeable crowd of his Welsh disciples who lived in Liverpool where he was a hero – and not only to most Welsh Independents. It was these lay people, many of them young and outspoken radicals, who were responsible for the gift of £1,245 which was handed over to Roberts in March 1868 at a large gathering in Hope Hall, Liverpool.

Michael Daniel Jones

The most prominent leader of the Utopia dream was Michael Daniel Jones (1822–98). On completing his theological studies, he went straight to America in 1837 and was ordained to the ministry of the Welsh Church in Cincinnati, Ohio. He formed the Society of the Britons to facilitate migration and acted as its secretary. But soon Jones realised that the Welsh language was suffering in the United States and that the Welsh were finding it harder to pass on the language to their children and grandchildren there than in London and Liverpool. When he returned to Wales he was totally convinced that it was necessary to bring the Welsh together on a specific piece of land in order to save their religious, cultural and linguistic heritage. 'Assembled together,' he said when on the verge of leaving Cincinnati, 'we should be much happier than dispersed as we are now; we would have a better ministry and our nation would be preserved from extinction.'

Another of the foremost pioneers of the settlement was Edwin Cynric Roberts. His vision struck a chord with many in Liverpool. By 1860 the idea had been thoroughly discussed and refined by two ordinary men: the compositor and printer Lewis Jones (1836–1904) and the stonemason Hugh Hughes (Cadfan Gwynedd or Hughes Cadfan, 1824–98).

Supporters of the Homeland

When considering the role of the Liverpool Welsh Homeland Committee, only a small number were totally committed to the cause. The members numbered twelve at most and every one was comfortably off and two of them among Liverpool's richest men, namely Eliezer Pugh and Peter Williams. Pugh made his fortune in cotton and Williams as a draper on a big scale. It is odd to think that none of the giants of the Liverpool Welsh Independent movement, such as Gwilym Hiraethog and Dr John Thomas, identified with the Homeland movement, for they had no time at all for Samuel Roberts or the pioneers of the Wladfa.

Captain Love Jones-Parry and Lewis Jones were sent out to the Chubut Valley and the pair returned to Liverpoool on 5 May 1863 to report back. They were much maligned for putting too attractive a spin on the territory, but, according to the historian R Bryn Williams, they both presented their observations to the Homeland Committee 'extremely fairly'. They gave valuable advice such as:

> You must remember the need for the first cohort of migrants to have enough
> provision for at least a whole year. But there are no words for me to go into detail
> or try to teach you.

Unfortunately, however, on his speaking tours around Wales, Lewis Jones lost his moderate tone and presented a rosy view of the situation. Exaggerating the charms of Patagonia was a weakness. Cadfan told the Liverpool Welsh in Lord Nelson Street Concert Hall on 4 August:

> ... there are there two green-crops to be had within a year: ... the fig trees and
> vines grow freely and perfectly in the open air.

Lewis Jones was a young man of twenty-five, as was Cadfan, with little experience of agriculture and blinded by the vision of the Homeland.

In 1865 an advertisement by the Homeland Committee appeared in *Y Faner ac Amserau Cymru* and other Welsh publications calling for migrants:

> The 700-ton ship *Halton Castle*, under the captaincy of Cadben Williams, will be sailing from Liverpool with the first cohort of emigrants to the Homeland on 25 April. Carriage: £12 for adults, £6 for children under 12, babies – 2 years free. Deposit: £1 for adults, 10 shillings for children to be sent to the Treasurer, Mr Owen Edwards, 22 Williamson Square, with the balance to be paid when the emigrants come to Liverpool to set out on the voyage.

The *Halton Castle* was a new iron ship and a lot safer than many leaving Liverpool for Brazil and Buenos Aires. The day dawned and it was evident that about 200 would-be migrants had reached Liverpool. But soon came the news that the *Halton Castle* had not arrived and no-one knew what had happened to it. This was a major crisis and it was necessary to set-to, without delay, to find another ship and to try to minister to the Welsh who had reached Liverpool. It was Michael D Jones and his wife Anne who shouldered this burden, with Eliezer Pugh ready to continue to pay for some of the group. Their opponents saw their chance to put an end to the proposed emigration. This disillusionment had its effect and the most needy among them began to turn back to Wales.

The dozen Liverpool Welsh stalwarts were not to be defeated. They decided to re-advertise, but this time with the bait, 'Generous help will be given to those who do not have enough money to pay their carriage. They should submit their names without delay.' Thanks to the advertisement, 163 men, women and children were found ready to set sail.

The brave passengers on the *Mimosa*

Most of those aboard the *Mimosa* were young; there were many children among them too. So was Lewis Jones's desire fulfilled? It was not older people who were on board the ship but young ones, adventurous and daring. Almost all of them felt that, despite their problems, their new world was a much better place than 'the hopeless servitude in which they lived in Wales'. Had that world been better, said Abraham Mathews, 'they would not have left and so the Homeland would not have continued, nor the Chubut Valley have been inhabited, nor the country explored, nor the Andes mountains have been discovered'.

Among the migrants were twenty Liverpool Welsh: George Jones,

David Jones, Hugh Hughes (Cadfan), Jane Hughes, David Hughes, Llewelyn Hughes, Jane Williams, Edward Price, Martha Price, Edward Price (junior), Martha Price (junior), William Davies, William Williams, Lewis Jones, Eleanor Jones, Thomas Ellis, John Ellis, Ann Owen, Elizabeth Wood and Dr Thomas Greene.

Remembering the *Mimosa* 100 years on

At the end of May 1965 hundreds came together in Liverpool to sail on the *Royal Daffodil* along the Mersey to celebrate the centenary of the establishment of the Welsh colony in Patagonia. Commemorations were led by Alderman D J Lewis, the mayor of Liverpool, and H Humphrey Jones, president of the Welsh Society.

Flowers were cast into the waters by a descendant of the settlers, Mrs Valmai Jones of Caergwrle, secretary of *Cymdeithas Cymry Ariannin* (The Welsh Society of Argentina). A religious service was led by the Rev. Nefydd Cadfan Hughes (a descendant of the pioneer Cadfan Hughes) who was born in Patagonia and was one of three who came to Wales to prepare for the ministry with the Welsh Presbyterian Church. The others were the Rev. R Bryn Williams and the Rev. Trebor Mai Thomas, who spent years as a missionary in India.

More celebrations in 2015

One hundred and fifty years after the *Mimosa* left the port, the Merseyside Welsh Heritage Society arranged a special festival from 29–31 May 2015 in Liverpool, and the large crowd that came together shared a feast of memories.

Chapter 10

A cluster of Liverpool Welsh medics

Liverpool was the first city in the UK to appoint a medical officer of health. The contribution of the Welsh to the development of world orthopaedic medicine has already been mentioned. Before the arrival of Evan Thomas, Hugh Owen Thomas and Sir Robert Jones, hospital orthopaedic practice was quite crude. From 1909, when Sir Robert Jones was appointed orthopaedic surgeon by the University of Liverpool, Liverpool Royal Infirmary became a centre of orthopaedic medicine.

The brilliant Dr Robert Gee

Dr Robert Gee was the brother of the printer Thomas Gee and his wife Mary Foulkes from the Vale of Clwyd. He welcomed the 1866 Public Health Act, which laid down guidelines for establishing hospitals for the poor and sick who suffered from infectious diseases which spread easily. He seized the chance to take a lead on this and worked with Dr Richard Caton and Dr Alexander Davidson in 1872. They established a private house in Netherfield Road as a hospital for young people from Wales coming to Liverpool by boat to follow educational courses, and consequently perhaps short of money to pay for treatment. In 1880 Liverpool Corporation made a grant of £250 a year on the understanding that twenty-five beds would be set aside for the medical officer of Liverpool with the cost kept down to seven shillings a week for these patients. There was much call for Dr Gee in other Liverpool hospitals and his death, along with that of Hugh Owen Thomas in 1891, were losses to medicine in general all over the city.

William Thelwall Thomas

Another very important surgeon among the Liverpool Welsh was William Thelwall Thomas (1865–1927). When he died suddenly in his luxurious home, Verdala Towers, Allerton, on Saturday, 10 September 1927, the news spread like wildfire through the Welsh community and, on Monday morning, 12 September, the *Liverpool Daily Post and Mercury* announced: 'The most famous surgeon Liverpool has produced has died suddenly.'

He was born in the town, the son of the photographer John Thomas of the Cambrian Gallery, and after studying in Glasgow and Liverpool became an assistant to Sir William Mitchell Bank, another of Liverpool's famous doctors. Dr Thelwall Thomas established his own practice, initially in Hope Street before moving to the well-known Liverpool medics' street, Rodney Street. In 1892 he was appointed assistant surgeon at the Royal Infirmary and became a surgeon in 1907. Six years later he was appointed a lecturer in general surgery at the University of Liverpool, and undertook this role for nine years until he was appointed Professor of Regional Surgery.

By then he was Liverpool's principal surgeon as well as being a professor of medicine. He was regarded as a star in the medical firmament, with the ability to analyse and act effectively. In his early years he was an active member of Fitzclarence Street Welsh Presbyterian Chapel and, for years, one of the consultants to the denomination's missionary society. He appreciated the chance to pay something back for his Welsh Calvinistic Methodist upbringing.

A surgeon's story: J Howell Hughes

John Howell Hughes became a familiar name to the Welsh in Liverpool and in north and mid Wales during the period after the Second World War. Born to a builder in a terraced house in Anfield, he graduated from Liverpool University in 1931. He started his career at the Royal Infirmary in Pembroke Place and became extremely successful as a surgeon. The Welsh flocked to him and Ward 8 became known as the Welsh Ward. It was an unusual ward; if one stood in the middle, one could see each bed and patient. He married a nurse called Myra and, when the new Royal Liverpool University Hospital began construction in the 1960s, he became the commissioning officer. It took many years to complete the hospital, and in the latter years he was its chairman.

Professor Owen Herbert Williams

Another renowned surgeon was Professor Owen Herbert Williams (1884–1962), who was born in Bootle to Owen and Jane Williams (née Evans). After the death of his father when he was eleven, his mother decided to return to her family in Llanfaelog, Anglesey. His potential was recognised at Beaumaris Grammar School, and in 1901 he went to Edinburgh University to study medicine, graduating in 1906. That year he was appointed as a surgeon to the Southern Hospital, Liverpool, where he served under well-known surgeons such as Dr Carter and Sir Robert Jones. In 1908 he moved to the Royal Infirmary as a registrar and house surgeon, working at the same time to win his fellowship (FRCS) from Edinburgh University in 1909, and his PhD from Oxford in 1911. He returned to the Southern Hospital and, apart from the First World War years, retained his connections there all his life. In 1919 he set up the Travelling Surgical Club for his co-medics who had served during the war. They made annual visits to European hospitals to keep up with the latest developments. In 1939 he was appointed Professor of Medicine at the University of Liverpool, and he retired in 1945. He served on the Regional Board of Welsh Hospitals, the Welsh Board of Health and on the Court of the University of Wales and University College Bangor. He received an honorary DSc degree from the University of Wales in 1952 and died at his home, 18 Sefton Park Road, Liverpool, on 6 March 1962.

The unconventional Dr William Williams

Another Welsh surgeon who was prominent in the Southern Hospital before Professor Herbert Williams was Dr William Williams. He had unusual ideas about how to treat typhoid fever and also gastric ulcers. According to Dr Williams, the patient had to be starved with no more than a pint of milk in twenty-four hours. He had remarkable success, far more than his colleague Dr Cameron, who believed in 'feeding up the patients'.

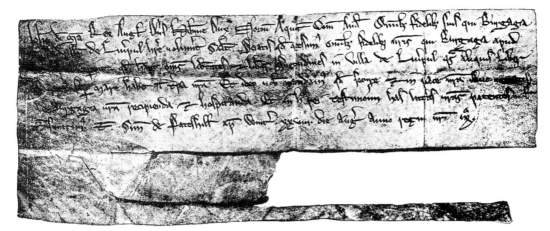

King John's Charter for Liverpool

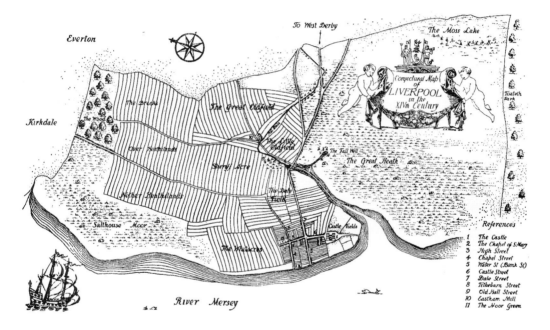

Liverpool in the
fourteenth century

Liverpool Castle

Toll house

Liverpool Tower

St Nicholas Church
from Mann Island

Map of Toxteth Park

Liverpool in the seventeenth century

London Road in the eighteenth century

Liverpool and its church

The Liverpool Welsh's first chapel, built in 1787 in Pall Mall

Pall Mall in the twentieth century

A John Gibson designed plaque of William Roscoe

Peter Jones (Pedr Fardd), the teacher and hymnwriter

Welsh Independents

The Rev. John Breese

The Rev. John Jones, Bethel

The Rev. Thomas Pierce

The Rev. William Williams of Wern

Tabernacle, Crosshall Street

The Rev. William Rees (Gwilym Hiraethog)

Bethel Chapel, Park Road

Orthopaedic Doctors

Evan Thomas

Hugh Owen Thomas

Health Centre, 11 Nelson Street

Elizabeth Thomas, the wife of
Dr H O Thomas

Robert Jones, sitting, with Huw Owen
Thomas and his cigarette

The Pioneers of the Liverpool Welsh's Religion and Culture

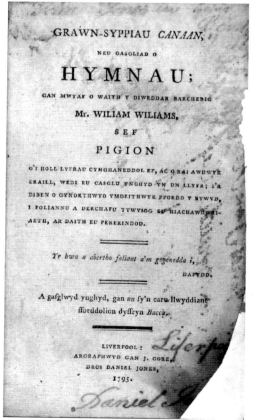

GRAWN-SYPPIAU *CANAAN*,

NEU GASGLIAD O

HYMNAU;

GAN MWYAF O WAITH Y DIWEDDAR BARCHEDIG

Mr. WILIAM WILIAMS,

SEF

PIGION

O'I HOLL LYFRAU CYNGHANEDDOL EF, AC O RAI AWDWYR
ERAILL, WEDI EU CASGLU YNGHYD YN UN LLYFR; I'R
DIBEN O GYNORTHWYO YMDEITHWYR FFORDD Y BYWYD,
I FOLIANNU A DERCHAFU TYWYSOG EU HIACHAWDWRI-
AETH, AR DAITH EU PEKERINDOD.

Tr hwn a abertho foliant a'm gogonedda i,

DAFYDD.

*A gasglwyd ynghyd, gan un sy'n caru llwyddiant
ffordddolion dyffryn Bacca,*

LIVERPOOL:
ARGRAPHWYD GAN J. GORE,
DROS DANIEL JONES,
1795.

Thomas Lloyd, the printer

Grawnsypiau Canaan, 1795, first hymnbook
of the Liverpool Welsh community

Matthew Jones, the coal merchant and
Calvinistic theologian

John Williams, a Welsh Presbyterian elder

Matthew Jones and his theological students

The Rev. Dr John Hughes

Thomas Lloyd, another Welsh Presbyterian elder

The Rev. Owen Jones

The grave of John Evans in Anfield Cemetery

The Rev. John Evans, Pontypridd

The Rev. J D Evans, Garston

John Gibson

The Rev. Dr John Thomas

The Rev. Noah Stephens

People in Publishing

The Rev. O L Roberts

The shop of Hugh Evans
in Stanley Road, Bootle

Hugh Evans, Printers and Stationers

Yr Angor executive committee in the 1990s. L–R, standing: H Wyn Jones, William Evans, E Goronwy Owen, Ken Williams, Hywel Jones, Walter Rees Jones, Ron Gilford. Sitting: Marian Prys Davies, Anne Jones, Dr D B Rees, Mair Jones, Lois Murphy. Only two are still on the committee in 2021, namely Mair Jones and the editor, D B Rees.

Emlyn Evans and Alun Williams of Gee Press, Denbigh, presenting a volume on preachers and preaching to the author in Liverpool in 1997

John Roberts (Ieuan Gwyllt), deputy editor of *Yr Amserau* (1852–58)

Codi yr Angor, 2019

Chapels

Great Mersey Street Chapel

Marsh Lane Chapel, Bootle

Trinity Road Chapel, Bootle

Heathfield Road Chapel,
near Penny Lane

Chatham Street Chapel

Princes Road Chapel

St Nathaniel's Hall

Smithdown Place, where
the Heathfield Road Chapel
cause started

The organ of Bethel Chapel, Heathfield Road, before it was sold to a family from Carno

Webster Road Chapel, which moved to Heathfield Road in 1927

Welsh Baptist chapel in Earlsfield Road, Wavertree

Maenan: poet and practitioner

Dr John Lloyd Roberts, known in literary circles by his bardic name Maenan, was a multi-faceted person with academic qualifications in science, medicine and surgery. He had BA, BSc and BS (first class) degrees as well as a doctorate in medicine, all from the University of London. He gained his MRCD (London), MRCP and PRCS (England) and made a name for himself at Guy's Hospital before moving to Liverpool, where his popularity as a clinical lecturer grew. Medical students flocked to him from all over Britain, attracted by his instructional skills. He was also one of the leading freemasons of the Welsh community: being master of ceremonies for West Lancashire and also master of the Cecil Lodge. Historians of the Liverpool Welsh have given little attention to masonic membership. Hundreds of middle-class Welsh belonged to the freemasons – builders, lawyers, ships' captains and ministers.

He retired from his medical work in 1923 and immersed himself in his literary interests, as a supporter of Everton Football Club, and in his lodge until his death in 1932.

Goronwy Thomas, bone doctor

Goronwy Thomas was born in Cyffylliog, Vale of Clwyd. His sister Besi Maldwyn was an author and his brother Dr J G Thomas was a family doctor in Denbigh. In the 1930s Goronwy Thomas attended the University of Liverpool, and after graduating worked with specialists such as Theodore Armour, Professor T P MacMurray and Bryan McFarland. During the Second World War he was appointed a consultant at Alder Hey Hospital and was also in charge of the orthopaedic service at Broadgreen Hospital. Later he became a consultant at the United Liverpool hospitals.

Other orthopaedic surgeons

One of Dr Goronwy Thomas's friends was Dr Tom Price (1914–67) who was a staff member and later orthopaedic registrar at the Liverpool Royal Infirmary. Dr Thomas's ability to communicate with children was exceptional and his only son, named after the famous bone doctor Hugh Owen Thomas, followed in his footsteps. He worked his whole career at hospitals in Wirral.

Another talented orthopaedic surgeon was Dr Hugh Osborne Williams

(1920–88), originally from Rhyl. The son of a family doctor, he attended the University of Liverpool to study medicine. He was appointed to David Lewis Northern Hospital. He served in the RAF during the Second World War and was later appointed orthopaedic registrar. In the same manner as Dr Goronwy Thomas, he was a committed teacher with particular talents as a surgeon and was much in demand for his services as consultant surgeon at Whiston Hospital in Prescot, Birkenhead and Wallasey.

Courageous career of Dr Frank Ieuan Evans

A doctor rather like Maenan was Dr Frank Ieuan Evans, who was born in Flint in 1900 but moved to Liverpool when his father was invited to become a family doctor in a Welsh-speaking suburb. He had an outstanding academic career at Cambridge University, gaining a first-class degree in natural sciences, with physics as his main subject. He volunteered during the Second World War and was in the forefront of fighting in the Far East. He won the Military Cross for his valour in Burma. He became a surgeon at Stanley Hospital, Bootle, with similar responsibilities at Birkenhead General Hospital.

Edgar Parry

Edgar Parry was a well-known surgeon, originally from Waunfawr, Arfon, who came to Liverpool to study before the Second World War and stayed in the city until his retirement. He enjoyed a number of years in retirement at Llandegfan, Anglesey, until his death in 1984. He was a consultant surgeon at Broadgreen and Waterloo hospitals and pioneered surgery of the arteries and veins.

Medical men who died prematurely

Living to a ripe old age was quite unusual in the history of the Liverpool Welsh doctors. In the Victorian era, Dr Hugh Williams (1849–1904) of Everton proves this point. He was born in Bryndu, Anglesey, and came to Liverpool as a sixteen year old to work as a pharmacist. His ambition was to be a doctor and so he set about studying in his spare time and at the University of Liverpool. He had experience as a house surgeon at Stanley Hospital before setting himself up as a family doctor in Breckfield Road North. He served his patients well and was very active in the Calvinistic Methodist chapel in Fitzclarence Street, where he was elected an elder in 1887. The Welsh community was devastated by his death on 26 July 1904 at the early age of fifty-five, and he was buried in Anfield Cemetery.

Similarly, in the 1920s Dr James Jones of Allerton, brother of Dr Emyr Wyn Jones of Rodney Street, had little opportunity to serve his adopted city. He endeared himself to the Welsh at Webster Road Welsh Presbyterian Chapel. His name is seen in the records of that chapel and he married the daughter of one of the elders, J W Jones the builder. A volume of his Welsh-language poetry was published in 1924 and he had an article published in *The Lancet*. He died at his home, Awelon, in Allerton Road, at the age of twenty-four, leaving a wife and young daughter.

The death of Dr Trevor Lloyd Hughes at the age of fifty-five in 1963 was an immeasurable loss to the health service across the Mersey region. The son of a Welsh Methodist minister, he shone as a medical student at Liverpool University, winning the gold medal in surgery and medicine and numerous prizes such as the Derby Exhibition, the O T Williams Prize, and Clinical School Exhibition. He won his MD with distinction and achieved first-class honours in his final examinations. He started his career in Middlesborough but returned to Liverpool in 1947, initially as executive medical officer for the Regional Liverpool Board and later in charge of all the Mersey region hospitals.

Another talented doctor who died prematurely – on 9 January 1973, the day before his sixty-second birthday – was Dr Raymond Winston Evans. He was born in Swansea to a Welsh-speaking family and arrived in Liverpool in 1947. He spent twenty-five years as consultant pathologist at David Lewis Northern Hospital and was regarded as one of the world's foremost authorities on cancer. He was awarded his PhD in 1959 – the same year in which his seminal book, *The Histological Appearances of Tumours*, was published – and a doctorate in science in 1970. For a term, in 1963, he taught at Texas University and in Chicago.

One of his contemporaries was Dr David Trefor Howell Evans (1920–84), a Welsh speaker from Caernarfon who became one of the outstanding pupils of Dr Watson Jones (the son-in-law of Sir Robert Jones) and Norman

Roberts. He was much admired in the world of orthopaedics for his surgical skills and spent many years at David Lewis Northern Hospital, Birkenhead General Hospital and Victoria Hospital, Birkenhead. He had the pleasure of seeing his own daughter, Dr Gaynor Evans, joining him as a surgeon.

Dr Gordon Lewis Mills (1930–83) came from Machynlleth and was admired by all who worked with him at the Royal Liverpool Hospital. He was appointed Professor of Geriatric Medicine at the university in 1977 where he was a much-loved lecturer. He died on 20 February 1983 after a long illness and at the age of only fifty-three.

Dr Eric Walker (1917–47) was born in Prestatyn and educated at Rhyl Grammar School and Liverpool University. His ability was noticed early in the medical world and he filled one important post after the other in Liverpool. He became a consultant in radiological care in the cardiac centre at Sefton General Hospital in Smithdown Road, then a radiologist at Liverpool Royal Infirmary and a lecturer in radio diagnosis at the University of Liverpool Medical School. He died at the early age of thirty.

Good Samaritans and much-loved medics

Dr John Owen gave many years' service to Liverpool. He was a native of Beaumaris on Anglesey but was educated at the universities of Liverpool, Cambridge and London. He became a first-class doctor in Rodney Street and a great authority on the nervous system and the lungs. He never charged people who were poor and in need. He caught influenza but refused to rest and died in February 1929 of pneumonia at the age of fifty-six.

One of his contemporaries was Dr Arthur Gruffudd William Owen of Gorwyl, Park Road North, Birkenhead, who worked as a doctor in Liverpool. He was senior residential medical officer at the David Lewis Northern Hospital.

Many Welsh doctors were, like Dr T E Jones and his brother Dr Bennett Jones, active within the Welsh chapels of every denomination. Another was Dr David Robert Evans of 1 Sandringham Drive, Sefton Park, who gave fine service to Belvidere Road Presbyterian Chapel. In the same chapel there was Dr William Robert Williams, of Warrington Welsh origins and a brilliant student at Liverpool University.

Dr R E Roberts of Marsh Lane, Bootle, became an influential man in Bootle, and was an elder at the Peel Road Welsh Presbyterian Chapel, Seaforth, a JP and mayor of Bootle in 1905–06.

The value of the University of Liverpool Medical School

Another prominent Welsh graduate of the University of Liverpool Medical School who deserves mention was Emeritus Professor David Alan Price Evans. He was a staunch Welshman, known in the Bardic Circle of the National Eisteddfod of Wales as Dafydd Baradwys (David from Paradise)! He was born in Birkenhead on 6 March 1927 and enjoyed a glittering academic career from Holywell Grammar School and on to Liverpool University where he won more university prizes than any of his contemporaries. He served in hospitals in Japan, Singapore and Korea after the Second World War, and also in Malaysia, treating tropical diseases. He served as senior medical officer and registrar at Broadgreen, Stanley and Northern hospitals and continued his research in the field of physiology. Over a period of forty years he contributed a large number of papers to medical periodicals throughout the world. To crown it all, in 1958–59 he gained another degree at Johns Hopkins University in Baltimore for original research into heredity. As a result of his discoveries he taught and lectured in thirty countries across the world. He spent more than twenty years as a lecturer, senior lecturer, professor and head of the University of Liverpool Medical School before going out to Saudi Arabia to work as superintendent of Riyadh Hospital in 1982. He took care of the royal family there for a quarter of a century. He kept a home in Liverpool and returned there for six months of the year. He died at the Royal Liverpool Hospital on 29 August 2019.

Professor Evans was succeeded at the medical school by another staunch Welshman, Professor Richard Edwards. It was he who installed the unique and sophisticated MRI scanner able to take detailed pictures of the inside of the human body. The scanner has been of immense help to Professor Edwards and his contemporaries in the study of muscle conditions, particularly muscular dystrophy.

Professor Robert Owen, too, made a key contribution to the university and is well remembered for his compassionate care of children and young people at Alder Hey Hospital and orthopaedic patients at the Royal Liverpool Hospital. He served for many years as the chair of orthopaedics and took the decision to add a Master's course for students from Britian and abroad.

Charismatic practitioners in the department at the same time included Dr David Enoch and the popular surgeon Wil Lloyd Jones. Dr Enoch worked for two decades as a psychiatrist there and at the Royal Liverpool Hospital. Dr Jones's profile as a surgeon without equal was raised by his work at Broadgreen, Lourdes and the Royal Liverpool. Today, the department is served by Professor Mari Lloyd-Williams who has achieved wonders in end-of-life care and is very supportive of the hospice in Woolton.

A medical specialist who has kept a close connection with his old department is Dr John G Williams. He enjoyed a notable career as a lung physician and was honoured by the Gorsedd of Bards for his contribution to Welsh life in Liverpool. He is chairman of the executive committee of *Yr Angor* and his contributions on various aspects of medicine are a pleasure to read. Both he and another specialist, Dr Rhys Davies of Aintree Hospital, ensure the Welsh medical tradition continues to flourish.

The all-rounder Dr Emyr Wyn Jones

The medic who was at the centre of Welsh life for the longest period was Dr Emyr Wyn Jones. The son of a Presbyterian minister from Croesywaun in Caernarfonshire, he graduated from the University of Liverpool in 1928 with first-class honours in surgery and medicine. After getting his MRCP (London) in 1933 and having decided that clinical medicine appealed more to him than pathology, he was appointed to the staff of the Liverpool teaching hospitals. In 1937 he was elected as one of the founders of the British Cardiac Society. His contribution to the world of medicine was enormous. In 1938 he was appointed to the Royal Liverpool Infirmary and was a physician for twenty years and in charge of the cardiac department for more than quarter of a century. In 1966 he became director of the Liverpool Centre for Cardiovascular Science and he had a clinic in Rodney Street. In 1967 he became administrative druid of the Gorsedd Bardic Circle and remained in the post for twenty years, having served seven archdruids.

The generosity of Sir Alfred Lewis Jones

There is one name that should be mentioned, although he was not a doctor. Sir Alfred Lewis Jones was primarily responsible for establishing the School of Tropical Medicine, as he was one of the leading merchants involved in the extensive trade between Liverpool and West Africa. He established the Alfred Jones Chair of Tropical Medicine and, when he died in 1909, donated an additional laboratory in Pembroke Place and a ward for patients suffering from malaria and tropical diseases at the Royal Infirmary. The Sir Alfred Lewis Jones Laboratory was used by the War Office during the First World War, to the delight of his friend David Lloyd George. In 1915 the Liverpool School of Tropical Medicine Auxiliary Medical Hospital was established, with 200 beds for soldiers suffering from dysentery and malaria – a well-deserved tribute to him.

Chapter 11

Photographer with an eye to the future

A man who had a wonderful opportunity to develop his talents in Liverpool was the photographer John Thomas (1838–1905) of the Cambrian Gallery. He was born on 14 April 1838 to David and Jane Thomas in Glanrhyd, Cellan, on the shores of the River Teifi. He was educated in Llanfair Clydogau and Lampeter before being apprenticed to a tailor in the town. He was the author of a very interesting essay, *Cyfrinachau yr Afon Teifi* (Secrets of the River Teifi). His father died in 1853, the year in which he left Cellan for the long journey to seek employment in Liverpool. The fifteen-year-old lad walked eight miles to Tregaron on the first day, through the picturesque village of Llanddewi Brefi, to find lodgings with Dafydd Jones the egg-carrier. The following morning, he set out with him for Llanidloes, a distance of forty miles, through Pontrhydfendigaid, Ffair Rhos, Pontrhydygroes and Devil's Bridge. From there he made for Eisteddfa Gurig, Llangurig and crossed Pumlumon Mountain on 8 May. According to the lad, 'we were up to our knees in snow'. Having reached Llanidloes, he relished the fire, the food and the snug bed that was provided for him.

From Llanidloes to Liverpool

The pair set out early from Llanidloes, to be in Newtown by the time the market opened so that Dafydd Jones could get rid of his eggs and the young man could catch a boat. Having reached there, the egg-carrier was in time, but the traveller was too late to get the fly boat on the canal that day, so John Thomas had to wait until the following day. He was there in plenty of time the following day to catch the boat, but he soon realised that it moved like a snail. Indeed, he admits, an elderly snail! It was pulled by two horses which would be changed quite often:

> Sometimes they would gallop, other times they would trot and within a few hours we were in Rednal, near Oswestry and there was the Great Western Railway to take us to Liverpool, arriving there before nightfall of the third day after leaving Glanrhyd.

Liverpool in the spring of 1853 was a very busy place. Here is how the young man from Cellan saw it:

> After landing in Liverpool, I thought, seeing everyone weaving in and out of each other and all looking very busy, it must be a fair day; but by the following day it was still a fair, and until this very day I've made my home in that fair.

He found work in a tailor's shop called Ingham and Morgan in Scotland Road, alongside Evan Herber Evans (1836–96) who was to become a theologian and preacher of great repute. Evans was born in Newcastle Emlyn and served in draper's shops in Rhydlewis, then Pontypridd and Merthyr Tydfil. In Liverpool, Herber Evans came under the influence of the Rev. Dr John Thomas, and in his chapel, Tabernacle, in Great Crosshall Street, he began his great life's work of preaching in 1857.

John Thomas married Elizabeth Hughes from Bryneglwys, near Corwen, and they had four children: Jane Claudia (1863–1934), who later became Mrs Hugh Lloyd; William Thelwall Thomas (1865–1927); Robert Arthur Thomas (1866–1932) and the doctor Albert Ivor Thomas (1870–1911).

Beginning of his life's great work

The momentous year in John Thomas's story was 1863, when he bought a camera and invited famous Welsh preachers like Henry Rees and John Hughes to sit for portraits. The managers of the clothing shop in Scotland Road were in poor health and the ambitious man from Cardiganshire realised he needed work to sustain him. Thomas saw a gap in the market and a chance to be a pioneer in a craft in its infancy. He worked for two years for one of the best-known Liverpool photographers, Harry Emmens, who had a studio in Seel Street, before opening his own Cambrian Gallery House at 53 St Anne Street. He was helped by his devoted wife and he employed his brother-in-law, Thomas Glwysfryn Hughes, to assist him.

A festival photographer

On Whit Sunday each year a preaching assembly was held in Liverpool, when the best preachers of the day would visit and there were large meetings in the huge Sun Hall, Kensington, which could seat 6,000 people. Edward Morris, Fraser Street, introduced him to a number of the visiting preachers, who received their portraits gratefully, especially when they heard it was free and that they could have a number of copies cheaply or for nothing to take home to show their family and congregations.

The attraction of Cambrian Gallery

The Cambrian Gallery became an attraction, especially for the prominent Welsh who came for a visit to lecture and preach. So, 1867 marked the start of the pioneering story of John Thomas as a full-time professional photographer. He travelled all the way to Llanidloes to the General Assembly of the Welsh Calvinistic Methodists to take pictures of the ministers and elders. The following year he visited the National Eisteddfod of Wales in Ruthin to take a photograph of the chairing and crowning of the winning poets. For the next thirty years he visited both these events regularly and many others, providing a wonderful permanent record of them.

Pictures of his beloved Wales

On his travels John Thomas tried to find both the famous and the not-so-famous. One of the periodicals popular with the Liverpool Welsh was *Y Cymru Coch* (The Red Wales). Its editor, O M Edwards, acknowledged the huge debt it owed to John Thomas over its ten-year life:

> His rich gallery has been open and welcoming to me. And so, instead of unusual
> pictures taken on a random basis, I had photos which had been taken carefully,
> at the best time of day: like the sun on Llansannan village or the lovely and sweet
> beauty of evening over the old Abererch churchyard.

A valuable legacy

Having realised the special worth of his unique collection, he picked out more than 3,000 plates and sold them for a moderate sum to O M Edwards. The historian–editor used them to illustrate his periodical and his valuable volumes in *Cyfres y Fil* (The Series of a Thousand).

When Sir Ifan ab Owen Edwards handed the collection to the National Library in 1930, he gave the nation a valuable gift. This collection is one of the best we have. John Thomas can be said to have begun the Welsh photographic tradition and, in Liverpool, he was followed by John Mills's company. Thomas died on 14 October 1905, at the age of sixty-seven. He did not want to be buried in the Teifi Valley, but rather in Anfield Cemetery, where his wife had lain since 1895.

Chapter 12

Growth of the middle class

Lord Mostyn was a fervent member of the Welsh Society which was formed after the National Eisteddfod came to Liverpool in 1884, a perfect example of the rise of the middle class. Scholars were invited to lecture every month, but ordinary people and their folk poets were not allowed unless they were well off and had the correct clothes to wear. Lord Mostyn was prepared to say that Liverpool – which was made a city in 1880 – was fast becoming the capital of Wales. Note, not the capital of north Wales, as the Liverpool radical John Bright proclaimed at a meeting in the Philharmonic Hall, but the capital of Wales.

The Rev. Owen Thomas – doyen of the middle class

Ministers, especially those much in demand like the Rev. Dr Owen Thomas of Princes Road Welsh Calvinistic Methodist Chapel, were exceptionally well off. His letters contained frequent references to dining in comfortable and luxurious homes. He wrote to his children in Treherbert on 10 May 1881:

> … our people are mostly of the working classes – but Providence was never kinder to me.

Well-to-do elders at Princes Road Chapel

One of the chapel elders and a pillar of the middle class in all its glory was Peter Williams. He came to Liverpool from Cefn Mawr, near Ruabon, in 1837, and built a fine business as a draper. In Toxteth Cemetery in Smithdown Road stands a memorial to him after his death in 1880 (the largest grave in the whole cemetery). He was one of the leading laymen in his denomination and was the first moderator of the Liverpool monthly meeting when the Welsh churches split from the English-speaking Welsh Presbyterian Council of Lancashire and Cheshire in 1864.

Another representative of the middle class was John Jones, of 4 Thackeray Street. He was born in Liverpool into a Welsh community surrounded by people of various nations. His son, J Harrison Jones, became an influential city councillor and was an elder at Princes Road from 1877 until his death in 1924. A school named after him stood near Edge Hill until the 1970s.

Another representative of the middle class was William Jones, 19 Berry Street, who was a leader in Princes Road Chapel for forty-six years. And perhaps the most noteworthy of all was David Roberts, 63 Hope Street, the father of the politician John Roberts, who came from Llanrwst as a young man and became the foremost timber merchant in the city.

The family of John Davies of Peel Road, and later Devonshire Road in Toxteth, is one that cannot be overlooked. His father David Davies had come from Llanilar in Cardiganshire to Liverpool in 1837 as an agent for a tea company. He set up his own business, in Cook Street initially, and formed Davies and Sons and Company Ltd in 1837, moving to Crosshall Street and later to School Lane. John Davies followed in his father's footsteps in the business and became prominent in public life in the city. He was a Liberal member of the town council and chair of the executive committee of the Liverpool National Eisteddfod in 1884. He married Gwen, the daughter of the powerful preacher, John Jones of Talysarn, in the Nantlle Valley, and they had six children. The family lived at 55 Peel Road and then Belvidere Road, moving in 1891 to 38 Devonshire Road, Princes Park, where the Merseyside Welsh Heritage Society erected a plaque to commemorate two of his outstanding sons, John Glyn Davies and George M Ll Davies. But in March 1891, tragedy struck that comfortable home which was used to welcoming the great Calvinistic Methodist preachers, when John Davies became insolvent. And this was why, a year later, he was dismissed from the *Sanhedrin* – the monthly elders' meeting – of Princes Road Chapel. Going bankrupt was an unforgiveable sin in the opinion of the middle class of the Liverpool Welsh chapels. The Methodists had no sympathy for people who failed to maintain the ethos of the respectable middle class and, after his insolvency, John Davies would make his way to chapel, alone, along the back streets past Rhiwlas, Madryn, and ten other streets with Welsh names. His wife Gwen sat in her silks with the children in the front row of the chancel, but John Davies had to slink in through the vestry door and sit on his own in the corner under the new organ. A noteworthy feature of the middle class, especially those Welsh people who were born, brought up and lived in Liverpool, was snobbery.

Critics of middle-class snobbery

Hugh Evans, the publisher in Bootle, admitted that 'in former times, there was a lot of class consciousness in the churches of Liverpool and district and that, amongst the members, a number of them had made a substantial amount of money and it had gone to their head'. In his book, *Gyrfa y Dyn Cyffredin* (The Career of the Common Man), J W Jones, a native of Caernarfonshire, speaks of leaving the quarrying districts of Arfon and frequenting Stanley Road Calvinistic Methodist Chapel in Bootle in 1890. His experience was simply one of being unable 'to breathe freely, as everyone and everything seemed so refined and formal to me from an unpretentious rural background'. Dr R Merfyn Jones argued that this class distinction within the Liverpool churches was partly responsible for the split in the Merseyside Welsh Calvinistic Methodists at the beginning of the twentieth century, and the establishment of a new denomination, the Welsh Free Church. So, we see that the Welsh middle class in Liverpool were keen to climb the ladder as high as possible.

Success in a strange city

As we have seen, failure in business was akin to a crime among the middle-class Welsh. John Glyn Davies and George Maitland Lloyd Davies were young boys when their father was bankrupted. Glyn Davies succeeded the German Kuno Meyer as head of the Celtic Studies department of Liverpool University in 1920, but did not want to live in the city as he detested middle-class snobbery and their right-wing political views. He would travel to Liverpool from Flintshire, and was nauseated when he had to conduct a seminar with young Welsh middle-class people such as Saunders Lewis. But, as a poet, he has an abiding place in the history of Welsh literature. To him, being a member of the Welsh middle class was like being in prison, especially when, in his early days, he worked for the Rathbone Brothers shipping company. It was like prison, too, to live in Liverpool, and heaven to be able to escape to the Llŷn Peninsula on his holidays and walk around Edern among the old Welsh sailors. You can see this in poems such as *Ar Fôr i Lŷn* (By Sea to Lleyn). His depiction of a Welsh Sunday on Llŷn is also memorable.

Professor Glyn Davies produced much important work but his greatest service to Welsh culture was his poems associated with the sea adventurer Huw Puw. The main appeal of his verse is longing (*hiraeth*) for home, but he is somewhat comforted by the fact that the same moon shines on both Llŷn and San Francisco.

Many will be familiar with the words of his sea shanty *Fflat Huw Puw*:

There's a sound in Porthdinllaen,
The sound of sails rising,
Pulleys creaking,
Dafydd Jones shouting,
I cannot stay at home all my life,
I must go to sea on Huw Puw's flat-bottomed boat.

In another poem he refers to the Liverpool middle class:

Dear souls, your world was easy.
A woman and carriages gleaming in the sunshine,
No shortage of wealth, all with snug homes
And worldly pride between you and the Earth.
Beloved souls, quiet with God
You left Huw Puw's flat-bottomed boat behind.

His brother George Maitland Lloyd Davies attracted attention as a pacifist and a conscientious objector in the First World War. The Fellowship of Reconciliation, established in 1914, and the peace movement made him an icon among the many Welsh people who came to see him as the leader of Welsh pacifists. One of his most prominent followers, the future president of the Welsh Nationalist Party and its first MP, Gwynfor Evans, said:

> And now the time has come for me to name the man who was the main influence
> on my life. That was George M Ll Davies, the pacifist, the Welshman I came to
> adore.

As soon as he could, Davies discarded the trappings of the middle class
which were so evident in his home and his chapel. He threw himself into the
mission school in Warwick Street where the impoverished Welsh gathered.
In 1923 he served a term as the MP for the University of Wales constituency.
He was there for less than a year and only once took part in a debate, but
preferred to confer with people who were keen to see a different and a better
world.

The life of Sir Alfred Thomas Davies

The Liverpool Welsh middle class was responsible for nurturing Sir Alfred
Thomas Davies (1861–1949), a good friend to the politician David Lloyd
George. He was born on 11 March 1861 in north Liverpool, the son of
William and Mary Davies. He was accepted at the University College of
Wales, Aberystwyth, and returned to Liverpool in 1883 as a graduate and
found work as a lawyer. For almost twenty-five years he practised in Liverpool,
specialising in licensing law, a very profitable area of business, since there were
so many taverns in the city. That is also how F E Smith (who became Lord
Birkenhead) made his money and a name for himself in Liverpool early in his
career. Alfred T Davies played a prominent role in the temperance movement.
He had the reputation of being a safe pair of hands in his field and served on
various committees and educational trusts in Liverpool. Because of his family
links to Denbighshire, he served on its county council and the education
committee from 1904 to 1907. In that year he was appointed first permanent
secretary of the Welsh department of the Welsh Board of Education and
remained in that post for eighteen years.

Alfred Davies should be remembered for an important campaign. In
1923 Warrington Town Council expressed its intention to drown the valley
of Glyn Ceiriog to create a reservoir. The plan was to submerge an Anglican
church, five Nonconformist chapels, two cemeteries, two schools, two public
houses, five shops, a forge, eighty-two homes, forty-five of them cottages and
farms, all comprising 13,600 acres. In 1923 there were two able opponents

ready to take on the enemy of the people of the Vale of Ceiriog. The first was a product of the Liverpool Welsh middle class, the influential civil servant Sir Alfred T Davies, with his office in Whitehall, London, and whose family roots were in the valley. The second opponent was Robert Richards of Llangynog, who was Professor of Economics at the University College of Bangor before being elected Labour MP for Wrexham. Alfred Davies managed to enlist the support of Lloyd George in the successful campaign. The former Prime Minister, who had knighted him in 1918, said:

> It is monstrous for English Corporations to come to Wales and drown our historic and beautiful valleys.

Sir Alfred thanked him publicly in 1948 (after the politician's death) in his book, *The Lloyd George I Knew*. A year later he died, on 21 April 1949 in Brighton, having kept a close connection all his life to his background in Liverpool among the middle-class Welsh.

Oracle of Welsh history – Sir John Edward Lloyd

Another who had a comfortable middle-class upbringing was Sir John Edward Lloyd. He was born in Liverpool on 5 May 1861, the son of Edward Lloyd, a wealthy businessman, and his wife Mary (née Jones) who, like her husband, came from north Montgomeryshire, near the small hamlet of Penybont Fawr. In those days justices of the peace were always middle class. Edward Lloyd was one of them and he was also a deacon at Gwilym Hiraethog's chapel, Grove Street Independent Chapel. Like others of the Liverpool middle class, he spent his summer holidays in Wales.

His son was well educated in Liverpool and went to the University College of Wales, Aberystwyth, and from there in 1881 to Lincoln College, Oxford. One of his contemporaries at Aberystwyth was the literary giant Owen M Edwards. Lloyd was remarkably successful at Oxford, gaining first-class honours in Greek and Latin and, the following year, a first in history. And, in the middle of his degree course, he won the main prize at the 1884 National Eisteddfod in Liverpool for a handbook on the history of Wales up to 1282.

He was appointed to his old college at Aberystwyth in 1885 as a lecturer in history and Welsh. He stayed there for seven years and, at that time, expressed a great interest in the Liberal Party campaign for a Welsh Parliament. The Young Wales movement became important to the Liverpool middle class. He moved in 1892 to the University College of Wales, Bangor, as registrar and to assist as a historian in the history department. He once said of those years that he would be lecturing in the morning, working as a registrar in the afternoon and researching in the evening. He became a highly organised man; wise, diplomatic and a committee man of the first order. It might be said that he was one of the most important committee men in Wales, thanks to his contribution to the proceedings of the Cambrian Archaeological Association, the Welsh Language Society, the Board of Celtic Studies and the National Eisteddfod Society. In 1899 he was appointed Professor of History in succession to Professor R H Reichel and that was the beginning of a prolific period as, in 1911, *A History of Wales to the Edwardian Conquest* was published: two dense volumes presenting a well-wrought early history of Wales. Here are the words of one of his chief admirers, Professor R T Jenkins:

> It is not too much to say that this book is a turning point in the study of Welsh history; it was the fruit of a thorough critique of the sources and a clear and readable exposition of the course of history during the age of the Princes.

These volumes continue to be readable and dependable, and though a great deal of new information has since been published, historians of the calibre of Professor Rees Davies and Professor Beverley Smith have both praised the output of this Liverpool Welshman. He was awarded a DLitt from Oxford University in 1918 and further honoured by that university when he was invited in 1931 to give the James Ford Lectures. He chose Owain Glyndŵr as his subject and the University Press published them all, another of his superb historical books. He was knighted in 1934.

More contributions by the historian from Liverpool

It is a great mistake to think of Sir John as an authority only on the early period; he was a fount of knowledge on the whole history of Wales. He was invited to edit the two volumes of the *History of Carmarthenshire*, published in 1935 and one of the treasures of any scholar's library. In 1937 he was invited by the Cymmrodorion Society to be the editor of *Y Bywgraffiadur Cymreig hyd 1940* (Welsh Biographical Dictionary to 1940). His experience as an academic scholar since 1885 was extensive and he contributed 120 biographical notes to the Welsh and English versions of the *Dictionary of National Biography*.

He was very keen to ensure that the dictionary would be helpful to anyone with an interest in the past; local historians as well as scholars. For him and his collaborator Dr R T Jenkins, the definition of a scholar was someone who had many books at his or her service and loved researching the past. He himself wrote more than sixty biographies, despite the difficulties of wartime. But at least it gave him and R T Jenkins, two Liverpool Welshmen, the opportunity of meeting every week. For we should remember that it was in the city of Liverpool, in the Toxteth area in 1884, that Jenkins was born before moving to Bala as a child.

Sir John died on 20 June 1947 and I remember going in the company of two friends who used to live in the city, Eurfryn and Sian Arwel Davies of Llandegfan, to Llandysilio cemetery, near Porthaethwy on Anglesey, to see the graves of the Rev. Henry Rees and John Edward Lloyd.

Characteristics of the middle class

Sir John Edward Lloyd, like Sir Robert Jones and Dr Thelwall Thomas, were fine examples of the Liverpool Welsh middle class for three reasons. Firstly their smart clothing, their Sunday best, whenever they appeared in public. On every occasion each would be well turned-out and trim. Secondly, they were good communicators in their fields, with clear, audible voices. Thirdly, the language, be it Welsh or English, was always grammatically correct and free from any vulgarity or lack of taste. These privileged men were products of the Liverpool Welsh of the Victorian era. Sir John did not try to gain popularity by lowering his standards. He was perfectly portrayed by Saunders Lewis in the last two lines of his long Welsh-language poem, 'Elegy for Sir John Edward Lloyd':

> But he, the lantern-bearer of the lost centuries
> Was no longer there; neither his lamp, nor his word.

Professor W Garmon Jones at Liverpool University

In 1893 John Edward Lloyd had married Clementina Miller from Aberdeen, a student who had been one of his pupils at the University College of Wales, Aberystwyth, and they had a son and a daughter. The daughter, Eluned Lloyd, came to live in Merseyside. In 1923 she married Professor William Garmon Jones (1884–1937), a Welshman from Liverpool and Birkenhead, and it was his proud boast that he was John Edward Lloyd's son-in-law.

Jones was born on 15 November 1884 in Birkenhead, the son of William Jones (of Jones, Barton and Co. Engineers, Liverpool) and Jane (née Jones) from Mold. Another offspring of the middle class, he was sent to King William School on the Isle of Man, as his parents intended to prepare him for a career in trade. He returned home and found work in a Liverpool office but, in 1903, was accepted into Liverpool University to read for a degree in engineering. He completed most of his course but, in 1905, fell under the influence of Professor J M Mackay and discovered his lifelong métier, history. He gave up engineering for history and in 1908 gained a first-class honours degree, also winning the Charles Beard Fellowship, created by one of the founders of the university and a multifaceted minister in the Unitarian Church. A year later he was awarded his MA and was immediately made a Fellow of the university. He played a key role in university life as a lecturer in the history department from 1913 to 1919 and then as professor from 1924 until his death in 1937. In 1928 he was appointed university librarian, and so it becomes apparent why there is such a fine collection of Welsh books in the university's Sidney Jones Library. In Birkenhead he became an elder at Parkfield Chapel where the hymnwriter, the Rev. John Gruffudd Moelwyn Hughes, was the Presbyterian minister. He died on 28 May 1937 and was buried in the family vault in Flaybrick Cemetery. A memorial to him, carved by Tyson Smith, was erected in the Cohen Library at Liverpool University.

One of his most able pupils was another of the Liverpool Welsh middle class, Professor Thomas Jones Pierce (1905–64). He was born on 18 March 1905 in Liverpool, the son of John and Winifred Pierce, a family involved with Edge Lane Welsh Presbyterian Chapel. He was sent to the outstanding Liverpool Collegiate School, where he showed great ability at history. He was accepted to study in the history department of the University of Liverpool where he got to know Professor W Garmon Jones. He graduated with a first-class degree in history in 1927 and won the Chadwick Scholarship and the W E Gladstone Memorial Prize. He was regarded as one of the most creative historians of his period and a pioneer in his field. He died on 9 October 1964 and his funeral was held at Anfield crematorium. His scholarly articles were collected into a large volume by one of his pupils, Dr J Beverley Smith, in a book called *Mediaeval Welsh Society* published in 1974.

The ideas of Saunders Lewis

John Saunders Lewis was another outstanding scholar and leader in Welsh life who was born and raised in the Liverpool middle class. He excelled in so many fields in his lifetime – regarded as a first-rate poet, Wales's greatest dramatist, a politician, and a controversial critic and journalist who has been the subject of fierce debate.

When he was born on 15 October 1893, a son of the manse, his cultured parents, the Rev. Lodwig Lewis, minister in Liscard Road, Seacombe, and Mary (granddaughter of the Rev. William Roberts, Amlwch, and daughter of the Rev. Owen Thomas) wanted to raise him in Welsh. The best way to achieve this was to have two maids from Anglesey to care for him – a sure sign of an important middle-class family. His mother died in 1900, leaving three small boys to be brought up by an aunt who moved from Bangor to fill the gap.

In response to Owen Thomas's biography, *Pregethwr y Bobl* (The People's Preacher) published in 1979, Saunders Lewis admitted that his mother, grandfather and he were completely possessed by the snobbish atmosphere of the Welsh folk in middle-class Liverpool.

> The conventions of the strong London and Liverpool middle class (and of the Princes Road elders) were his standards and those of his children, yes, and of the only living grandchild – not by my choice, but a fact.

And sometimes the members of this class fell out within both sacred religious and social circles. Take Saunders Lewis's confession about J Glyn Davies: 'My personal relationship with Glyn Davies was very short, and fiercely quarrelsome.' And Glyn Davies's daughter Elen said of Saunders: 'His name was mud in our house.'

Yet there was a close connection between J Glyn Davies and J Saunders Lewis, both products of the Liverpool Welsh middle class at its best. Lewis's grandfather, Dr Owen Thomas, was minister at Devonshire Road and Davies remembers him spending Sunday at his home in the company of two other ministers, Dr David Saunders, the first minister of Princes Road, and Edward Matthews, of Ewenny in the Vale of Glamorgan. John Davies, his father, would sit at the head of the table in the splendid dining room, with Edward Matthews next to him and J Glyn Davies, a young man of seventeen or eighteen, opposite the other two preachers. Owen Thomas would steer the conversation and would mull over the old days with his father.

When Lewis set about preparing his MA thesis at Liverpool University he asked for support and guidance from Davies. In his preface to the book, *A School of Welsh Augustans: Being a Study in English Influences on Welsh Literature during part of the Eighteenth Century,* he writes of his debt:

> First to my teachers at Liverpool, and especially to Mr J Glyn Davies who suggested to me this course of study, and whose generous and inspiring criticism saved me from pitfalls and made my progress possible.

And he also notes:

> Oliver Elton, my teacher in Liverpool, was a cold, punctilious Oxonian scholar to the last degree; but it was Elton who said to me [about J Glyn Davies]: 'In spite of everything, you know, he is, he really is, a genius, and these are not so many.'

And one could give the same compliment to Saunders Lewis himself. His scholarship covered so many fields: literature, theology, psychology, sociology and politics. It is little wonder that Dr R Geraint Gruffydd said he was in no doubt that the University of Wales never, in all its history, had a more brilliant member of staff. His field at the time was Welsh literature and he produced valuable studies of William Williams Pantycelyn, shorter studies of the novelist Daniel Owen, J Ceiriog Hughes and a host of poets and literary figures such as Dafydd ap Gwilym, Islwyn, Dafydd Nanmor, Tudur Aled, Goronwy

Owen, Ann Griffiths, Robert ap Gwilym Ddu, Emrys ap Iwan and Owen M
Edwards. He immersed himself in the recognised classics of Europe in at least
four languages: Latin, French, Italian and English were at his fingertips. He
benefited from his teachers at Liverpool University and from the leadership of
French giants such as Paul Claudel, the poet and dramatist; François Mauriac,
the novelist; Jacques Rivière, the literary critic, and especially Étienne Gilson,
the historian and philosopher. In contrast to many of his contemporaries, he
succeeded in creating literature out of his critical writings.

One cannot completely understand Saunders Lewis without taking
account of his life within the Liverpool middle class. In the suburban life of his
Merseyside youth, in Wallasey, Seacombe and Liverpool, he became aware
of Catholicism and fierce Irish nationalism. He was privately educated, like so
many children of the Welsh middle class. After he met and fell in love with
an Irishwoman called Margaret Gilchrist, Ireland became meat and drink to
him. The poets of the Emerald Isle occupied hours of his time. The Irishman
with whom he venerated was Thomas Kettle (1880–1916), who advocated an
independent Ireland and was a close friend of the world-famous author James
Joyce. And, like Kettle, Saunders Lewis joined the army.

He got to know young people from the Liverpool middle class like
Gwilym Peredur Jones, the son of J H Jones, the editor of the weekly
newspaper *Y Brython* and subsequently Professor of Economic History at
Sheffield University. Peredur was chair of the Welsh Students' Society
at Liverpool University, Saunders was vice-chair and Jennie Thomas of
Birkenhead, who herself became a writer, was secretary. On the executive
committee was Richard Alan Morton (1899–1977), who became a lecturer
and professor at the university and a world leader in the field of biochemistry.
Here were five young Welsh exiles in Liverpool, debating and collaborating
whatever their background or religion.

It was during this time that the truth struck him – when he was arguing
with his father. Suddenly, his father turned to him and said to him as he
sat at his desk in the library: 'Look here, Saunders, you will never come to
anything unless you return to your roots.' He was brought back to earth
completely. Here was his fundamental weakness: forgetting that his roots in
the Welsh community in which he was born and nurtured were responsible

for his ardent nationalism. Despite his estranged affections towards Liverpool from time to time, it was decided, when the Merseyside Welsh Heritage Society was inaugurated in 2000, to erect a plaque on his home in Wilton Road and to hold a service emphasising his contribution and his self-sacrifice to the Welsh nation. He was loved and he was hated, acknowledged and rejected, but in the end he remained the most famous son of the Merseyside Welsh middle class.

Chapter 13

Literary figures

The exile's longing for Wales

Longing for Wales is a strong element in Liverpool Welsh poetry, as indeed it is in Welsh poetry itself. It is part of human experience, as Elias Davies maintains in an *englyn* composed when he was working in Barclays Bank in Egremont – for him it brings dark hours and pain, sleepless nights and tears.

There is a brilliant example of the power of this emotion in a *cywydd* composed by the Rev. Goronwy Owen in 1753 after a short time as curate of St Mary's Parish Church, Walton. It is a verse about longing for Anglesey and it clearly underlines the fact that he was very conscious of being an exile in Liverpool. Translation cannot do justice to this superb poem, but he expresses the feeling that he is a man of no significance and a foreigner to the land of Anglesey, a stranger to both his language and his poetic muse. Where he once played, very few people still recognise him. Even talking about it causes deep longing (*hiraeth*).

The message of Hugh Evans

We hear the same message time after time, and there is a fine prose example from a Merionethshire man of letters, Hugh Evans (1854–1934), who came from Llangwm in 1875 to Liverpool. Were it not for his longing for the area known as Uwchaled, the disappearing crafts and customs, the old world ceasing and his strong radicalism, he would not have written the classic *Cwm Eithin* which appeared in 1931 at the end of his productive life as a highly successful publisher. It is a much sought-after Welsh classic, for the fifth impression was published in 1949, the year after it was translated into English by the journalist E Morgan Humphreys under the title *The Gorse Glen*. Hugh Evans is the best example of a follower of Samuel Roberts (SR) of Llanbrynmair, the fierce pro-tenant, anti-landlord radical. *Cwm Eithin* is an uncompromising volume of propaganda on behalf of the hard-pressed tenants in the uplands of Wales. Here is the exile, in Bootle, reclaiming a lost culture and recounting in perfectly clarity his childhood haunts in Merionethshire and Denbighshire and the wool-gatherer Mari Wiliam calling to see his family:

> It was worth seeing her coming, one pack of wool tied to her back, something like a pillowcase stuffed full of wool; another pack under each arm like a cushion cover. My old uncle would be thrilled to see her coming and we boys made sure to be in the house that evening after supper, as one of the delights of the year was hearing my uncle asking Mari about all the doings of the families she would have been calling on.

Support for the creative artist

Goronwy Owen, who spent only two years as a curate in Liverpool, raises another point: that the writer and poet have to have some sort of support, not so much financial but rather social. He wrote to Richard Morris, one of the Anglesey Morris brothers, who did so much to preserve and promote Welsh literature from their London base in the eighteenth century:

> You ask why I have let the muse go rusty [in Walton]. By God, if I could get a reasonable price for it I would sell it. What is the point of the muse when a man is in nakedness and poverty? And who has the leisure to meditate when he is going from one affliction to the other in spiritual and bodily fatigue?

The sweet muse of Peter Jones

From the cultural vigour of Pall Mall, the first chapel set up by the Welsh community in 1787, came one of the earliest poets, Peter Jones, who was born on 17 September 1775 in Garndolbenmaen and died in Liverpool on the last Sunday of January 1845. He was the son of William Jones, also known as William Jesus, a folk poet. His son moved to Liverpool as a young man and, by 1799, was an elder, and despite the fact that the relationship between him and his fellow elders could be tempestuous at times, he made a huge contribution to the Liverpool Welsh community. The work of Pedr Fardd, as he was best known, can be seen in his volume *Mêl Awen* (The Muse of Honey), published in Liverpool in 1823 and containing a variety of metrical verses on topics such as innocence, brotherly love, the greatness of love. His *cywydd* 'The Deliverance of Israel and the Defeat of the Egyptians' was a prize winner at Brecon Eisteddfod.

However, his chief contribution was as a writer of hymns. The main theme is the salvation which is in Jesus Christ, but he also recounts his experiences as a believer, safe in the midst of peril, and confidence of victory in the suffering of his Saviour:

> Ere the creation of the world,
> Ere the creation of the sky
> With sun and moon and stars above
> Shining on us from on high,
> The Trinity a way prepared
> That man by sin be unimpaired.

The pen of Gwilym Hiraethog

A hymnwriter of the same standard is the Rev. William Rees (Gwilym Hiraethog, 1802–81). The love of God in Christ is the theme of his greatest hymns such as '*Dyma Gariad fel y Moroedd*' (Here is Love like the Seas). William Edwards (1848–1929) of Cardiff translated the verse into English:

> Here is love, vast as the ocean,
> loving-kindness as the flood,
> when the Prince of Life, our Ransom,
> shed for us His precious blood.
> Who His love will not remember?
> Who can cease to sing His praise?
> He can never be forgotten
> throughout heav'n's eternal days.

It was first published during his ministry in Liverpool in the volume *Per Ganiedydd* (Sweet Singer, 1847), his selection of hymns by William Williams (1717–91) and which contained an appendix of his own hymns. This hymn was sung regularly both in English and in Welsh during Evan Roberts's

Revival (1904–05). The scholar Professor Pennar Davies maintained that it was the finest hymn in the Welsh language.

Gwilym Hiraethog was active as an eisteddfod poet, winning a host of prizes, and won the crown for his poem on the subject of peace at Madog Eisteddfod in 1851. But his chief poetic work – on the subject of 'Emmanuel: the Essence of the Works and Government of God' – is a Welsh-language masterpiece filling 759 pages! David Adams (Hawen), one of the Liverpool poets, compared him to John Milton in terms of 'the strength of his convictions, his deep love of freedom… his hatred of violence and oppression… his sympathy with down-trodden people and nations, and in his spiritual devotion'. Indeed, to Hawen, the Welshman surpassed the author of *Paradise Lost*. Another of Hiraethog's important works is *Tŵr Dafydd* (The Tower of David), containing the psalms set in song and composed when he was sick.

Other Liverpool hymnwriters

During the nineteenth century there were a number of other hymnwriters within the chapels such as Minimus, who was mentioned in the chapter on mission, and John Owen Williams (Pedrog, 1853–1933), a minister with the Independents. He came from Llanbedrog to Liverpool in 1878 to work for a shareholding company and was soon an assistant preacher with the Methodist Church. He was attracted to the Welsh Independents in 1881, becoming a member of Kensington Chapel. Despite having had no theological training, he was ordained as a minister in 1884 and remained there for forty-six years until his retirement in 1930. By then the chapel was known as Pedrog's Chapel! He won the National Eisteddfod of Wales chair on three occasions, in Swansea (1891), Llanelli (1895) and Liverpool (1900). The latter chair can now be seen in the city hall. He was in demand as an adjudicator at eisteddfodau in Liverpool and the surrounding areas, in Wales and at the National Eisteddfod. He won a host of chairs at eisteddfodau and his best work is worth reading.

One of the Liverpool poets, Robert Owen Hughes (1893–1967), composed an *englyn* in his honour, describing him as a crowned leader in the world of literature and religion, a guide to contemporary poets and a very gentle philosopher.

A poet-preacher who is sometimes forgotten is the Rev. John Hughes

(1850–1932), a contemporary of Pedrog and a minister at Fitzclarence Street Welsh Calvinistic Methodist Chapel. He came to Liverpool from Machynlleth and was very busy ministering, preaching, theologising and composing poetry in both languages. In English he published *Songs of the Night* (1885) and *Tristora* (1896), and in Welsh *Dan y Gwlith* (Under the Dew, 1911), which contains his hymns.

Hawen and Pedr Hir

The Rev. David Adams (1845–1923) was a very forceful minister known in Welsh circles as Hawen. In 1895 he came from Bethesda in Arfon to be a minister at Grove Street Welsh Independent Chapel. He was extremely busy supporting eisteddfodau and, indeed, in 1884, won at the Liverpool National Eisteddfod with a treatise on the German philosopher Hegel, who was an influence on Karl Marx. He made an extensive contribution in the fields of poetry, philosophy and theology, and some of his hymns remain in circulation.

Two years after Hawen arrived in Liverpool, another eisteddfod-goer, Peter Williams (Pedr Hir, 1847–1922), arrived to minister to Balliol Road Welsh Baptist Chapel in Bootle. He stayed there until his death on 24 March 1922. Some of his hymns can be seen in various anthologies and the hymn he composed when he was just twenty, '*Bydd Canu yn y Nefoedd*' (There will be Singing in the Heavens), is still sung today.

Literary giants from the Thomas family

Among the Liverpool writers from the Nonconformist ministry, the contribution of the brothers Owen and John Thomas is worth noting. Owen Thomas's major literary feat is *Cofiant John Jones, Talsarn* (Biography of John Jones of Talsarn) which was published in 1874. His grandson, Saunders Lewis, deemed the biography to be a masterpiece of Welsh prose.

> This stands alone as a completely new biography in Welsh. Owen Thomas does not belong to the tradition of the biographers who preceded him. He was a scholar, studying mainly ecclesiastical history, modern English literature including historians and novelists and the history of the development of Protestantism in Wales. He loved the great English biographers, especially Boswell and Lockhart;

The Birbeck Hill impression of the *Life of Samuel Johnson* was his favourite book in his library.

He also wrote a biography of Henry Rees, minister of Chatham Street, and though not in the same league as the biography of John Jones, it is nevertheless valuable. His brother Dr John Thomas (1812–92) could be regarded as one of the pioneers of the Welsh novel with the work published in *Y Tyst a'r Dydd* in 1879 under the title 'Arthur of Llwyd y Felin' and later published as a book. I have a copy of it and his style is very attractive. He also wrote biographies: *Cofiant y Tri Brawd* (Biography of the Three Brothers, 1881); *Cofiant John Davies, Caerdydd* (A Biography of John Davies, Cardiff, 1883), and *Cofiant Thomas Rees, Abertawy* [sic] (Biography of Thomas Rees, Swansea, 1888). He and Thomas Rees wrote *Hanes yr Annibynnwyr Cymraeg* (A History of the Welsh Independent Churches) while he was minister at Tabernacle Chapel in Great Crosshall Street where he served from 1854 to 1892.

The efforts of the Rev. Griffith Ellis

One of Owen Thomas's admirers and good friends was Griffith Ellis (1884–1913), the minister of Stanley Road, Bootle, for thirty-eight years. He made a huge contribution after arriving in the midst of the Welsh people of Liverpool and Bootle following a brilliant career at Balliol College, Oxford. Certainly his most popular work was his tribute published in Welsh in 1898 to Prime Minister William Ewart Gladstone. There was significant demand for the book as Gladstone was an idol to the cultured Welsh. He is the only writer from Liverpool to have written a biography of Queen Victoria in Welsh, published in 1901, the year of her death.

Literary preachers among the Welsh Wesleyan Methodists

A prominent feature of the literary preachers who moved to the Liverpool region was that they remained in their new homes for a long time, the exceptions being the Wesleyan Methodist church ministers who moved either every three or five years. The Welsh in the city enjoyed the company and contribution of some of their most distinguished ministers, for example David Tecwyn Evans (1876–1957) who was in Liverpool and Birkenhead during the First World War. It was in Liverpool that he translated the well-known hymn by George Matheson (1842–1906) 'O Love That Wilt Not Let Me Go' for a community hymn-singing event in Bala in 1916. It was here, too, that he translated Charles Wesley's popular hymn 'Jesu, Lover of my Soul' and it was published in the March 1917 copy of the periodical *Cymru* (Wales), edited by Sir Owen M Edwards.

Another versatile Welsh Wesleyan minister and writer was the Rev. Edward Tegla Davies who, in August 1928, came from the Manchester circuit to the circuit of Mynydd Seion, Princes Road, one of the loveliest chapels in Liverpool. He described Mynydd Seion thus:

> … like an old gentleman who has seen better days – with the same bearing, the same walk, the same silk hat and frock coat, but the hat has begun to go brown and the coat is rather bluish-green with shiny elbows and the trousers browning at the knees.

His great literary work during his period in Liverpool was his translation of *Pilgrim's Progress* by John Bunyan, published by Hughes and Son. It was a volume of 341 pages and the Rev. J D Dyfnallt Owen of Carmarthen paid it this tribute in *Y Tyst:*

> Since the days of Stephen Hughes, many attempts have been made to turn John Bunyan's thoughts into Welsh. All are agreed on one thing: until now there has been nothing like Tegla's translation, newly published by Wrexham Press. Tegla's translation is much simpler, direct and idiomatic.

He received an honorary MA from the University of Wales in 1928 for his contribution to literature, and the multitalented writer moved to Bangor in 1931.

Liverpool Welsh writers of the twentieth century

Professor Gwilym Owen was a son of the manse, and had a notable career as a science professor. His father, the Rev. William Owen, was the minister of Webster Road Calvinistic Methodist Chapel in Wavertree. At the beginning of the First World War, Gwilym moved to New Zealand – this was a huge loss to Webster Road Chapel in Liverpool where he had been elected an elder in 1911. On his return from New Zealand he was appointed a professor at University College of Wales, Aberystwyth, and later deputy principal. But his great contribution was as a writer, presenting science through the medium of Welsh.

Later he was followed by Owen Elias Roberts of Childwall who worked as the principal scientist at Broadgreen Hospital's laboratory. He was a leader in both Anfield and Heathfield chapels and won the prose medal twice in the National Eisteddfod at Aberystwyth in 1952 and Ystradgynlais in 1954. Through his writings on science, he expanded the vocabulary of the Welsh language and his books are testimony to his skill as a writer.

Another writer who won the prose medal at the 1978 National Eisteddfod for *Y Ddaeargryn Fawr* (The Great Earthquake) – a fictional autobiography of the Danish philosopher and theologian Søren Kierkegaard – was Professor Harri Williams. He was a prolific writer and a product of Douglas Road Welsh Chapel, Liverpool.

One should mention the output of the Rev. D D Williams, the minister of David Street Welsh Presbyterian Chapel and later Belvidere Road, as he won National Eisteddfod prizes for his studies. One of the most important was his biography of Professor Thomas Charles Edwards, who was a minister in Liverpool before moving to be the first Principal of the University College of Wales, Aberystwyth, and later followed his father, the Rev. Dr Lewis Edwards, in charge of Bala Theological College. The work was published on behalf of the society of the National Eisteddfod in Liverpool in 1921. His biography of the Rev. Thomas John Weldon, published in 1925, was a controversial work in its day.

Probably the writer and historian who still remains significant to us is the Rev. John Hughes Morris (1870–1953). He had no higher education, only Chatsworth Primary School in Edge Hill, Liverpool. However, as a young man, he was appointed to the office of the Foreign Missions and served in Falkner Street from 1892 until 1949. He was the editor of *Y Cenhadwr* (The Missionary) from its inception in 1922 and also of the English publication *Glad Tidings*. His main achievement was his work as a historian of the missionary endeavour, and his *History of the Foreign Mission of the Welsh Calvinistic Methodists until 1904* is a mine of reliable information, published in English in 1910. In 1930, in Liverpool, a more popular book, *Ein Cenhadaeth Dramor* (Our Foreign Mission), was published and he also wrote and published small attractive booklets in Welsh on pioneers such as Thomas Jones, William Lewis and T Jerman Jones. He wrote two excellent volumes on Welsh Calvinistic Methodism in Liverpool and district in *Hanes Methodistiaeth Liverpool, Cyfrol 1* (Brython Press, 1929) and Volume 2 by the same press in 1932.

Another writer of distinction was the Rev. Iorwerth Jones of Gorseinon, one of the most prominent Welsh Independents of his generation. He was a product of Bootle and Liverpool. After the bombing in 1941, the Great Mersey Street Welsh Independent Chapel moved to Trinity Welsh Independent Chapel, Bootle. He came from a cultured family but his father worked in the docks. We get a lively picture of Welsh life in Kirkdale and Bootle in his book *Dyddiau Lobsgows yn Lerpwl* (Days of Lobscouse in Liverpool), describing the interwar years. The value of the work is that, apparently without intending to, it challenges the ideas of historians like D Tecwyn Lloyd and Gareth Miles who argue in their studies, mainly of Saunders Lewis, that the Liverpool Welsh were purely middle class. Iorwerth Jones shows that there were a host of cultured working-class Welsh in the city. The Welsh community in Great Mersey Street Welsh Independent Chapel were working class, and this was a chapel that had been well served by exceptionally talented ministers such as Peter Price, a fierce critic of the 1904–05 Revival; J Lewis Williams, a highly distinguished poet in eisteddfod circles, and the poet Simon B Jones (one of a well-known family of poets – Bois y Cilie – associated with Llangrannog in south Cardiganshire). But Simon B Jones stayed for only two or three years (1923–26), a year longer than David Emrys James (Dewi Emrys) who became a minister at the Welsh Free Church in Bootle in 1903 and won the chair at the National Eisteddfod of Wales in Liverpool in 1929.

The next two authors, Emrys Roberts and Namora Williams, are associated with Edge Lane Welsh Presbyterian Chapel. Namora Williams could write animatedly and memorably as we see in some of her essays in the periodical *Y Bont* (The Bridge). She was born in Liverpool, her father coming from Groeslon and her mother from Nantmor. She was educated in the city and at Liverpool University and was a teacher at Merchant Taylors Girls' School in

Crosby, along with many other Welsh speakers such as Megan Williams, Pat Williams and Dilys Jones. In 1986 she published a valuable study of one of the cultured country-folk of Merioneth: *Carneddog a'i Deulu* (Carneddog and his Family) – a gem of a book.

Emrys Roberts was the son of poet John Henry Roberts (Monallt). Three poets, Monallt, Deudraeth and Collwyn, worked together in the same cotton warehouse for years, all three skilled in metrical verse. Emrys Roberts, who was born in 1929, was named after the chaired poet at the Liverpool Welsh National Eisteddfod held at Sefton Park, namely the Rev. David Emrys James. Both his father's talent and that of Dewi Emrys were conferred on the infant! His unusual book about his father as a poet, *Monallt: Portread o Fardd Gwlad* (Monallt: Portrait of a Country Poet), is unique in our literature and explains the close relationship between father and son. Emrys Roberts has poems in *Gwaed y Gwanwyn* (The Blood of Spring) which speak of his Welsh-language childhood in Liverpool and includes a tribute to the Welsh teacher Olwen Williams (née Jones) of Anfield. She later married the eminent writer Harri Williams (1913–83), a hymnwriter and translator of hymns. As a labour of love Olwen taught the language to the children of Welsh families on a Saturday morning. This is a free translation from my pen of the original poem of Emrys Roberts:

> Scorn lay in the employers' eyes
> In wealthy Liverpool
> Seeing you on your confused way
> With your little parcel of books.
>
> Who but an insane teacher
> Unpaid would cheerfully go,
> Saturday mornings without fail
> To the alien chapel vestry?
>
> And we children, so disrespectful
> Of your sacrifice, loyal Siprah,
> Who brought to the place of dust and death
> The crystal excitement of a river.

What did we know of the heavy oppression
Of powers out to destroy us?
But deep in the lonely lady's heart
Were the scars of the enslavement.

You bathed us completely in the Welsh,
And carefully fed us
With the Mabinogion and with song
Your voice nourished and sustained us.

We knew not of the lost treasures
In the Israel of your memories,
All we in Egypt had been born
Who listened so reluctantly.

Today I do not know how
O pure midwife, without bitterness
You were able to keep us alive
In the unrelenting captivity.

But I know, when in cruel mischief
We sniggered under our breath
Where your thoughts were
As you gazed through the windows.

The eisteddfod tradition

The eisteddfod tradition was important – the Eisteddfod of the Ordovices, named after Celtic tribes living in Britain before the Roman invasion, was held from 1840 until the end of the century. The National Eisteddfod of Wales came to Liverpool in 1884, 1900 and 1929 and to Birkenhead in 1878 and 1917. The latter became famous as the Eisteddfod of the Black Chair when the winning poem was by Ellis Humphrey Evans (Hedd Wyn, 1887–1917), a young poet from Trawsfynydd. He wrote half the poem, entitled *Yr Arwr* (The Hero), in Litherland military camp before going to France and being killed at the Battle of Pilkem Ridge on 31 July 1917. The chair he should have occupied as the winning poet became known as the Black Chair of Birkenhead.

Eisteddfod founder and star of the Ordovices

One of the most important eisteddfodau of the nineteenth century was the Eisteddfod of the Ordovices. One of the founders was the Anglesey tailor Evan Evans who used the bardic name Eta Môn. He came to Birkenhead from Bethesda in 1865, and persuaded his fellow Welshmen of letters, such as William Owen, to form the Welsh Society which gave birth to the Literary Society of the Ordovices. He came from Llanfair Mathafarn Eithaf and gave many years of unpaid service as secretary of an eisteddfod which provided a platform for poets from Wales, Liverpool, Lancashire and Cheshire. Richard Davies (Tafolog, 1830–1904) took the first prize at the Ordovician Eisteddfod for a metrical verse on the subject of prayer.

In Liverpool itself there were groups of poets competing in these eisteddfodau – such as the builder William Williams (Gwilym Mathafarn); Gabriel Williams; Hugh Jones (Trisant), another cultured builder; Tanadlog, whose wife was a sister of the powerful-preacher the Rev. John Evans, a native of Eglwysbach in the Conwy Valley; Carog; Caradog of Anglesey, a Kirkdale pharmacist; and Rowland Williams (Hwfa Môn, 1823–1905), a Welsh Independent minister and chaired bard at the Birkenhead Eisteddfod in 1878. Another poet was Edward Davies (Iolo Trefaldwyn, 1819–87) who won the chair at the Ordovician Eisteddfod in Liverpool in 1870 for his poem *Goleuni* (Light).

We should also note the Rev. J Myfenydd Morgan, an Anglican priest who hailed from Blaenpennal in Cardiganshire; R W Jones (Diogenes) from Garston; Griffith Griffiths; Robert Parry (Madryn); as well as Gwaenfab and Llwynog who were all greatly involved. R H Davies (Erfyl, 1789–1858) also promoted the eisteddfodau. He was disabled and, towards the end of his life, served in the Welsh press in Chester, printing Welsh books for David and John Parry. Another colourful literary figure was Robert Herbert Williams (Corfanydd, 1805–76), the author of the tune '*Dymuniad*' (Desire). He kept a clothing shop in Basnett Street on the corner of Williamson Square and won a notable prize at the Ordovician Eisteddfod in 1869 for his treatise on the failings and virtues of the Liverpool Welsh.

Other eisteddfodau and various bards

In the years following 1870 and up to about 1930, eisteddfodau were established on both sides of the river. There was the Scotland Road Eisteddfod and the Bootle Eisteddfod, Lewis Eisteddfod in Renshaw Street and important eisteddfodau on the outskirts such as Widnes Eisteddfod and *Y Glomen Wen* (White Dove) Eisteddfod in Birkenhead. In 1918, at the end of the First World War, *Undeb y Ddraig Goch* (Union of the Red Dragon) was set up, a patriotic movement largely in the hands of poets and writers. The union organised a host of activities: an annual St David's Day celebration, preaching meetings, concerts, Welsh-learner classes and also classes in Welsh strict-metre verse. In 1921 the *Undeb y Ddraig Goch* Eisteddfod was established by the journalist R J Rowlands (Meuryn). Welsh was the sole language of the eisteddfod, with emphasis on the nationalist aspirations and ambitions of the *Cymru Fydd* (Young Wales) movement. The founders of the Union of the Red Dragon were Rolant Wyn Edwards (Hedd Wyn's uncle); bookseller J R Morris; the pacifist and nationalist Dan Thomas; poets William Morgan (Collwyn) and J E Roberts (Ap Heli); the medical practicner R T Williams and the estate agent Cledwyn Hughes. The lectures in Hackins Hey were important, with Saunders Lewis, as a university postgraduate student, attracting a large number of people to enjoy weekly classes in literary criticism. D R Jones was the president of the Union of the Red Dragon and R J Rowlands the secretary.

But the arrival of the Union of the Red Dragon was a source of contention among the Liverpool Welsh. The wealthy middle class felt it was an attack on them and their Welsh National Society, which met monthly in Colquitt Street and carried out its activities mainly in English. One of the Liverpool eisteddfod-goers who attacked them vehemently was the Rev. W A Lewis who had been involved with *Eglwys Rydd y Cymry* (Welsh Free Church) along with the influential Bootle-based R Vaughan-Jones. The Red Dragon eisteddfodau were of great benefit to poets and writers in 1920s Liverpool, and some of Wales's foremost bards competed for its chair, among them the Rev. William Morris, J M Edwards of Llanrhystud and Evan Jenkins of Ffair Rhos near Pontrhydfendigaid, Cardiganshire.

The prime instigator of the eisteddfod movement was R J Rowlands (Meuryn) together with O Caerwyn Roberts (Caerwyn) whose work as

Master of Ceremonies was highly accomplished. The Union had moved away from cultural matters by 1928, and by then had been more or less swallowed by the executive committee of Plaid Cymru.

Gwilym R Jones

Gwilym R Jones published his first volume of poetry during his period in Liverpool. He lived in Gredington Street in Dingle which contained a number of Welsh people, and attended Princes Road Chapel. He achieved the feat of winning the Crown at the National Eisteddfod of 1935 and the only National Eisteddfod Chair by a Liverpool poet during this time, at the Cardiff Eisteddfod of 1938 when two of the three judges had connections with Liverpool, namely Professor T Gwynn Jones (who had been a young journalist on *Y Cymro*) and Saunders Lewis. Gwilym R Jones was also editor of *Y Brython* from 1931 until publication ceased at the start of the Second World War.

Gwilym Meredydd Jones

Gwilym Meredydd Jones came originally from Glanrafon in Edeyrnion and made a particular contribution in the world of drama and short stories. His first novel was *Dawns yr Ysgubau* (The Dance of the Sheaves of Corn), based on the Old Testament Book of Ruth, and published in 1961. He got to grips with the Liverpool of the 1970s especially in the book *Ochr Arall y Geiniog* (The Other Side of the Coin) and in that fine story *Yr Ymwelydd Annisgwyl* (The Unexpected Visitor). He had similar stories in *Gwerth Grôt* (The Value of a Groat, 1983) and he produced the novels *Yr Onnen Unig* (The Only Ash Tree) and *Drymiau Amser* (Drums of Time), as well as a volume of short stories, *Chwalu'r Nyth* (Destroying the Nest), which was published after his sudden death in 1992. He also contributed extensively to the local Welsh-language community papers, *Y Bont* and *Yr Angor*.

Master of metre – Gwilym Deudraeth (1863–1940)

One of the most prominent poets among the Liverpool Welsh was William Thomas Edwards (Gwilym Deudraeth). He worked in a cotton warehouse but followed the classes of the well-known educationalist J J Williams, who was a teacher at Granby Street School in Toxteth and later appointed deputy director of education for Birkenhead Corporation. Two volumes of his work, *'Chydig ar Gof* a *Chadw* (Something to Remember and Keep) and *Yr Awen Barod* (Impromptu Verse), were published at the request of his many admirers. Poetry came totally naturally to him and he taught the complex internal rhyming form of *cynghanedd* to the poet Elis Aethwy, the son of the minister at Newsham Park Chapel. He was beset by a number of weaknesses, such as a fondness for beer and gambling, but he could compose an *englyn* for any occasion – and even in English. Here is his memorable couplet to the bookie:

> But after a bitter bet
> The bookie kicked the bucket.

He was buried in Allerton Cemetery on 23 March 1940, and for more than sixty years there was no headstone there. In 2003 the Merseyside Welsh Heritage Society succeeded in persuading undertakers Pearson-Collinson in Allerton to erect, at a reasonable price, an impressive headstone worthy of him with an appropriate *englyn* by Dic Jones of south Cardiganshire who came with the nephew of the poet, Trefor Edwards (London), to the unveiling.

Charm of Gwaenfab's muse

Robert Roberts (Gwaenfab, 1850–1933) from Bala worked with Gwilym Deudraeth in the cotton industry. While quite young he went to sea and worked as a stoker with the Cunard company; it was heavy work at which the boys of Scotland Road excelled. Departing on his travels out of Liverpool, he grew fond of the city and, after getting married in 1880, decided to settle in Bootle where he spent thirty years before moving back to Bala. He was the grandfather of the entertainer and very able conductor of our generation, the late Emrys Jones of Llangwm.

Gwnus and Madryn

Owen Parry (Gwnus, 1873–1954) lived in Bootle but hailed from Cefn Gwnys farm, Llithfaen. He was an agent for the Prudential insurance company and became an official and a manager within the company. One of his great friends among the poets who wrote *cynghanedd* was Robert Parry (Madryn, 1863–1935) who spent most of his life in Liverpool. Owen and his wife Elizabeth Catherine Parry (née Williams) had nine children. In the early years he worked with the company of J E Davies, Master Carters, and later with Monk and Newall doing similar work. Towards the end of his life he moved to the shipbuilders Harland and Wolff. His poems can be found in *Y Brython* and he won chairs at many Liverpool eisteddfodau.

The poems of R Lloyd Jones

The work of the *cynghanedd* poet R Lloyd Jones (1883–1968) was seen regularly in the Liverpool Welsh-language press. He was from Penmachno, son of the local poet Dewi Machno and, after working some time as a quarryman and mechanic, moved to Liverpool and found work until retirement at Cammell Laird shipbuilders. His funeral was held at Anfield Crematorium in December 1968.

Teachers of local poets

J R Morris (1874–1970) is considered a teacher among the Welsh bards of Liverpool and he was prominent in every cultural movement in the city. He and his poet friend Rolant Wyn were partners in a bookshop in Renshaw Street before leaving for Wales and setting up an interesting second-hand bookshop in Pont Bridd, Caernarfon. Morris was a member of Princes Road Chapel for twenty years; for most of that time the Rev. H Harris Hughes was there, and for a portion, the ministry of the prince of Welsh preachers in the 1930s, Griffith Rees.

William Morgan (Collwyn, 1882–1952), from Carno in Montgomeryshire conducted two evening classes on Welsh literature under the auspices of Liverpool University, and was a good friend of Gwilym Deudraeth. He was a coalminer in south Wales before moving to Liverpool to work, like so many other poets, in the cotton industry.

Llanowain and his contemporaries

One of the most prominent composers of *cynghanedd* in the post Second World War period was Owen Trevor Roberts (Llanowain). He lived in

Liverpool for thirty-six years and led a very interesting life. He was in the merchant navy for twelve years, and when his ship was torpedoed during the war Roberts spent sixteen days in an open boat before being rescued. He lost his wife Bet (originally from the Blaenau Ffestiniog area) and married again to Miss Mair Jones (Telynores Colwyn), who was the principal harpist with the Liverpool Philharmonic Orchestra. The couple made their home in Ruthin. Liverpool's Modern Welsh Publications published two volumes of his poetry: *Cerddi Llanowain* and *Ail Gerddi Llanowain* which appeared in the 1970s. He published a novel, *Helynt wrth ddal Morfilod* (Adventures Catching Whales) and *Englynwyr Glannau Mersi* (Merseyside *Englyn* Composers, 1980).

One who worked alongside Llanowain in north Liverpool was the Rev. R Maurice Williams. He edited the magazine *Y Bont* where many of his own *englynion,* as well as those of Llanowain, appeared between 1959 and 1979. For twenty-seven years, from 1952, the poet-preacher 'RM' was minister at the Welsh Presbyterian churches of Crosby Road South, Waterloo, and Peniel, Southport. He was the son of the poet and harpist Ap Berth from Bethesda (one of R Williams Parry's friends).

It was Williams who nurtured the poet R J Roberts – who came from Blaenau Ffestiniog to live in Wavertree – the author of two volumes of poetry and a writer of *englynion* who won many prizes at eisteddfodau in Liverpool and Wales.

Towards the end of his life John Roberts moved from Lleyn to Allerton and he too wrote skilful *englynion* for *Y Bont*. These four were among the last *cynghanedd* bards among the Liverpool Welsh in the twentieth century.

Chapter 14

Welsh builders in Liverpool

An early pioneer, William Jones

One of the first Welshmen to make his mark was William Jones (1788–1876), who was born in Ty'n y Graig, Cerrigydrudion, the eldest son of William and Catharine Jones. They had seven children but, in spite of that, William was educated in Chester and served his apprenticeship in the Pentrefoelas area. He moved to Liverpool in 1815, where he spent sixty years or more. He was responsible for building some of the main streets of Liverpool: Parliament Street, Upper Parliament Street, Duke Street and Upper Duke Street. Of the streets he built, the most splendid was probably Catharine Street, named after his mother, who had been so supportive of him in his early years. He himself made his home there in number 35, and the preacher Dr Owen Thomas lived in number 46. He had sixty people working for him, most of them Welsh, but he rejected a job request from the young Welshman, John Morris, who himself became an important builder.

Certainly one of his great contributions was building the railway stations between Liverpool and Manchester for George Stephenson, when he laid one of the railways for the *Rocket* in 1830. His nephew, also named William Jones, of Tafarn y Llew, Cerrigydrudion, took over the business, but he didn't enjoy the same success as his uncle.

William Jones was the first of the Liverpool builders to use his wealth for the benefit of his birthplace. He built a school and a schoolhouse in Uwchaled and bought the farmhouse of Pen y Bryn, which he bequeathed to the school so it could benefit from the rent. Every year he would give a tea party for the school children, and there is a window in Cerrig Church to commemorate him.

Raw materials for the building industry

North Wales was, of course, famous for its raw materials, particularly slates. There were quarries in Caernarfonshire and Merionethshire which transported slates to harbours like Porthmadog, Caernarfon and Port Dinorwic for shipping to Liverpool. Hundreds of slates were needed to make a roof, 400 to 500 at the very least, and the slates from the Penrhyn and Ffestiniog quarries were considered to be first class. Sandstone and lime were readily available from Flintshire, close to Chester, while Parys Mountain, near Amlwch, was an important source of lead, zinc and copper. With all this on their doorstep – slates, gravel, bricks and stones from Trefor and Penmaenmawr – Welsh builders in Liverpool had access to the finest raw materials.

Builders connected with Princes Road Chapel

Their cultural background formed a bond between the builders. Princes Road Chapel was famous for the number of builders among its membership. For example, Daniel Daniel (1834–1911) of Amberley Street was an excellent precentor and was elected an elder in 1882. He came from Castell-y-Cregin in Cardiganshire and from 1869 onwards he was responsible for building a number of houses in the Toxteth area, Upper Warwick Street, Churchill Street, North Hill Street, Upper Parliament Street and Amberley Street, and even some of the magnificent houses in Princes Road. As a joiner he liked to do the woodwork himself, but he was fortunate in having the help of Manoah Evans (1830–1909) of Mulgrave Street. He worked on his own, so when Daniel Daniel needed a first-class craftsman in North Hill Street, Upper Parliament Street and Upper Warwick Street, he relied on Manoah Evans, a hard-working member of Princes Road Chapel. Manoah could not bear sloppy workmanship and he believed that every builder should do the woodwork. But he had a kind heart and was a generous treasurer of the Princes Road Chapel Poor Society. He was responsible for building houses in Claribel Street in Princes Park, one side of Beaconsfield Street, and a cluster of houses in Mulgrave Street, where he himself lived. He moved his business from Toxteth to the suburb of Aigburth and built houses in Allington Street and Bryanston Street.

Another builder who made his mark was Hugh Jones (1834–1904), a native of Llandwrog, near Caernarfon. The youngest of twelve children, he lost his parents when he was only twelve and came to Liverpool in 1858 to work for a building company. He was keen to educate himself and attended evening classes at the Mechanics' Institute in Mount Street. There he met the architect Richard Owen and they became good friends. He set up on his own and began building Thackeray, Tennyson and Arnold streets, all off Parliament Street. He bought seven acres of land between Lodge Lane and Alt Street and built more than 300 terrace houses there.

A family of builders

There was another Hugh Jones (1852–1915) who was a member of the same chapel at that time. Hugh Jones, Mulgrave Street, as he was called, came from Holyhead. His expertise was in plastering and he worked on his own. He had plenty of work before venturing to join his fellow Anglesey builder, John Lewis, of Cemaes, in renting a yard and large shed to store his machinery in Upper Parliament Street. From there he received his first contract to build Mulgrave Street and Kimberley Street near his favourite chapel, Princes Road. He had a discussion with the Corporation about the road surfaces and he suggested laying cobbles, but granite setts, however, for busy streets like Selborne and Granby. This was a good move because it made the streets less noisy. Hugh Jones seized his opportunity and, together with his three brothers, John, William and Edward, he started a company under the name Jones Brothers. The company concentrated on two areas, Edge Hill and Aigburth. They bought a large factory in Spekeland Street and pulled it down in order to build streets called Sirdar and Luxor. Later, his son Edward of Alexandra Drive joined him as a partner. Liverpool Corporation had great faith in him and, after condemning a number of streets, they asked the company to build new ones. There was much activity in Aigburth and he built four estates, namely Woodlands, Briarley, Valleyfield and Mossdale. He became an income tax and land tax commissioner, a member of the Toxteth Board of Guardians, and one of the founders of the Young Wales Club in Upper Parliament Street.

His son, Edward R Jones, was a pioneer in the building trade, one of the founders of the Liverpool Housing Building Company, together with William

Jones and J W Jones. He believed that the slums should be demolished and better houses built, old properties renovated and homes built for the poor at a low rent. In 1915 he built a house that was heated with gas, using a system he had seen on a visit to Utica, New York State. He also built houses that were totally dependent on electricity. Although brought up in Princes Road Chapel, he concentrated on missionary work, particularly in Kent Square. His daughter Leah with her husband Clement Evans, and also their sons, John and Ted Clement-Evans, were involved in surveying, building and selling houses. So five generations have been involved in the building industry and the sixth, Gaynor Clement-Evans, of Aigburth, is still running a property management business to this day. It is an incredible story, the only example of a single Liverpool Welsh family retaining its involvement with the building industry for such a long period.

Better living conditions in terraced houses

The Welsh had a great influence on the planning of the streets and terraced houses. From the 1840s onwards terraced houses were built in the suburbs and in the town centre, particularly in Vauxhall, as a result of the efforts that were made from 1842 onwards to upgrade homes. Two men in particular – W H Duncan, a doctor, and Samuel Hughes, a builder – were determined to make sewerage a priority. A private member's bill had been put before Parliament in 1842 enabling corporations such as Liverpool to take the lead. The aim was to build new homes and to impose strict conditions on other buildings. These were the first steps to improve the standard of urban living. Probably the most important stimulus was the Liverpool Sanitary Act of 1846, which was a huge advance on the Liverpool Health and Town Act of 1842. Every street had to be at least thirty feet wide, instead of twenty-four feet, and the ceiling of every cellar had to be at least three feet above the level of the pavement. Another requirement was that the owners had to install pipes to carry waste to the main sewer. To ensure that these improvements were all carried out, an engineer and a so-called nuisance inspector were appointed. This was the decade in which Liverpool was changed for the better in the field of house and street construction and the environment. Several Welsh builders saw a business opportunity and developed what became known as Welsh streets and Welsh houses.

The contribution of the Welsh to the building of Liverpool

It was Welsh builders who introduced the four-roomed house on two storeys. It was quite different to what was available previously and the working class welcomed these new terraced houses with a small back garden and their front door opening, not on to a narrow street but a wide one. They were houses built from high-quality raw materials from Wales. By the next decade, the Welsh were building six-roomed houses with three bedrooms, which were better still. These houses became very popular and sold in the 1850s for £140 to £160, rising to £180 to £220 in the 1870s.

John Hughes expands his empire

The style of house built by the Welsh was exported to other cities. Take for example John Hughes (1863–1936) of Moneivion, Green Lane, Allerton, originally from Llanrhuddlad, Anglesey, whose company was responsible for housing estates in Liverpool, the Kenton Estate in London and the Shirley Estate in Birmingham. Hughes constructed all kinds of buildings – cottages, detached houses, rows of houses, flats and shops. His construction of the Kenton Estate was regarded as his greatest achievement, as he incorporated churches, schools, play centres, boulevards, and a railway station. J R Jones, his contemporary and fellow elder at Heathfield Road Chapel near Penny Lane, paid this tribute to him regarding the Kenton Estate:

> In short, one of the satellite towns of London has been brought into existence through the enterprise and determination of a Welsh builder born of humble circumstances on Anglesey.

Economic heart of the town

Kirkdale – or Llangwm to the Welsh – was considered to be the economic heart of the community because of the factories, the warehouses and the starting point of the Liverpool-Leeds canal. The place was buzzing with foundries, cotton warehouses and various storehouses. One of the large mills was Kirkman's Union Cotton Mill, which was known for years as the Welsh

Factory, as the vast majority of its workers were Welsh. In addition there were older industries like the sandstone quarries at Bankhall, where again most of the workers were Welsh. There were a number of stone quarries on the high ground above Netherfield Road, which supplied materials for the public buildings that were being built. There was a constant demand for building land.

One of the Welsh builders who was an expert at this was Robert Evans of Roscommon Street. He was heavily dependent on John Roberts, West Derby, a distinguished architect. Their greatest accomplishment in 1855 was building houses in Boundary Street between Great Homer Street and Scotland Road. By this time the rural atmosphere had long gone, with the docks and warehouses an integral part of the landscape.

Two building families from Anglesey

An undisputed pioneer in developing Kirkdale was David Hughes (1820–1904) from Cemaes, Anglesey. He came to Liverpool in a small sailing boat from Amlwch, a journey which took three days. He was employed as a joiner by the important builder Owen Elias, but he was ambitious and, after saving £80 from his paltry wages, he ventured into the building industry, concentrating on Kirkdale. After building a good number of streets on a large piece of land between the northern docks and Stanley Road in Kirkdale, he saw the potential of Everton, where his friend Owen Elias (1806–80) was engaged in building on a grand scale. Elias, who came from Llanbadrig on Anglesey, seized on the excellent opportunity he saw for building between Great Homer Street and Heyworth Street. Soon afterwards David Hughes also began building in Everton, and between them – but not together – they built hundreds of houses and made Everton a centre for the Welsh. More Welsh than English was spoken in the streets, and foods, books and periodicals from Wales were sold in the shops. Nearly every shop window had an advertisement for a concert or a preaching meeting to be held in one of the churches or chapels.

David Hughes concentrated on Anfield, just as Owen Elias and his son William Owen Elias (1850–1917) did in Walton. Elias named the streets he and his son had built in Walton using the letters in their own names for the initial letter of the street. For example, Oxton, Winslow, Eton and Neston after the letters of the father's Christian name; then Andrew, Nimrod and Dane after the conjunction 'and', with Wilburn, Isman, Lind, Lowell, Index, Arnot and Mandeville, following the letters of William's name. These are to be found between County Road and Goodison Road. Later, William used the name of his eldest son Alfred in a similar fashion – starting with Aspen Street and ending with Dyson Street, thus commemorating three generations of builders who benefited greatly from the industry.

Everton was a pretty village when Owen Elias and his two bachelor brothers, William (1808–84) and Edward (1814–87), moved there. The two bachelors lived in Everton Valley, near the church of St Chad, and Owen in Water Street initially, before moving to a small mansion called Mere House in Mere Lane. By then he was known as 'The King of Everton'. All five builders were active members of Welsh Calvinistic Methodist churches. Thomas Hughes adapted a room in Walmsey as a missionary chapel and, when it ran out of space, his brother David built Cranmer Street Chapel at his own expense, and from there the congregation later moved to the new Anfield Road Chapel. Thomas Hughes also erected, at his own cost, a building in York Terrace for members who had moved from the chapel in Burlington Street, before Netherfield Road Chapel was built. There was no end to Thomas Hughes's generosity to the Welsh Calvinistic Methodists. Because he saw an opportunity around West Derby Road, he built a chapel and a schoolroom in Lombard Street and presented them as a gift to the Calvinistic Methodist denomination.

Owen Elias had the same generous nature as Thomas and David Hughes. He designed the chapel in Burlington Street and contributed towards the cost. Several years later he erected a schoolroom in Arkwright Street at his own expense for the use of non-Welsh-speaking Welsh people. The church moved later to Everton Brow, where the wood merchant William Evans was in charge and Elias was honoured by being elected president of the Assembly of English Causes, which were under the auspices of the Presbyterian Church of Wales. Evans played a prominent part in the life of Liverpool as a councillor and alderman. At least sixty per cent of the houses in Everton were built in the days of Owen Elias and his brothers, along with David Hughes and his brother. It is little wonder that one of Liverpool's historians, James Picton, called Everton the 'Welsh Goshen' – the place in Egypt given to the Hebrews by the pharaoh.

The streets of John Williams, Moss Bank

An exceptionally intelligent man in the building industry in Everton was John Williams (1817–1906) of Moss Bank. He moved from the Conwy Valley to Liverpool in 1837 where he spent seventy years, and built on a large scale for sixty of them. His wife Eleanor Jones (née Williams) from Abergele was the mother of nine children and her eldest son, W H Williams, became Lord Mayor of Liverpool. He built not only in Everton, but also around Sefton Park, Lodge Lane, and Princes Road, as well as in Anfield. His company built two streets near Goodison Park and named them Leta and Gwladys after his granddaughters.

Over-development in Everton, West Derby and Kensington

The greatest weakness of building in Everton was that it was overdone. As early as 1860 there were complaints that so many streets were a concern for the environment. By 1900 there were further complaints that the four-roomed houses lacked basic facilities. This is Thomas A Roberts's analysis of the situation:

> Thousands of these regulation houses, mainly of the four-roomed type, lacked
> the basic amenities of mains water, mains sewerage and gas, and had to share
> a communal WC. Even when gas and electricity were commonplace in other
> districts, such housing lingered on without the benefit of either until demolished
> after the Second World War.

The same story was to be heard in West Derby and Kensington. Robert Evans (1832–1919) from Llannerchymedd, together with Robert Edwards of Bootle, made an important contribution in Kensington. They formed a partnership after being commissioned by Owen Elias to help him build houses. They moved from there to Kensington and Fairfield, building street upon street of terraced houses, and then they moved on to Dingle.

Building boom in Toxteth

The same reconstruction that took place in the 1840s in Kirkdale and Everton was repeated in the suburb of Toxteth. Two decades later a new model was available, namely the six-roomed house, and by the next decade an average of 600 houses per annum were being built in the borough of Toxteth. Frequently one Welsh company would build on one side of the road and another would take charge of the opposite side. Manoah Evans was responsible for one side of Beaconsfield as well as for Granby Street and Princes Park. He was originally from Llanarth, Cardiganshire, and made a huge contribution to the building of Anfield, Edge Lane, Fairfield, Dingle and Wavertree. He was a staunch Welsh Independent and a deacon at Tabernacle Chapel, Belmont Road, Anfield, and a scholarship is offered in his name at Aberystwyth University.

Indeed, most of the builders in Toxteth were Welshmen. For example, the Williams brothers from Abererch, namely Griffith Williams (1833–86), Robert Williams (1834–1918), Richard Williams (1841–1911) and Elias Williams (1842–1902). Griffith Williams was a joiner, apprenticed with his brother Richard in Llaniestyn and Morfa Nefyn. He built in Upper Warwick Street, Pickwick Street and Dorrit Street in Toxteth, but more of his work is found in Everton (St Domingo Road, Melbourne Street) and in Anfield (Oakfield Road, Brick Road, Esmond Street, Rocky Lane and many more).

Robert and Richard Williams worked together in Dombey Street in Toxteth, but on a larger scale in Kirkdale, and when their brother John Williams joined the business, they expanded to Walton (Walton Lane, Sleepers Hill, Stonewall Street and Saxon Street).

Elias Williams's work can be seen in Upper Warwick Street and Dorrit Street. At a later stage he joined his brother Griffith and William Rowlands to form a construction firm known as Williams and Rowlands, concentrating on the borough of Anfield.

William Williams (1839–1915), Eversley Street, concentrated on Parliament Fields between Princes Road and Upper Parliament Street.

To us today, the best-known streets in Toxteth are the Welsh streets, which local people have campaigned to retain in spite of the Corporation's demolition plan. They have been preserved to a large extent because one of the Beatles, Ringo Starr, was born in 9 Madryn Street. They were built originally for Welsh families working in the building industry, with Welsh names like Rhiwlas, Powis, Elwy and Dovey. Eleven such streets can be seen within walking distance of Princes Road Chapel and Princes Park. Teilo Street was built by the important leader of the Welsh Independents, Evan Evans (1854–1924), Borrowdale Road. He was a deacon and treasurer of the Welsh Independent Chapel in Park Road, Dingle. He and his brother John Evans were responsible for building Credington Street in Dingle and Sandhurst Street in Aigburth, and streets where many of the members of Edge Lane Welsh Calvinistic Methodist Chapel lived, namely Whitland Road and Manton Road in Fairfield. But perhaps the most famous street he built in Toxteth is Teilo Street, built for wealthy families and within easy distance of the town centre.

A self-sufficient building industry

It is interesting to note that the Welsh established a self-sufficient building industry. In Toxteth they had a huge advantage because David Roberts had the foresight to open a timber yard in Fontenoy Street in 1834, later expanding to Fox Street. But what made him a key figure was the purchase, by him and his brother, of Parliament Fields from Lord Sefton and then, with other like-minded people, developing the land into a Welsh suburb. David Roberts laid conditions on the land he sold, namely that there was to be no public house within the area and that is why the road between Princes Road and Penny Lane used to be a teetotaller's walk, with Brookhouse in Smithdown Road the only public house.

Arranging capital for building

Initially Welsh builders had no need to worry about raising capital. There were plenty of banks and building societies on hand. However, capital became a problem at the end of the 1850s when the number of houses built in Liverpool doubled to 66,000. Keeping their companies afloat became a perennial problem for the builders, as there was so much competition from railways and industrial companies. A number of astute members of the Calvinistic Methodist denomination saw an opportunity to invest in building while offering interest to anyone willing to lend money to building societies.

And that is how chapel building societies came into existence, with names such as Clarence Street Building Society, Chatham Street Building Society and Crown Street Building Society. Other companies were established and run by leaders of the Welsh community – the Working Men's Calvinistic Methodist Trust, the Liverpool and Birkenhead Building Society and the City of Liverpool Permanent.

The Cambrian was established in 1863, and among the trustees were the estate agent Owen Roberts (1818–86) and Robert Owen Evans (1810–72) of Everton Valley – a builder who stood as a Liberal in the Scotland Road ward and on another occasion in Everton but failed to beat the Tory challenge. He persuaded another Anglesey man, Councillor William Williams, to join the Cambrian Company.

Another founder member was Thomas Hughes (1805–80) of Atherton Street, Everton, brother of David Hughes, and they were two of the most important builders of the century. The next founder member was John Jones (1814–1900) of Elm Bank, Anfield. He was born in Bodffordd, Anglesey, and married Ann Elias, Owen Elias's sister, and he concentrated on the two suburbs of Anfield and Walton where he built scores of houses. William Williams (1813–86) had a huge influence on Liverpool as a builder and councillor. He was a first-class craftsman from Llanfachraeth and he supervised the houses that were built in Newby Terrace, Everton. He was the first Welshman to build the enormous warehouses in the north of the city. He expanded the suburb of Waterloo and was given numerous contracts to build bridges on the Birkenhead and Chester railway line and other places in England, as well as in Milford Haven in south Wales. He also cut the channel through the rocks in the Menai Straits. With R W Rowlands he also completed work in Scotland. He intended to dig a tunnel from Dover to Calais, but that dream was not realised for more than a century. He believed that, as an exceptionally successful businessman, he had a duty to make a contribution to the life of the city, and he was one of the first Welsh builders to be elected to the town council, representing the Liberals in the Scotland Road ward from 1863 until 1877 when he lost his seat. He was re-elected for the St Paul's ward, where many Welsh people lived, in 1877 and retired in 1880. He gave sterling service to the Calvinistic Methodists in the churches of Rose

Place, Whitefield Road and Newsham Park and contributed generously to the building of Fitzclarence Street Chapel. It was he who donated the handsome pulpit on which the following words were inscribed: 'Donated by William Williams, town councillor, as a gift to the Lord and to adorn His holy place.'

The ambition of Owen Williams, Toxteth

It was the chapel people who ran the building societies. One of the most important was Owen Williams (1842–1902). He was brought to Liverpool in his mother's arms in 1815 from Llanfair-yn-Neubwlch, Anglesey, and lived in 4 Warwick Street, Toxteth. By the age of twenty he was a greengrocer; then he invested in second-hand bookshops, but by 1840 he was an estate agent. He established a company under the name of Owen Williams and Sutcliffe, operating from their office in Victoria Street. His work can be seen throughout north Wales and north-west England. Lord Mostyn invited him to investigate the feasibility of developing a copper mine on the Great Orme. He went there from Liverpool in 1849, but the main attraction was the possibility of building houses in the shadow of the Great Orme. He developed plans for the construction of a town and it was these that were used to develop Llandudno as a holiday resort. He acted on behalf of a railway company to develop factories in Horwich, and he was the surveyor who planned Treaddur on Anglesey and parts of Rhyl, particularly the wide streets and the parade.

Samuel Evans (1868–1938) of the Chatham Society

Samuel Evans made a substantial contribution to the Chatham Street Building Society during his time as a member of Chatham Street Chapel and after he had moved to Anfield Chapel. He built many houses in Anfield. It was his company that was responsible for Harrow Road, Finchley Road, Hornsea Road and Wilmer Road, and before that, he and Hugh Jones (a native of Cemaes, Anglesey) had been building in Everton.

The Venmore family

In the wake of the building boom, a number of estate agencies were formed, such as W and J Venmore. William Venmore (1849–1920) and James

Venmore (1850–1920) were born in Llannerchymedd, Anglesey, but when they were both young men they moved to Liverpool to work in the office of one of their uncles. After gaining experience in business management and the construction industry, they established an estate agency which continues to this day as Venmore Thomas and Jones. William Venmore made a huge contribution to the Welsh and religious life of Liverpool. He was the secretary of Cranmer Street Church. After the congregation moved to a new chapel in Anfield Road in 1878, he was elected an elder. He died in 1920.

The incredible story of John Drinkwater

John Jones (Drinkwater, 1853–1936) was the eldest of nine children born in Carreglefn, Anglesey. He left school at thirteen to work as a farm labourer and later went to Rhosybol to be trained as a joiner by a master of the craft, Hugh Griffiths. When he felt confident in his own ability, he ventured to Liverpool and received much help, such as from the Elias brothers, David and Thomas Hughes, and John Jones of Elm Bank, Anfield. He was a faithful member of Netherfield Road Chapel before moving to Toxteth and attending Princes Road Chapel. Subsequently, he was one of the fifty members who left to establish David Street Chapel. In 1887 he moved his business to Smithdown Road and joined Webster Road Chapel, married Catherine Parry from Gorslwyd, and set up home in Barrington Road. She died in 1887 after seven years of marriage, leaving him with two sons to rear. He became a builder on a grand scale in the Sefton Park area, Smithdown Road, Earle Road, Princes Park and Penny Lane.

He was no different from many builders and his fellow elders in placing great store on temperance. When some of the Irish labourers employed by him would ask for extra pay on a Friday night so that they could enjoy a pint of beer, his inevitable reply was 'Drink water' – and hence his nickname.

John Jones was one of a group of builders who attended Webster Road Chapel. His partner in the early days was John Hughes of Moneivion and they were the founders of the construction company, Jones and Hughes, with its headquarters at 13 Whitechapel – a partnership that lasted thirty years. It was they who planned and built housing estates like Westdale in Wavertree, Longmoor in Fazakarley, Queen's Drive Estate in Walton, Breeze Hill Estate in Bootle, Cabbage Hall Estate in Anfield and Prenton Estate in Birkenhead. They would buy land and develop it on a huge scale.

In 1906 he built a small mansion for himself and his family at Mayfield in Dudlow Lane, Allerton. It is worth seeing to this day, as it is a testament to the success of the Welshman from Anglesey. His son, W H Jones, also became a builder in Liverpool and Birkenhead, while his brother, J R Jones, was an estate agent, and a historian of the Liverpool Welsh building industry.

Another Jones, another builder

Another elder at Webster Road was John William Jones (1868–1945), founder of another well-known company. He was the lynchpin of the company J W Jones and Sons, 158 Allerton Road. Born in Cae'r Hafod, Cyffylliog, in the Vale of Clwyd, he came to Liverpool in 1886 to work as an apprentice with David Roberts and Son. He spent eight years as a joiner with other firms before venturing on his own. He married a girl from Llanrhaeadr-ym-Mochnant and they had four sons and a daughter, all of whom were involved in the business. J W Jones served on the Liverpool council from 1932 to 1938 and, like John Jones, was one of the generous founders of Heathfield Road Chapel, Penny Lane. He was treasurer for many years, as was his youngest son Howell, who married Gwen, the daughter of the Rev. E Tegla Davies.

In 1900 he set up his own office and yard in Trentham Avenue, near Sefton Park Station. Richard Jones joined him as a partner and they worked together until Richard Jones's sudden death. Up until the First World War they concentrated on the areas around Sefton Park and Allerton and they built impressive streets in Allerton, such as Tanat Drive (to register his thanks to his wife from Tanat Valley) and Garth Drive, where he moved to live in the largest house there, called Hiraethog. His expertise can be seen today in Garth Drive, particularly in the differing designs of the houses, hardly any of them being the same. He concentrated on pleasant suburbs like Childwall and Calderstones, but his company also worked in Anfield, Woolton and Norris Green. He succeeded in overcoming difficult times by offering painting and other building services.

His move to the middle of Allerton Road in 1923 marked the company's golden age as he was building on a large scale in West Derby (the estates of

Larkhill and Lisburn), Springwood in Allerton, a large part of Speke, where there are 20,000 houses, as well as hundreds of houses in Huyton and Bootle. He had contracts from local authorities and enterprising companies with their own plans. He won a contract from the Ministry of Works to take charge of public buildings in 1923, which kept the company occupied for the next fifteen years. They had enormous opportunities, having been chosen to build the main Post Office in Widnes, rebuild the Customs House, and given charge of maintaining the historical buildings of Croxteth Hall and Speke Hall. During the Second World War the company had a special relationship with the Government, which was crucially important in rebuilding Liverpool after the merciless Luftwaffe bombing of 1940–41. The company restored thousands of houses that had been damaged during the Blitz, and after the war began building in suburbs like Childwall, Allerton and Gateacre.

Contemporaries of J W Jones

The same year that J W Jones was elected an elder at Webster Road Chapel in 1811, another builder, Henry Williams of Grovedale Road, was also elected. He had moved as a twenty year old to Liverpool from Moelfre, and found work as a joiner in the construction industry. Seven years later, during a difficult period in the building industry, he lost his job. He seized the opportunity to sail from Liverpool to Hamburg and from there to Rangoon in the Far East. He was a joiner on board ship and spent seven years as a sailor. He returned to Liverpool in 1898 to resume his work in the building trade, and this time he formed his own company. He concentrated on Wavertree and Mossley Hill, which were near to his home.

One of his co-elders was George Jenkins (1859–1946) of Karslake Road. He was a native of Cilgerran in Pembrokeshire, and had led a very interesting life, having emigrated to the United States of America where he worked as a stonemason in Denver and Colorado from 1887 to 1893. He then returned to Liverpool. He and his company built in Aigburth, St Michael's, Dingle, as well as in Wavertree.

Also in Karslake Road lived Thomas Roberts, who had come to Liverpool from Ysbyty Ifan as a bricklayer. Like George Jenkins he, too, had been to America, but only for a year. On his return to Liverpool he was employed by Welsh companies, and when a builder was needed to erect the chapel-house at Heathfield Road, he was appointed foreman of a group of men who worked for nothing, as did Roberts. He collected around him stonemasons, joiners and plasterers like Isaac Roberts of Towers Road, who was a fine poet and wrote under the name of Ap Carrog. He called on Roberts one day, and finding him ill in bed immortalised the situation in an *englyn*.

Dewi Clwyd and his industrious family

One of the earliest builders in Liverpool was Robert Davies (1812–75), better known by his bardic name Dewi Clwyd. He built ten houses in Liverpool as early as 1839 but it is not known in which part of the city. From the 1840s to the 1860s he lived in 44 Saxon Street, West Derby Road. He felt lost, being surrounded entirely by English people, and wrote about himself in a memorable line, 'He and his family are pilgrims among the English'.

But whether he was a pilgrim or not he reared a sufficiently large family to keep him exceedingly busy. He had eight sons and four daughters, with seven of his sons working in the building industry. Dewi Clwyd built more than twenty houses in Tuebrook, and his sons built on a large scale in the area of Rock Ferry, Birkenhead and Wallasey.

A family firm before the bankruptcy court

It would be a mistake to give the impression that every Welsh builder in Liverpool was a success. In 1887 the Lewis brothers, originally from Cemaes, Anglesey, came before Mr Registrar Cooper in the Liverpool Bankruptcy Court. The company had been established in 1851 by the brothers Lewis, all joiners, with its headquarters in Taylor Street in the neighbourhood of Scotland Road. Their main business was building houses, shops and storerooms, financed by the excess of the rent they received over their mortgage debt. The brothers John, Robert and William were monoglot Welshmen, according to the bankruptcy court records. The only one who understood enough English to be represented was Hugh Lewis. They owed £5,810, while their assets only amounted to £2,641. The case was adjourned and, as far as one can tell, they continued to operate.

John Lewis, the builder

A first-class builder who went through a difficult period was John Lewis (1875–1944) of Courtland Road, Allerton. He hailed from Darowen and came to Liverpool in 1896 looking for work, which he found as a joiner in Waterloo. After starting his own business in Clubmoor, he built flats and houses in Muirhead Avenue and Lewisham Road, but his best work is seen in Allerton, particularly the police and fire stations and the houses near Allerton Library. He was commissioned to work on the tower of Speke Airport and he built the Liverpool stadium in the area around Pall Mall, which was called Liverpool Town. He built cinemas and schools and attended Welsh Presbyterian chapels in Waterloo, David Street and Heathfield Road.

An enterprising tale in the building of Liverpool

The story of the Welsh builders is amazing. They succeeded in transforming Liverpool from a small town to a large city and Welshmen were the main builders in the Victorian era. They were crucial to the development of Liverpool and suburbs like Everton and Allerton – from Anfield to Speke, and from Mossley Hill to Huyton. There is no suburb in Liverpool where the Welsh did not build. Thomas A Roberts, a lecturer at York University, quite rightly said in 1986:

> The Welsh were the most able, well-equipped and best connected to provide the necessary resources in the quantities demanded and ensure continuity of supply, whether in terms of manpower, materials or finance. And provide they did, in increasing volume and numbers.

Chapter 15

The Liverpool Welsh
and the sea

The harbours of north Wales and Liverpool

For centuries, Liverpool had been an attraction for the Welsh because of its boats and ships and the eighteenth century was an important era in that relationship. There was particular emphasis on trade between the borough and the Anglesey ports, especially Amlwch, Beaumaris, Dulas Bay and Moelfre. By 1787 there were sixty-two small ships sailing between Amlwch and Liverpool, carrying copper from Parys Mountain to their headquarters in St Helens. Ships travelled into Runcorn port and carried coal from the Lancashire coalfield back to Caernarfon and Anglesey.

William Thomas, an early shipowner

One of the Welsh who made a significant contribution to the world of ships was William Thomas (1838–1915). He was a native of Llanrhuddlad, Anglesey, and came to Liverpool at the age of seventeen. He set up his own business in 1859 when he was only twenty-one. His company, William Thomas Sons and Company of Liverpool and London, became famous in the shipping world. Some of his ships had Welsh names like *Prydain* (Britain) and *Gwynedd*, and the *Queen of Cambria* sailed regularly to New York in 1893.

He will be remembered not only as a very successful businessman but also as an elder in three different Calvinistic Methodist chapels in Liverpool. In 1845, at the early age of twenty-seven, he was elected to lead at Pall Mall Chapel. He moved to north Liverpool in 1879 and played an important role in the Welsh life of Bootle and was one of the founders of Peel Road Calvinistic

Methodist Chapel in Seaforth. He was also elected an elder in Stanley Road Welsh Calvinistic Chapel in 1887 and was there until 1901 when he moved back to the city and became a member of Chatham Street Welsh Calvinistic Methodist Chapel.

He also stood as a Liberal in local elections. In 1889 he won the Mersey ward in Bootle and became a powerful figure on Bootle Town Council, and in 1892–93 he was the town's mayor. He was chair of the finance committee for nine years and a councillor for thirteen.

His son, Sir R J Thomas, was part of the shipping insurance world in Liverpool before becoming a Liberal Party MP for Wrexham (1918–22) and MP for Anglesey (1923–29).

The Cambrian Line

Another successful shipping firm at the time was the busy Cambrian Line owned by Thomas Williams. The *Cambrian Warrior* sailed back from Saigon to Liverpool on 10 August 1893, while the *Cambrian Princess* sailed from New York to Java two days later. The *Cambrian King* sailed from Liverpool to Melbourne, Australia, and came back to port in London on 11 September 1893. The previous day the *Cambrian Monarch* had set sail from the Far East for Britain, just as the *Cambrian Prince* was arriving in the Far East. This ship sailed on a long voyage from Bangkok on 1 September, firstly to the port of Rio de Janeiro before turning around and making for Liverpool. On 21 September the *Cambrian Chieftain* sailed from Newport to the port of La Plata, Argentina, as the *Cambrian Queen Anfa* arrived on 18 September. The last of his ships was the *Cambrian Hills*, which plied its trade between Antofagasta, Chile, and Liverpool.

All these boats depended heavily on Welsh mariners, but it is unlikely that any Welshman sailed so often or so far as George Paynter (1822–1911), a native of Amlwch. He went on 355 voyages back and forth over the Atlantic. He travelled to Aleppo in Syria, to Cuba, China and Java, serving aboard steamships like *Africa*, *Australasian*, *Canada*, *Kedar*, *Abyssinian*, *Persia*, *Bothnia* and *Algeria*. In forty-five years at sea he was never involved in a shipwreck.

Sir Alfred Lewis Jones

One of the successful Welsh people involved in the maritime world of
Liverpool was Sir Alfred Lewis Jones (1845–1909) from Carmarthen,
who began his career on board ship at the age of fourteen, though he
made only one voyage. Financial difficulties forced the family to move
to Liverpool. Alfred managed to persuade a captain working for the
African Steamship Company to take him on as a cabin boy. He made
an impression on everybody on that journey and, when he came back
to Liverpool, the captain praised him and he was offered work as a clerk
with the marine company Laird and Fletcher. It was a small office which
employed thirteen people and the Welshman fell heavily under the spell
of the Scotsman Macgregor Laird. He stayed with the company, receiving
support to study at night school, and was able to hold the household
together after his father died in 1869. Two employees, Alexander Elder
and John Dempster, were important to his career and, when they left
the company, one in 1866 and the other in 1868, he had a better chance
to climb the ladder. By 1870 he was in a very comfortable position and
earning wages of £125 per year.

He decided to establish his own shipping company in an office above the
bank at 6 Dale Street. The shipping business grew, and he leased a number
of sailing ships to carry goods to West Africa. This new step was quite
revolutionary; he made more money in his first year trading on his own than
he had made in the previous eighteen years. The following year he bought
some of the ships that were leased to him so that he could carry more goods.
He was arranging voyages to distant countries in West Africa, but he saw that
the days of sailing ships were coming to an end; he had to have a steamship
to transport a heavy tonnage of goods. He got rid of his sailing ships and
chartered a small steamer. The companies that monopolised the trade, the
African Steamship Company and the British and African Steam Navigation
Company, were astonished by the Welshman's boldness and protested at this
new competition. But the owners of the Elder Dempster company knew
more than most how able he was, and also how ambitious, so he was offered
a partnership in their company. From his home in West Derby he welcomed
the invitation, and his own company disappeared overnight. In October 1879

he once again joined up with his two ex-colleagues, Alexander Elder and John Dempster.

Partner in Elder Dempster company

He remained a junior partner with the two Scots until 1884 but he was the driving force behind the company's success. He soon secured an excellent agreement from the British and African Steam Navigation Company. This meant a revolution at the port of Liverpool, as, from then on, Elder Dempster would be responsible for all the ships bound for West Africa. Alfred Lewis Jones began arranging and supervising most of the professional trade between Britain and the countries of West Africa. Jones was in his element, and as the months passed it was quite clear that it was he and no-one else who had the upper hand among the directors.

Elder Dempster had offered a junior partnership to a Cornishman, W J Davey. He had arrived in Liverpool, aged eighteen, in 1871 and found work as a clerk in the shipping company. There he fell under Alfred Lewis Jones's influence. By 1884 the Welshman was confident enough to take over the Elder Dempster company. He did not think for a moment that Elder or Dempster would agree to his daring suggestion but, to his great surprise and that of W J Davey, the two Scots agreed to break all links with the company they had created.

There was a lot of mystery surrounding this coup. In an interview in the *Sunday Strand* in November 1903, Alfred Lewis Jones gives the impression that, by 1884, he held a good number of shares in the company so that he could easily take affairs into his own hands. Another suggestion is that he had persuaded sufficient friends who were shareholders to back him in the takeover. However, an obituary to him in *The Times* on 13 December 1909 gives a different version: Alfred Lewis Jones had offered such a large sum of money to the two founders of the business, they could do nothing but accept.

In charge of West Africa

The determined Welshman had the advantage of having nurtured a close relationship with the two most powerful shipping companies in England

and Scotland. It was clear to him that he should keep close links with both companies. He set about amassing shares in the African Steamship Company and, by 1900, after a quarter century of transactions, he was a majority shareholder. He was literally the company's principal director. He continued to buy shares in the company until his death in 1909. By then he had 26,325 shares out of a total of 33,732, each worth £20.

Successful to the end

After 1891 the Elder Dempster company became executive representative for the African Steamship Company, as well as maintaining responsibility for the well-being of the British and African Steam Navigation Company. Alfred Lewis Jones managed to keep hold of the professional market and the West Africa trade. The only other company over which the Welshman failed to have the last word was the German company Woermann Shipping of Hamburg. This company had some obvious advantages, but Alfred Lewis Jones managed to get it to agree not to compete with him in British ports.

There was a bold attempt by the Royal Niger Company and the African Association Ltd to undermine the undoubted success of one of the most successful shipping magnates in the Liverpool Welsh community. Alfred Lewis Jones had to use all the diplomatic and financial skills available to him to come to an honourable arrangement with these new competitors.

The proportion of goods transported by sea had fallen forty per cent between 1889 and 1895, and more and more shipping companies were looking enviously at the success of Alfred Lewis Jones and his company. So, he encountered fierce battles on numerous fronts. He succeeded in opposing a merger between the Royal Niger Company and the African Association and sought the agreement of the Woermann Company in Germany to create a co-operative system to regulate ships sailing to Africa. This was a particularly important step. Firstly, it was agreed that the Woermann Company would not call into British ports, although British companies had permission to discharge cargo in European ports. Secondly, the price of carriage from New York to West Africa would be the same as that from Liverpool. Goods to be carried from New York across the Atlantic to Liverpool and thence to Africa would be at the same rate as those carried from the Mersey to Freetown. This meant that the shipping companies within the agreement were defended against ships from America. Also, goods from America were sold in West Africa very cheaply. British merchants were very annoyed that the agreement did not allow sending goods from anywhere in Britain into West Africa. The ships had to sail to Liverpool and be re-exported but, unlike American competitors, they had to pay the full costs of carriage and transfer of goods from one ship to another.

Fingers in many pies

Despite his triumphs up to this point, Alfred Lewis Jones continued to be an anxious man. The African Association and the Royal Niger still existed, and he devoted his energies to subduing them. He knew the Colonial Secretary Joseph Chamberlain very well and, in January 1896, he persuaded the politician to nullify the Royal Niger Company's charter. This meant that the only large company beyond his control was the African Association, but he managed to cast doubts on the pronouncements of the chairman, John Holt.

He also saw the need for banks in West Africa. A limited company, the Bank of British West Africa, was established on 30 March 1894 and he owned 1,733 of the 3,000 shares. Almost all the rest were in the hands of his two partners, Sinclair and Davey, and his representative in Lagos, George Neville. He was made head of the bank and it was soon in profit with branches being set up in different countries in the region.

Another industry in which Alfred Lewis Jones took a great deal of interest in was coal. He bought coal mines in the Maesteg area that employed around 1,000 miners producing on average about 5,000 tons of coal per week. The coal from Elders Navigation Collieries was used to fuel his ships. The coal was brought to Port Talbot docks where the Elder Dempster ships loaded up enough tonnage to take them to West Africa.

Alfred Lewis Jones was also the man who popularised the banana in the north of England. He had seen the possibilities of these as a youngster when he visited the Canary Islands. He sent carts full of bananas around the Liverpool streets, giving them away on his first visit but then selling them cheaply. Thus, he popularised the banana in Liverpool, Lancashire and the rest of the north of England.

His last years

So great was Alfred Lewis Jones's influence that he had constant calls for his help from movements and societies, hospitals and the University of Liverpool. The government called upon him for advice and information. He thought very highly of Joseph Chamberlain and believed he had done more in his twelve years as colonial secretary than his predecessors had in fifty years. It was Chamberlain who suggested that he should be knighted and so this Welshman became Sir Alfred Lewis Jones.

He was lucky to have his sister, who was a young widow with a small daughter, to look after him in West Derby and later in Cressington Park and then, in his final years, in a big house in suburban Aigburth. On 14 January 1907 he was in Jamaica on a business trip when an earthquake destroyed the town of Kingston, killing thousands of people. Sir Alfred Lewis Jones was staying at Myrtle Bank Hotel but managed to get out uninjured. Despite that, the experience affected him greatly and, when he arrived home in Liverpool he was much more inward-looking and taciturn. It was obvious to his sister and family that he was ageing prematurely. He was advised to take a break for a few weeks but could not be persuaded to do so.

At the end of November 1909 he went on his usual train journey from Liverpool to London. He caught a heavy cold that day. On 30 November he gave a dinner as president of the Liverpool Chamber of Trade in honour of Sir Hesketh Bell, the governor of northern Nigeria. A fortnight later, on 13 December 1909, he died, leaving a huge legacy of £600,000 – one of the richest merchants in the history of the Liverpool Welsh.

His legacy

One of Sir Alfred's greatest admirers was Winston Churchill who said of him: 'Sir Alfred Lewis Jones is a candid man, and never so candid as when he tries to conceal his thoughts.'

David Lloyd George described him memorably. He said, 'He could only be compared to the Atlantic Ocean, unfeeling and restive; he was not really a man who lacked the common touch but self-sufficient and such a man as he not even Wales could produce more than once in a generation.'

Others believed that Wales did in fact produce two, and Alfred Lewis Jones was described as 'the Lloyd George of the business world'.

There is a fine monument to him on Pier Head, and for a century or so his name was on Garston Hospital: the Sir Alfred Jones Memorial Hospital. The hospital was rebuilt but there is still an extensive memorial preserved to the life of Sir Alfred and his generosity. He is also remembered in the lovely Springwood Anglican church, built with the money that, as the grandson of an Anglican clergyman in Wales, he left to the Anglican Church of Mossley Hill where he worshipped.

Chapter 16

Controversy gives birth to a new denomination

One of the loveliest chapels in the city of Liverpool is the Calvinistic Methodist Chapel in Chatham Street. It was opened in 1860 and the congregation merged with two other chapels in 1950 to form Eglwys y Drindod (Church of the Trinity) in Princes Road. The building was bought by the University of Liverpool and has been cared for by them ever since. The Merseyside Welsh Heritage Society had the chance to erect a plaque there in 2002 to mark the ministry of the Rev. Henry Rees between 1860 and 1869. It was through him that the chapel became very well known because, as one of his chief admirers, Dr Owen Thomas, said at his funeral:

> In our view, it was in him that the pulpit reached the greatest peak of perfection ever in our land.

The controversial Rev. William Owen Jones

However, the minister who made the chapel the source of much controversy among the Welsh of Liverpool and north Wales was the Rev. William Owen Jones. He was originally from Chwilog, in the Dwyfor area of Gwynedd, the son of a well-off family and well educated at University College of Wales, Bangor, and St John's College, Cambridge. In 1890 he was called to Waunfawr Chapel in Caernarfonshire and, within three years, received a further call to minister to the famous Chatham Street Welsh Calvinistic Methodist Chapel in Liverpool. By 1895 he was regarded as one of the up-and-coming pulpit giants.

Unfortunately, W O Jones had his weaknesses. He tended to be rather authoritarian in his attitude to some of the most cantankerous and difficult elders in the elders' pew. He was tempted to drink at night in his lodgings, mainly whisky. And he threatened more than once to resign from the pastorate. Indeed, he did so four times, twice to the elders and twice to the congregation, but his resignation was not accepted since he was perfectly acceptable to most chapel-goers.

Conflict between the minister and elders

Matters came to a head in April 1899 when the elders decided to discipline one of the members and expel him from membership of Chatham Street. W O Jones showed considerable courage in his stance. He could not agree to excommunicating one of the members of Christ's church and he was supported by two of the most influential elders, Eliezer Pugh and Nathaniel Bebb. On 18 July, in the *seiat* (group meeting), the minister presented his defence and the majority of those present voted in his favour. But he had acted unconventionally and ignored the Calvinistic Methodist rulebook, which stipulates that such a matter is the prerogative of the elders, not the congregation.

Some elders therefore felt he should have presented the matter firstly to the elders' meeting and from there, if necessary, to the presbytery. For some months both sides were relatively forbearing but it was clear that a majority of the elders wanted him to resign. Four of them wrote a letter to the presbytery without informing the minister. When W O Jones heard this, he felt that he had been publicly condemned in his absence and offered his resignation. A fortnight later there was a meeting at Chatham Street to discuss this unfortunate disagreement. There was no love lost among the leaders and it was decided to ask the local presbytery to send arbitrators.

The presbytery steps in

The first arbitrator to be appointed was the Rev. Dr Hugh Jones, the minister at Netherfield Road from 1871 and an exceedingly popular preacher. The other was his friend, the Rev. John Williams, minister of Princes Road since 1895 and another forceful preacher. Dr Jones was considered a capable man, skilful in dealing with people and this was his golden opportunity. He visited Chatham Chapel on 24 November 1899 but nothing very startling was mentioned. Since his arrival at the church in 1893, the minister had been allowed to preside at the sacrament on the first Sunday of the month but, by November 1899, William Williams had asked other ministers to be responsible for the sacrament. The Rev. W O Jones again submitted his resignation in these words:

> I want you to tell the church next Sunday that I am breaking my link with the church for good. I cannot reconsider the matter, so there is no point in the church passing any resolution. I want to be released at once.

The letter was not read, as there were still hopes W O Jones could be persuaded to change his mind. W O Jones was in despair and had decided to go to Wales for a while to renew himself in body and in spirit. Before leaving Liverpool he made the following announcement:

> I do not feel I can say anything more relating to the resignation but I have left the whole case in the hands of two or three other ministers so that, together with you, they can consider it and decide as they see fit.

The ministers he had in mind were clearly Dr Hugh Jones, John Williams and Griffith Ellis, who were to meet the elders. However, the elders decided there was no point in meeting them and agreed to accept his resignation.

A turn for the worse

By now, tales were spreading that the Rev. W O Jones had a number of moral failings and, by 28 March 1900, it was decided to set up another committee to investigate the whole matter. Two days later a committee of four ministers and four elders met at the Chatham Street buildings. The chairman was the Rev. Dr Hugh Jones and the tribunal sat for three-and-a-half hours. The minister was asked why he was resigning, and he was honest enough to tell them that he was tired of the conflict, and at times felt sick in mind and body. There was a lot of pressure on him to stay, especially from those who respected him and saw his ability in the pulpit and elsewhere. After another session the committee pronounced:

> Having listened to the causes of strife amongst the officers of Chatham Street
> Church, we are unanimously agreed that, under the circumstances, it would
> be better for the Rev. W O Jones BA to carry out his decision to resign as the
> minister of the church. After long and detailed discussion with the minister and
> the elders, and having listened to all the evidence brought before us in relation to
> the complaints against W O Jones habitually drinking alcohol, it was decided there
> was no need to take this any further. At the same time, we felt that the complaints
> brought against Mr Jones reflect unfavourably upon him and his response to them
> unsatisfactory insofar as we considered them.

It was agreed that, on Sunday evening, 1 April 1900, he would present his resignation to the congregation with at least four of the eight members of the committee present. However, rather than read out the clear pronouncement as prepared, Dr Hugh Jones presented an outline of the decision without notes or a resolution. When called upon to tender his resignation, W O Jones refused on the basis that Dr Hugh Jones had complicated and bungled everything. He asked the congregation to reject his resignation. The vast majority of them agreed.

The minister continues to receive support

The committee met the following day, calling on the presbytery to make arrangements without delay to arrange a number of Liverpool ministers to help out with the needs of Chatham Street Chapel. On 6 April the presbytery passed this resolution:

> Because of what has happened at Chatham Street and after discussion in both
> committees, we urge the monthly meeting to carry out further investigations into
> the complaints against W O Jones in relation to alcoholic drink.

The presbytery set about arranging a new committee to debate the whole issue again, pleasing no-one in the long term but splitting the Calvinistic Methodist cause on Merseyside. The evidence the committee heard varied widely. Some witnesses were in favour of W O Jones but there were many more against him.

On 9 July 1900 the Liverpool committee revealed its findings after many hours of hearings and debate:

In the light of the investigation we have undertaken, together with the testimony brought before us, our unanimous feeling is that we are forced to believe that the Rev. W O Jones has been guilty, on a number of occasions, of conduct unfit for a minister of the Gospel, and so we have decided that he should not be allowed to carry out such an important role amongst us at all.

There was now civil war within the chapels of Merseyside. Two leading legal firms were ready to prepare for the inevitable legal action. Rees and Hendley were acting on behalf of W O Jones and the legal firm of Elwyn D Symond, a member of the Princes Road Chapel, on behalf of the Liverpool Presbytery. But the situation was extremely confused, for not only was the Liverpool Presbytery divided, but others as well. Out of twenty-seven presbyteries in the North Wales Association, at least seven favoured the minister. Waunfawr Chapel in Caernarfonshire, his first pastoral ministry, took his side, and even in Chatham Street Chapel, 255 members – more than half – supported him. A petition in his favour was prepared and signed by 2,000 Welsh church-goers asking for mercy and for permission for him to carry on his ministry in the city.

Supporters of W O Jones

One of the influential supporters of W O Jones was Isaac Foulkes, the publisher and editor of the weekly paper *Y Cymro*, who allowed him to defend himself in its pages. By the end of 1900 he had many supporters and on 12 January 1901, seventy Welsh speakers came together to the Hackins Hey Hall to form what became known as the Committee for the Defence of W O Jones. In January 1901, Seacombe Welsh Presbyterian Chapel, where the Rev. Lodwig Lewis (Saunders Lewis's father) was minister, voted to support W O Jones, and Parkfield Chapel, Birkenhead, followed its example. There was a petition in Stanley Road Chapel, Bootle, and 515 of the members signed in favour of the Rev. W O Jones.

On 23 April 1901, an appeal committee under the chairmanship of the Rev. William James, of Manchester, was established. This comprised three ministers and four elders, together with three observers on behalf of the Liverpool Presbytery and three others to be chosen personally by W O Jones. There were fifteen sessions in all, and eighty-nine witnesses were to be called, forty-three of them members at Chatham Street Chapel.

Reporting back

Their report was presented to the North Wales Association of the Presbyterian Church of Wales at Seion Chapel in Oswestry on 26 September 1901. Dr William James presented in detail the conclusion reached by the committee, namely that W O Jones did not deserve to be a minister of the denomination because of his moral failings in one called to perform sacred work.

W O Jones had enthusiastic supporters, and the Committee for the Defence of W O Jones met to discuss the verdict and the way ahead. A public meeting was held and the most important item on the agenda was the intention to establish a new denomination and to arrange services in Hope Hall in Mount Pleasant. There, on Sunday, 14 July 1901, the first services of the new denomination were held. Five hundred Welsh people came to a prayer meeting in the morning, and in the evening an English service was held, when 2,000 people turned up. This was the first service W O Jones had preached in for a year.

A new denomination – the Welsh Free Church

On 21 July, W O Jones announced that the first church of Eglwys Rydd y Cymry, the Welsh Free Church, had been incorporated and based at Hope Street Hall. It had a membership of 450, and the following Sunday he was invited to be its minister. He set about setting up Sunday schools throughout the city, naturally in Hope Hall but also in Smithdown Road, Everton, High Park Street and Birkenhead.

Founder and editor of *Llais Rhyddid*

W O Jones set about designing a magazine for the new denomination. The periodical was called *Llais Rhyddid* (The Voice of Freedom) and he was the natural choice for editor. It came out monthly from 1902 to 1912 and then quarterly from 1912 until its disappearance in 1920. By the time of the publication of the first edition, the Welsh Free Church had established a chapel in Garmoyle Road in Wavertree and another chapel in Merton Road, Bootle. The poet, the Rev. David Emrys James, better known as Dewi Emrys, was invited to the ministry of Merton Road Welsh Free Chapel. He left the denomination of his father and his family for the new church, but his stay was short, and he moved back to the Welsh Independents in the Merthyr Tydfil area where his situation was still insecure. By 1903 there was a flourishing Welsh Free Church chapel in Donaldson Street, Birkenhead, with 1,200 members. Hope Hall's congregation had moved to a new home in Canning Street, very close to the old church in Chatham Street.

The new Welsh Free Church remained a divided denomination, with the majority brought up in the Calvinistic Methodist tradition. By 1920 its day was done, and the chapels of the Free Welsh Church were handed over to the Welsh Independents. The Rev. W O Jones remained as minister of Canning Street Chapel until his death on 14 May 1937.

Chapter 17

The effects of the
Religious Revival 1904–05

At the beginning of the twentieth century Liverpool had England's largest Welsh community. There were more Welsh speakers in Liverpool than in Wrexham, Swansea, Newport and Cardiff put together. Close to the city centre there were thriving Welsh chapels such as Princes Road, Chatham Street, Grove Street and Bethel in Park Road. And such was the pattern across the city, from north to south, to the middle of the suburbs of Walton and Anfield and from Everton to south Liverpool. At the beginning of the twentieth century all of these chapels had extremely capable ministers, well-qualified academically, products of Oxford, Cambridge and the University of Wales.

The role of the Rev. John Williams in the Revival

One of the most talented preachers was the Rev. John Williams, the minister of Princes Road Chapel, the man known as Dr John Williams, Brynsiencyn. It was he who was responsible for nurturing a preacher called the Rev. W F Phillips who was prominent in his opposition to socialism in the south Wales Valleys from 1905 to 1920. He was also responsible for bringing Evan Roberts to Liverpool. As the Rev. W Morris Jones, the minister of Crosshall Street Chapel (and later of Llansantffraid in Montgomeryshire) said of him: 'He threw his whole body, soul and spirit into the work.'

Three ministers, John Williams, W M Jones and William Owen, minister of Webster Road Welsh Calvinistic Methodist Chapel, arranged a meeting for the young people of the Welsh chapels of south Liverpool in Webster Road

Chapel. John Williams chaired the meeting, delivering a gripping address. Some of the fire of the Revival took hold in these young people. A gifted young woman called Llinos Moelwyn prayed for a Revival in a powerful manner. The fire was kindled and spread from one Welsh chapel to another in south Liverpool.

The Revival and the new denomination

The Revival spread among the new denomination. On Tuesday, 22 November 1904, in the thriving Donaldson Street Free Church chapel, the congregation began to debate whether preaching or singing had more influence on the worship of the church when they were all moved powerfully by the Holy Spirit. Young and old were fired by a new intensity they had not experienced before, and one of the young people broke into song, singing a hymn from the eighteenth-century Methodist Revival: '*Duw mawr y Rhyfeddodau maith, Rhyfeddol yw pob rhan o'th waith*' (Great God of wonders! Every aspect of Thy work is wondrous). The young of Donaldson Street chapel went on praying until 11 p.m. that night. It was the same the following Thursday and the Revival took a remarkable hold on the majority of the large congregations of the recently-formed Welsh Free Church.

A crusade in Crosshall Street and Edge Lane

Two of the founders of the 1904–05 Welsh Revival had strong links with Liverpool. The Rev. Joseph Jenkins, of New Quay, served as the minister at the English-speaking Welsh Presbyterian Chapel in Spellow Lane, while the Rev. David Howell, of Llawhaden in Pembrokeshire, was the vicar of St Bede's in Toxteth. The mission of two Americans, Charles Alexander and Reuben A Torrey, was held in Liverpool when the excitement of the Revival was being felt in Welsh chapels of every denomination. An enormous pavilion was erected in Edge Lane Park to hold 11,000 people over Christmas 1904 and the New Year.

W O Jones promotes the revivalist spirit

The Revival took hold of the controversial Rev. W O Jones also, who took the initiative by holding preaching meetings in Sutton Oak Interdenominational

Welsh Chapel, between St Helens and the smaller township of St Helens Junction, along with his co-evangelist, the Rev. David Davies, on Boxing Day, 1904. W O Jones's great hero, like that of David Davies, was the young miner and theological student Evan Roberts of Loughor, near Llanelli.

According to W O Jones, Evan Roberts was a tool in God's hand to fulfil an extraordinary ministry among the Welsh. Such was his faith that he travelled by train to Swansea to catch sight of the revivalist in the flesh. This was his experience after seeing him at a Revival meeting in Swansea:

> After seeing him and hearing him, one can form a clearer perception of the Old Testament prophets and the New Testament Apostles. Thanks be to God for another of the Welsh prophets.

The tragedy of the Liverpool mission was that the Rev. W O Jones was forced to change his tune and his opinion of the revivalist, as Evan Roberts was swayed to take the side of the much stronger Calvinistic Methodists against the Welsh Free Church. There was bitter friction between W O Jones and Evan Roberts, and others. As a result, the Revival of 1905 on Merseyside suffered enormously.

Evan Roberts prepares to visit

Evan Roberts worried greatly before setting out for the Liverpool mission. He prepared himself spiritually for a whole week 'in complete silence' in the home of a friend in Neath, and then for over another week in Cardiganshire, especially in Newcastle Emlyn where he had been a student for a few weeks. From there he went home to Loughor to give away his money – £200, to clear the debts of the small chapel known as Pisgah, Bwlchymynydd, where he was a greatly-admired teacher and superintendent of the Sunday school during his days as a coal miner; £100 to pay part of the debt of Moriah Welsh Calvinistic Methodist Chapel in Loughor, and another £10 to a fellow ministerial student, David Williams of Llansamlet. These gifts added up to a considerable sum, equal to tens of thousands in today's money. And then, on the platform at Loughor railway station, on his way to the distant city of Liverpool, he put his hands in his pocket and discovered he had not shared out all his money. He presented the rest to his brother Dan Roberts to give to a poor elderly woman who lived near his home. Thus, when he arrived at Liverpool Lime Street Station at the end of his journey, he was penniless.

His sister Mary travelled with him, along with the singers, Annie Davies of Maesteg, and the Rev. Dr D M Phillips of Tylorstown in the Rhondda Valley, and his niece, Edith Jones Phillips. They stayed in comfortable lodgings at 1 Ducie Street, a very convenient location for the 'Welsh Cathedral' of Princes Road Welsh Calvinistic Methodist Chapel. The landlady was Mrs Margaret Edwards and very soon word spread in Toxteth as to where the young man was staying.

The unique Liverpool mission

The campaign in Liverpool was different from anything that had happened hitherto. In the mining valleys of Glamorgan he had been working on his own, but the meetings in Liverpool and Birkenhead had been carefully arranged by the executive council of the Welsh Free Churches in the city. Before he arrived a large team of volunteers from the Welsh chapels canvassed every home in Liverpool, Garston and Birkenhead, finding 30,000 Welsh speakers within these communities, 4,000 of them lapsed as far as church attendance was concerned, and many of them non-believers. Seventeen meetings were arranged in different centres in south Liverpool, central Liverpool, Bootle, Birkenhead and Seacombe.

The first meeting, 29 March 1905

The campaign was opened in John Williams's church in Princes Road Chapel, Toxteth, on Wednesday, 29 March 1905. The building held 1,500 and was packed to the rafters – in fact, there were more people in the vestry and outside than inside. Such was the pattern everywhere. The huge Sun Hall in Kensington, which held 6,000, was full. Posters of Evan Roberts were to be seen in hundreds and hundreds of windows of Welsh-speaking homes throughout the city. Some of the most prominent ministers of English chapels in the city flocked to see and listen to the Welsh rejoicing in the works of the Almighty in their own language. One of those affected by the ardent religious emotion was the Rev. John Watson, a Scot who looked after

Sefton Park English Presbyterian Church and wrote novels under the name Ian Maclaren.

Disagreement among the denominations

However, there was a fly in the ointment and that was the Welsh Free Church. The conflict and quarrelling between the new denomination and the more established ones – the Calvinistic Methodist Church, later known as the Presbyterian Church of Wales, the Baptist Church, the Welsh Independents and the Methodist (Wesleyan) Church – were evident at the meetings held in Birkenhead. Evan Roberts went so far as to claim in one meeting that it was necessary to 'cleanse this place', as some of those present were unable to forgive. One of the young leaders of the Welsh Free Church rose, praying passionately for God to subdue the stubborn people who were not ready to work together in a brotherly manner. But Evan Roberts failed to display the generosity W O Jones had emphasised in his articles about him. He continued to proclaim that the Holy Spirit was being defied, and that there were many religious Welshmen in exile refusing to forgive their fellow Welsh Christians. The following day, on 1 April, in Shaw Street Welsh Wesleyan Chapel, Liverpool, completely without warning, the revivalist raised a storm of protest. He said that the Holy Spirit had left Liverpool bereft, as there were five people present that day who were jealous of the triumphant work done in the Revival. The congregation was disturbed, to say the least, and the Rev. John Williams tried to calm them. In his wisdom, Williams suggested the meeting should come to an end, but Roberts did not agree with him that day. And, as W O Jones acknowledged, the rhetoric and eloquence of one of the giants of the pulpit was unable to silence the young man from Loughor.

A monoglot English minister rose, asking kindly for more English in the service, remarking that these services were not held in Wales but in an English-speaking city (all the public meetings in Liverpool and Birkenhead were held in Welsh). He argued that a goodly portion of the congregation was unable to understand Welsh at all. Roberts's reaction was simply: 'If the Spirit agrees, you may have more English. I listen to the Holy Spirit and he speaks to me in my native tongue.'

Invited to meet the Lord Mayor

On 7 April, prominent Welshmen such as the secretary of the Liverpool Campaign, Councillor Henry Jones, and the chairman, William Evans of Anfield, a former city councillor, arranged an official reception with the Lord Mayor of Liverpool, Councillor John Lea, in the Mansion House. John Williams presented the young revivalist with these words:

> Allow me, Lord Mayor, to present to you Mr Evan Roberts, the servant of the Lord Jesus Christ.

There was room for only five guests at the top table and there sat the Rev. John Watson, Evan Roberts, the Rev. J A Kempthorne, the Anglican rector of Liverpool, the Lord Mayor and John Williams. This was a completely new experience for the revivalist, an ex-miner of only twenty-six. The cream of Welsh and English Nonconformism had been invited to the Mansion House for the lavish reception. These included, for example, John Morris, the builder and elder at Princes Road Chapel, and his fellow elder, Alderman J Harrison Jones. There was the religious and generous layman, Herbert Radcliffe, and the revolutionary socialist, the Rev. Dr C F Aked, minister of Pembroke Place English Baptist Chapel. It was he who spoke on behalf of the guests to praise the revivalist for coming to Liverpool and to thank the Lord Mayor for his hospitality. It was a disappointment to the chattering classes that Roberts refused to say a word in public at the reception.

Large congregation at Sun Hall

Six thousand people came to Sun Hall, Kensington, to listen to Evan Roberts later that evening. From beginning to end, he was agitated and tired and irritable. At one point he accused an unnamed person in the congregation of being wicked. He was obviously at the mercy of his subconscious and forces he could not explain. One thing is certain, he frightened the congregation when he said his accusation, at the command of the Holy Spirit, was aimed at a minister of the gospel. Two of the city's Welsh-speaking ministers rose to their feet. The first was the Rev. Hugh R Roberts, minister of Edge Lane Welsh Baptist Chapel, and the other, the Rev. O L Roberts, minister of the Independent Welsh Tabernacle Chapel, in Belmont Road. The latter was very influential and one of the six representatives who had travelled to Dowlais near Merthyr Tydfil to persuade Roberts to come to Liverpool.

When the two ministers protested in public, their voices were drowned by the crowd shouting, 'Shame'. Evan Roberts was seen slipping out through the back door with his sister and Miss Annie Davies.

More meetings

On 10 April, in the large Westminster Road English Congregational Chapel, the Rev. W O Jones of the Welsh Free Church led a prayer meeting. He sought the strength to forgive completely, so that all unpleasantness and differences could be forgotten. Evan Roberts was in tears hearing the earnest intercession for forgiveness and reconciliation as in the Gospel. Another forceful minister who had come from Merionethshire also took part in the service. This was the Rev. Gwynoro Davies, Welsh Calvinistic Methodist minister of Jerusalem Chapel, Barmouth, since 1887.

On Tuesday evening, 4 April 1905, Evan Roberts was taking part in an emotional meeting at Mynydd Seion Wesleyan Methodist Church in Princes Road. The church was packed. Evan Roberts appeared on tenterhooks and his words caused a great commotion:

> God gave me this message. The message concerns the Welsh Free Church. It is a message directly from God – 'The foundations of this church are not on the rock but rather on the sands'. That is the message.

The men of the press were all ears and delighted with this outlandish pronouncement. Gwilym Hughes went straight to interrogate W O Jones in his home in Percy Street. He was deeply hurt and started to denigrate Evan Roberts to the journalist.

There was more to come, especially at a meeting arranged for a Friday evening in Chatham Street Chapel where the trouble over the Welsh Free Church had begun. The meeting was chaired by the minister, the Rev. Richard Humphreys, successor to W O Jones. Evan Roberts was present but sat like a statue without saying a word. But in time a young minister, the Rev.

The effects of the Religious Revival 1904–05

Daniel Hughes, rose in the elders' pew, with anger in his voice, turning to the revivalist and asking him publicly:

> Have you reconciled with your brother before coming to the meeting this
> evening? Why do you play with sacred things like this?

The minister was referring to the unfortunate relationship between W O Jones and the revivalist, which was the talk of the Welsh. There was heated debate between Hughes and a number of ministers who supported Evan Roberts. When the revivalist rose to try and address the men, his words were drowned by shouting from both sides.

It was time to bring the overheated meeting to an end and that is what Richard Humphrey did in his own leisurely style. That night, there was a great deal of chatter into the early hours at Percy Street, the home of W O Jones and his family; for it was there that Hughes stayed. Within a few months, on 1 October 1905, Daniel Hughes moved from Chester to minister at a Liverpool chapel belonging to the Churches of the Disciples of Christ, the denomination in which President Ronald Reagan was brought up. But before he left Percy Street he wrote a strongly-worded letter, published in the *Liverpool Courier*, suggesting that the public work of Evan Roberts and his co-workers was chicanery and that he was showing particular mastery of the arts of hypnotism and telepathy, that is, reading the thoughts of his audience.

Soon after, the Rev. John Williams arranged for Evan Roberts to go to 88 Rodney Street to be examined by four doctors, all well-known specialists in the Liverpool medical world. One of them, Dr William McAfee, was a great admirer of the reformer and there are numerous examples of his wanting to be alongside Evan Roberts during his mission in Liverpool and his stay afterwards in north Wales. The verdict of the four, James Barr, William Williams, Thomas A Bickerton and William McAfee was:

> We find him mentally and physically quite sound. He is suffering from the effects
> of overwork, and we consider it advisable that he should have a period of rest.

The mission comes to an end

There were two subsequent revivalist meetings to bring Roberts's visit to an end: on Saturday evening, 15 April, in Liverpool and on Monday evening, 17 April 1905, in Birkenhead. It was clear that Evan Roberts was happy enough to leave on 18 April. A great crowd of Liverpool Welsh ministers, elders and deacons and their wives came to wish him well on the platform of Lime Street Station. John Williams and Evan Roberts were together, along with the two young women, Annie and Mary, who had thrilled the crowds with their spiritual songs.

The influence of Evan Roberts in Liverpool

Thanks to Evan Roberts, the temperance movement was strengthened. Indeed, Liverpool's chief constable said Roberts did more good in his three weeks in the cosmopolitan city than anyone else or any other movement in three years.

The Rev. William Henry, minister of Waterloo Welsh Calvinistic Chapel, Crosby Road South in north Liverpool, said: 'A new church was constituted in Laird Street, Birkenhead, in the ardour of the Revival which is felt so strongly in Parkfield Welsh Calvinistic Church and the mission rooms belonging to it.' This is particularly interesting, as the subject of the Welsh Free Church had been a hindrance in the Liverpool meetings while, in Birkenhead, the Revival was a means of spurring on at least two new religious causes for the Calvinistic Methodist denomination.

Another effect was the inevitable increase in attendance at Sunday schools in many Nonconformist chapels. It is said that the membership of Welsh Calvinistic Methodist Sunday schools in the Liverpool Presbytery reached 7,173, an increase of 606 in a year. The Rev. R Aethwy Jones, minister of Newsham Park Chapel, added that it had to be remembered that 'a multitude of lapsed members made up that increase' in the Sunday schools.

Another effect was an increase in the membership of the chapels. There were at least 750 individuals who joined Welsh Calvinistic Methodist chapels. The sacred music that resulted from these meetings became a topic of great wonder to a host of the city's residents.

The main weakness of Roberts's mission was the wrangling over the existence of the Welsh Free Church denomination and its future. The Rev. R R Hughes, biographer of the Rev. John Williams of Princes Road Chapel in Toxteth, blamed the latter powerful preacher for what happened:

> He always believed in the great preacher, the great meeting and the great service and, in his desire to see the churches and the whole city of Liverpool baptised and aflame with the Spirit, he planned it thus. His heart often overruled his head and so it was in this case.

Another critic was Alderman Joseph Harrison Jones of 99 Ullet Road, Sefton Park, an elder at Princes Road (he was elected in 1887) who believed that the saga of the Welsh Free Church had spoilt the whole purpose of Evan Roberts's visit to the Liverpool Welsh.

The Rev. John Williams's departure from Princes Road Chapel for Brynsiencyn on Anglesey, nine months after organising the visit, was a heavy blow to Liverpool Welsh Nonconformism. In the words of the Rev. R Aethwy Jones:

> Mr Williams was of great service to the Liverpool Presbytery and its monthly meeting and its various committees during his eleven-year stay in the city and, through his strong and evangelical ministry, was an adornment to the Welsh pulpit in the city and a means of blessing to all the churches.

He did not mention his responsibility in 1905 for arranging the visit of the revivalist and his team. Evan Roberts was a man on fire for the Gospel, as he said himself at a meeting in Shaw Street Wesleyan Welsh Chapel in the city: 'Man was saved by Christ so that all could be saved, as one person escapes from a shipwreck to save the rest of those in despair.'

Chapter 18

War, politics and the Black Chair (1910–19)

Liverpool as the capital city of north Wales

When Hugh Evans first published *Y Brython* (The Briton), he put it quite simply thus:

> It is possible that it is within the Mersey region that one has the highest number of Welsh folk in one area.

Liverpool had the facilities and activities to attract north Walians in their thousands. If surgery was required, there was a large number of hospitals in Liverpool as well as Welsh-speaking doctors and nurses to care for them. The diaries of John Evans of Beaconsfield Road, Toxteth, give an idea of the number of Welsh speakers who used Liverpool hospitals at the beginning of the twentieth century. He was a regular hospital visitor, and from April 1893 until 1908, he made 1,607 hospital visits and comforted 4,352 Welsh-speaking patients.

The century opened with the arrival of the National Eisteddfod of Wales. One of the city's ministers, the Rev. J O Williams (Pedrog), won the Chair for his ode *Y Bugail* (The Shepherd). Another important event was Dowlais Male Voice Choir winning the main choral competition under the baton of Harry Evans. But one of the most important results of hosting the National Eisteddfod was the promotion of the eisteddfod movement across the Mersey region, and also the creation of a choir that still exists today, the Liverpool Welsh Choral Union. Over the next decade eisteddfodau of every sort sprang up on

Merseryside. By 1907 these included the New Brighton Musical Eisteddfod and the Eisteddfod of the Temperance Society, called Good Templars, which was held in Central Hall, Renshaw Street, on Boxing Day.

The children's choir of Everton

Exploring the history of these Welsh choirs is a delight – for example, the Everton Village Children's Choir was based in one of the strongholds of Welsh life in Liverpool. The choir was formed in 1899 along with the Welsh Baptist Chapel Band of Hope in Everton Village by a young enthusiast called R T Edwards. He was only twenty-one at the time but keen, as a member of the chapel, to help children who came to the Band of Hope to understand the meaning of temperance and to raise the standard of choral singing in the next generation. Thanks to the foresight of its Welsh and English supporters, the Liverpool Children's Musical Festival was established. By 1907 the children's choir had received so much attention and had won so many prizes that it was able to take over Oak Hall in Oakfield Road, Anfield. The choir enjoyed success across the Mersey region and in eisteddfodau in Wales. It won the main choral prize at the National Eisteddfod of Wales for three successive years – Rhyl (1901), Caernarfon (1902) and Swansea (1903). After that, the conductor decided that it should concentrate on concerts and forget the world of competitions.

Liverpool Welsh Choral Union

Following the 1900 National Eisteddfod, the Liverpool Welsh Choral Union was established that year, thus resurrecting the choral union linked to the Welsh maestro J Ambrose Lloyd. The choir decided to invite Harry Evans of Dowlais, near Merthyr, as choirmaster, and this was the beginning of a wonderful period in his life and that of the choir. He became a distinguished music judge who was invited to competitions in every part of Britain and Ireland.

Welcoming the Welsh Baptists

The Mersey region's Welsh Baptists were very active in preparing for the Welsh Baptist Union's visit to Liverpool. The Union had previously visited

Liverpool in August 1874 when the Rev. Dr Thomas Davies, principal of its theological college in Haverfordwest, was president, but it had many more delegates when it returned to Liverpool in 1903. Accommodation was arranged for more than 600 delegates, but only 400 turned up, which was extremely disappointing for the local officials, the builder Owen Owens (chairman), D Roberts of Everton (treasurer) and John Davies (secretary). All the meetings were held in the large Welsh Baptist chapel in Everton Village and meals in the extensive schoolhouse of the Fitzclarence Street Calvinistic Methodist Chapel.

The politics of the Welsh and Young Wales

Politically, most of the Liverpool Welsh were Liberals. They were very much encouraged by Gwilym Hiraethog and John Thomas, two Welsh Independent ministers who were powerful advocates for Liberalism. Thomas was one of those who spotted the potential of the young David Lloyd George as a politician. In 1889 he, along with Thomas Ellis, MP for Merionethshire, was invited to a meeting at Hope Hall on the subject of 'The Disestablishment of the Church in Wales'. After the meeting there was supper at the home of Dr Owen Thomas, John Thomas's brother. Others joined the three of them and Lloyd George was fiercely rebuked by Dr Owen Thomas for mocking the parson and the sexton with their formal liturgy in the empty parish church. 'That is not how one should talk about the ministers of God,' were his sobering words from the head of the table.

Lloyd George was twenty-six when he was elected to the House of Commons in 1890. Thomas E Ellis was thirty at the time, and had already been in Parliament for four years. These two were the heroes of the Liverpool Welsh Liberals. Indeed, Liverpool Liberals were in the vanguard of the movement which developed under the name Young Wales – *Undeb Cymry Fydd* in Welsh. It was a movement that supported young Welsh politicians in their vision of devolution. Although W E Gladstone was a native of Liverpool and an icon to the Welsh nation, generally the Liverpool Welsh were more sympathetic to the idea of a secretary of state for Wales, the establishment of a land commission, and the implementation of temperance legislation alongside improvements in secondary schooling and university education than the world-famous politician was.

The Liverpool Welsh, surrounded by Anglicisation and imperialism, yearned for cultural nationalism. According to O E Roberts, 'Welsh nationhood was even more important than Liberalism in their opinion,' and this persisted into the second decade of the twentieth century. However, prominent Welsh men and women wanted to start a Young Wales society in rooms above a shop on the corner of Granby Street and Arundel Street in Toxteth. It opened on 24 January 1893, and one of its active Welsh members was Herbert Lewis. He came to Liverpool in 1885 as a lawyer in partnership with Alfred T Davies, who later became very influential in the field of education in Wales. Herbert Lewis stayed with his uncle Edward Lewis, who came to Liverpool as early as 1836 to establish a clothing business. For about forty years Edward Lewis ran the Ragged School for street children, completely paid for out of his own pocket. In November 1887 Herbert Lewis took the chair at a large meeting of Liverpool Welsh where Tom E Ellis made an important speech, suggesting the creation of an assembly elected by the people of Wales. He was far ahead of his time.

President of Undeb Cymry Fydd in Liverpool was Herbert Lewis, with other notable Liberal politicians, Tom Ellis, Lloyd George and Ellis Jones Griffiths, as vice-presidents. During the last years of the nineteenth century and the first of the new century, they set about establishing branches of the Young Wales movement in other parts of Liverpool, primarily in Anfield and in Bootle and Toxteth. The Toxteth branch moved to larger premises at 150 Upper Parliament Street. Owing to the failure of the Liberals, principally D A Thomas, a prominent leader in south Wales, and Lloyd George in the north, to unite the Liberal Party, the Young Wales movement lost its drive. The vision was lost. Lloyd George devoted his time to winning more power within the British Liberal Party. But, in Liverpool, the Welsh stayed in the club and, in 1910, they set out to buy the building in Parliament Street. A number of people took fivepenny shares until they achieved their target of a thousand pounds. During 1910 the building was purchased, money was spent on renovating and painting it and installing electricity. The women's branch, which had been separate, was unified with the men, with the advantage that it became a centre for all the Welsh in Liverpool city. What had started off as a powerhouse of the Liberal Party became more or less a cultural centre where lectures, concerts and games were held regularly. There was a concert room in the club, and a library was set up with local Welsh periodicals and papers for members to read.

By 1910 the Young Wales Club was a centre of activity – Welsh people coming to the city to work were warmly welcomed, but it was always made clear that its principles stemmed from the vision of Tom Ellis and Lloyd George in the 1890s. The club supported movements in the city which aligned themselves to Welshness and Welsh politics. In 1914 the leaders wanted to commemorate and emphasise the place of Liberal Party principles in the life of the club. It was decided that no-one could become a member unless, firstly, he or she was Welsh in origin and, secondly, would further Liberal beliefs. But within a few months the situation changed completely, and the First World War disrupted every section of society. There was no longer a requirement to be a member of the Liberal Party, but Young Wales continued to be a forum for discussing topics of the day as well as a home-from-home for sporting activities.

The efforts of John Edwards as a socialist pioneer

Social circumstances for very many people in Liverpool during the first years of the twentieth century were pitiful, to say the least. At least 1,000 inhabitants died of starvation every year. The newly-formed Labour Party was the most active in providing support for the needy.

The Welsh did not escape poverty and unemployment but, in general, they were better off, as the chapels organised societies to keep an eye on their welfare. And it was among the Liverpool Welsh that one of the most important socialists was raised – John Edwards (1861–1922), brought up in one of the chapels to middle-class parents. Little is known about his early years, but we do know that he lived for some time in Stoneycroft and then West Derby and, at the end of his life, in Roby. In his later years he joined the Unitarians, a religious denomination which did amazing work during his lifetime for the poor in particular. It must be noted too that David Lloyd George's father had been a teacher at the Unitarian school in Liverpool for eight years. William

George spoke with admiration about the achievements of the denomination, and as a man of the left enjoyed his stay in the city.

Edwards was a member of the Liverpool Socialist Society, which met weekly in a café in Dale Street where many of the leading lights of the socialist world came to address them, such as William Morris, Edward Carpenter and the propagandist and editor, Robert Blatchford. By 1892 the local Socialist Society had joined with the Liverpool Fabian Society and John Edwards became its president. Edward Pease, a well-known London Fabian, sent a letter of praise to John Edwards.

> Your Society certainly seems to be doing a great deal of work, and Liverpool
> is rapidly removing the disgrace which it had for so long of being the largest
> town in which there was the least Socialist agitation of any in England ... with
> congratulations on your energetic propaganda.

The Fabians under Edwards made a significant difference, and in 1893 a branch of the Independent Labour Party was established. Both branches worked together. Indeed, John Edwards had been a founder member of the Independent Labour Party in Liverpool, along with J W T Morrissey and Robert Manson. Although John Edwards has not received the attention he should have from the political historians of Liverpool, his presence was felt in every progressive circle and among socialist societies. He played his part as one of the Liverpool Welsh who raised the plight of ordinary people, and promoted the socialist ideas which circulated in the port of Liverpool.

One of those who came to know Edwards was the syndicalist Lorenzo Portet, who came to Liverpool as a language teacher. Even more important were the Irish socialists, James Connolly and Jim Larkin, who played a key part in the development of syndicalism among the Liverpool dockers, a high proportion of them being militant Celts, both Welsh and Irish. One of the unofficial centres of the Labour movement was the English Baptist chapel in Pembroke Street, where C F Aked was minister. He was a bastion of the left and one of those who welcomed the revivalist Evan Roberts to Liverpool. The Clarion Society attracted thousands to the Labour movement.

Liverpool experienced one strike after another and, in 1911, blood was shed on the streets during a strike by railwaymen, and soldiers were sent to restore order. One policeman was killed, and twenty others were injured. On 15 August 1911 two protesters were shot dead when 3,000 people attacked a van carrying arrested strikers to Walton Jail. The strike was very harmful financially to Liverpool Corporation. The Conservatives – and in particular the city's leader, Sir Charles Petrie (1853–1920), one of the most fervent members of St Anne's Anglican Church, Aigburth – attacked Edwards and his comrades. Petrie saw no virtue in the Independent Labour Party (ILP), or in the Labour movement, and suggested that those who organised the strike wanted to see anarchy in the city. By their deeds Liverpool people would suffer ill health, disease and even death, he argued.

Edwards worked closely with his friend, the minister of the Hope Street Unitarian Chapel, H D Roberts. He was first and foremost a Christian socialist, a chapel secretary who organised tirelessly during the transport strike of 1911 which paralysed the city. Edwards chaired a great number of meetings and gave his support unreservedly to the militants. From the First World War onwards, the Welshman experienced a great deal of ill health and suffered from rheumatism. He died at Albion Villa, Roby, on 12 February 1922. His pioneering work was not in vain and one can clearly see his socialism in his articles for *Liverpool Forward* and in his pamphlets, the best of them being *Socialism and the Art of Living* (Liverpool, 1913).

Another Labour pioneer, Jonah Evans of Runcorn

Another Labour man who shared the idealism of John Edwards was Jonah Evans (1826–1907), precentor in the Runcorn Welsh Presbyterian Chapel and a pioneer of the Co-operative movement. He left his birthplace, Froncysyllte, to work as a labourer, first on the railway from Chester to Warrington, and then in Runcorn docks. However, his great contribution was as a founder of the Runcorn and Widnes Co-operative Society in 1862. He was the general manager from 1879 until his retirement in 1904.

Tom Price's Australian career

In June 1909 news reached the Liverpool Welsh that one of its sons, Tom Price (1852–1909), had died. He was an influential leader in the world of trade unionism in southern Australia. He emigrated from Liverpool to Adelaide in

May 1883, and in 1893 was elected a Labour member of the government in South Australia. He became secretary of the Labour Party in 1900, and leader in 1901 and, in 1905, Prime Minister of South Australia in a coalition government of Liberals and Labour.

Support for the suffragettes

A section of socialists in this period pleaded the cause of the suffragettes in Liverpool and throughout the country. The government was dragging its feet and the Liverpool Welsh were divided on the question. The well-known socialist George Lansbury lost his seat in the Bow and Bromley election in London in October 1912 over this sensitive issue. Edward Hughes, of Anfield, expressed his views on Lansbury's failure to keep his seat in a cynical and cutting verse in the *Liverpool Echo*:

> To Mrs Pankhurst you may be
> A gallant 'beau' and comely;
> Still, with such charms it seems to me,
> You're not the 'beau' for Bromley.

The First World War and its consequences

The Liverpool Welsh played a prominent role during the First World War. The Young Wales society was shaken to its core and a number of members were lost in the war. David Lloyd George was their hero and, although he was somewhat disappointed in the response to his campaign for volunteers, he was an extremely ambitious politician who saw that the war could help his career. He devoted himself to achieving victory over Germany and frequently attacked Prime Minister Asquith for being cowardly and slow to respond to events. Lloyd George was the Munitions Minister from 1915 to 1916 and War Minister from July to December 1916. He called on the Liverpool Welsh to rally and face the German threat in battle, finding the strongest support among the young men of Stanley Road Presbyterian Church in Bootle. They published a church booklet naming the 205 members of that church who had volunteered; twenty-six members lost their lives on the field of battle. Thirty-one members of Webster Road Welsh Chapel joined the armed forces. The first among them to be lost was John David Jones, of Bective Street, who had joined the Royal Welch Fusiliers. He was killed in the Battle of Mons in September 1914, just over a month after the start of the bloody conflict. The response of the minister, the Rev. William Owen, was:

> The church is called upon to minister to the suffering and comfort those who mourn; we must ensure that her touch is light and her heart tender enough to fulfil her important duties.

And that was the usual response from the centres of the Christian faith, especially among the ministers. They organised food parcels diligently, and this task was more than enough for the Rev. H Harris Hughes, minister of Princes Road from 1909. His health broke down and he was confined to his home and extremely weak for some months. His affliction stemmed from his concern for the 179 young men from Princes Road (including six from Upper Warwick Street Mission School) called into battle. Twenty of them made the ultimate sacrifice.

Care for soldiers at Waterloo Presbyterian Chapel

The Rev. William Henry, the minister of Waterloo Presbyterian Chapel, prepared detailed newsletters for those soldiers who left behind parents and family. After all, two of his sons took part in fierce fighting in France. In his 1914 report the father and pastor said:

> A goodly number of our young men have enlisted and, by now, some of them are on the battlefield and they have all the support and prayers we can muster on their behalf. The church's interest in them was evidenced in a very happy way on the night of an Organ Recital in November, when each of them was presented with a Gold Pendant and a copy of the New Testament. And we are glad to look at the crafted and beautiful Roll of Honour prepared by Mr W S Roberts and placed in the chapel porch.

The Roll of Honour listed forty-one names. The list grew from year to year, twenty-four in 1915, thirty-two in 1916, thirty-eight in 1917, and forty-one in 1918. Waterloo Chapel was very caring towards soldiers who came to the military camps in Liverpool, especially the one in Litherland. In 1915

War, politics and the Black Chair (1910–19)

William Henry speaks of the provision for Welsh-speaking soldiers from Wales in Waterloo Chapel rooms on a Friday evening and Saturday afternoon:

> It is clear that the leisure meetings every Friday evening for Welsh soldiers who were in various local camps give great enjoyment both to them and to us. And putting one of our rooms at their disposal every Saturday afternoon is a step in the right direction. It is great joy to us that a goodly number of Welsh soldiers frequent the Prayer Meetings and the *seiat* and participate in them. This proves that they were raised in thriving, welcoming churches in the country.

Most of these were boys from Litherland camp and, after David Lloyd George was made Prime Minister in December 1916 in circumstances which caused tension, strife and deep division within the Liberal Party, there was increasing pressure for volunteers. It was, by then, compulsory for men under forty to enlist.

One of the Welsh who arrived at Litherland camp in January 1917 was the shepherd poet from Trawsfynydd, Ellis Humphrey Evans (Hedd Wyn, 1887–1917). A son of Yr Ysgwrn, Trawsfynydd, he had been forced to enlist at the beginning of 1917. He joined the 15th Battalion of the Royal Welch Fusiliers. The writings of a soldier from Seven Sisters in south Wales, Private J B Thomas, give an idea of how he spent his time at the camp. The major in charge of training was English, so Thomas was used as an interpreter as so many were more or less monoglot Welsh:

> It was a pathetic sight to see those who had been forced to enlist, coming from vital work on the farms, leaving their loved ones at home, as hardly any of them were cut out to be soldiers.

Ellis came second in the Chair competition at the National Eisteddfod in Aberystwyth in 1916 and made up his mind to compete at the Birkenhead National Eisteddfod in September 1917. He had started work on his ode on the theme of 'Hero' when he was at home tending his sheep at Yr Ysgwrn, then wrote more during his short stay in the camp before being allowed to return home on 27 March to do the ploughing, as the government wanted farmers to produce more food. When he returned to Litherland ten weeks later, he was moved to another part of the camp and it was then he wrote an *englyn* to the camp, where he speaks of the sea of helmets, the red-cheeked lads from the Welsh countryside full of thunder, and the camp recognisable to all who passed as the home of soldiers waiting to be sent to war.

He kept his friendship with J B Thomas, meeting regularly in the YMCA and twice attending socials for Welsh soldiers at York Hall in Bootle. He offered a word of thanks on that occasion on behalf of the soldiers for the kindness shown to them by the Liverpool Welsh Society. On a Sunday afternoon Hedd Wyn would attend Sunday school and stay for the evening service at Marsh Lane Welsh Independent Chapel, Bootle. In June 1917 he left Litherland for France, and was killed in the Battle of Pilkem Ridge on 31 July. Two Welshmen from Birkenhead also fought alongside him – Robert Roberts, son-in-law of the editor of *Y Brython*, J H Jones; and Cecil Roberts, a deacon at Woodlands Road Chapel.

In September 1917, with thousands having come together to the National Eisteddfod at Birkenhead, the three judges awarded the Chair to the soldier-poet Hedd Wyn. When Archdruid Dyfed announced from the stage that the poet had been killed in the war, David Lloyd George, Sir John Morris-Jones, the Rev. John Williams of Brynsiencyn (three who had been recruiting keenly) were seen with tears streaming down their cheeks. The chair was covered with a black shroud, to the grief of the crowd of 18,000. J B Thomas gave thanks for the *englyn* Hedd Wyn had penned for him in Liverpool on 6 March 1917. It speaks of Thomas's cheerfulness, his gift for talking, his influence and his character, unsurpassed by anyone else in the camp.

Another literary soldier

Hedd Wyn was a conscripted soldier, unlike one of the most talented sons raised in the Merseyside Welsh community. John Saunders Lewis (1892–1985) was a son of the manse and grandson of Dr Owen Thomas of Princes Road. Lewis joined the army as soon as he could, despite having started on his academic studies at Liverpool University. On 3 September 1914 he went to a recruitment meeting at the Students' Union in Bedford Street, Liverpool, and the following day joined the 3rd Battalion of the

King's Liverpool Regiment, the Liverpool Pals as it was called. On his recruitment form he put 'Presbyterian' under the religious denomination heading. Then he added 'Welsh, Yes' after it. He was keen to find himself among his fellow Welshmen as he was 'the son of a Welsh minister of religion' and, as a university student, he hoped to have a commission in a Welsh regiment.

He joined the 12th Battalion of the South Wales Borderers and was awarded a commission as a sub-lieutenant in 1916, then made a full lieutenant on 2 February 1916. As he said in one of his essays, he experienced the coldness and brutality becoming a part of his personality.

> Iron bore deeply into the nature of men who were previously mild. I saw this once, when I was returning from the lines, with the water reaching our loins: a lad fell and the one following him stood on him to get a firmer foothold. At those times, as many were drowned as were killed, with no-one answering or noticing when someone called for help. It was the earth which triumphed and killed us.

One April morning Lewis was in the middle of a battle and this is his graphic description:

> The artillery and machine guns awoke, there was harsh shouting and swearing and voices that could only be heard from a soldier; the ground was trembling, the sky a mixture of flashing fire and black darkness, men in front of us, falling as they ran, the occasional body keeping up its speed for a moment, we like sheep before the storm, all moving the same way, some wincing at the slaughter, others fumbling, their faces in the grass and, above their heads, unseen, the pale day spreading across the heavens and the dawn breaking on blind, ant-like humanity.

His youngest brother, Ludwig, was killed on 7 July 1917 in France. Lewis was wounded in his left leg and spent time at the Red Cross hospital in Rouen, then in London, and then at Luton Hoo Hospital on the outskirts of Harpenden. From Luton Hoo he was taken to the Isle of Wight and back to the 3rd Battalion before being transferred to hospital in Liverpool. There he spent Christmas 1917 before rejoining his battalion in Hightown near Liverpool. For him, the consequence of the war was a passionate desire to 'do something for Wales along the lines of Ireland'. He wanted to follow in the footsteps of Owain Glyndŵr, but in that he was in a minority.

According to his mistress Frances Stevenson, Lloyd George visited the battlefield for a few weeks, and paid the price, for he suffered when he came back from insomnia. He confessed: 'I am too sensitive to pain and suffering and this visit has almost broken me down.'

Of the nearly 900,000 British military personnel who lost their lives in the First World War, 35,000 are listed in the Welsh Memorial Book. The Welsh Presbyterians lost 209 young people from churches in Liverpool and district. The loss was one of the biggest blows to Liverpool Welsh centres, and it was decided to commemorate the dead in a spirit of thanksgiving. Stanley Road Chapel in Bootle placed a memorial column near the chapel. It is called the 'Soldiers and Sailors Memorial' and is made of solid granite from Aberdeen.

Few pacifists among the Liverpool Welsh

There were few examples of any of the chapels in Liverpool and district having raised pacifists. The two exceptions were George Maitland Lloyd Davies (1880–1949), who was born, brought up and educated in Liverpool, and the medical student, Emyr Wyn Jones, later a cardiologist at Liverpool University Hospital. Davies became secretary of the Fellowship of Reconciliation when it was formed in 1914. He was imprisoned many times because of his unyielding opposition to the slaughter in Europe and to military conscription in 1916. Quaker pacifism won new credibility, though the Fellowship of Reconciliation and Quaker ideology was an important influence on at least one of the sons of Princes Road Chapel. Emyr Wyn Jones became a campaigner for peace within Chatham Street Chapel, among his fellow countrymen in Liverpool, and later with the Quakers. A number of pacifists were imprisoned in Walton Jail during the First World War and one of them was John Jones (JJ), of Llangoed, a country poet and historian.

Losses of the war of the Black Chair

Supporters of the Young Wales movement in Liverpool realised that the First World War had not progressed the cause of decentralisation in Wales.

More than 200 young Liverpool Welsh were lost, and the sisters of the Liverpool Welsh societies and congregations took great care in sending parcels and frequent letters to the lads. Many Welsh women worked in Liverpool hospitals, some voluntarily and others as paid workers. One of these was Gladys Davies (née Roberts, 1894–1993). She was the daughter of plasterer Isaac Roberts who worked for a Welsh company in the city. In 1914 she married a young Liverpool Welshman, John Iorwerth Davies. They had a son, Ifor, who became a teacher at Quarry Bank School and a clergyman in Flintshire. Iorwerth Davies was injured at the Battle of the Somme and came home to his family as one of the wounded. He died of his injuries in 1922.

Memorials to the fallen soldiers

Memorials were placed on the walls of chapels and churches, and a memorial was prepared for all the soldiers and sailors who fell in the war. The Rev. Daniel Davies, minister of Webster Road Welsh Calvinistic Chapel, described the importance of the memorial in these words:

> It remains testimony to the love of the church for its young men and their
> appreciation of their service and sacrifice for their country. 'They were a wall for
> us, night and day.'

But perhaps it is the long and sincere poem of Megan Lleyn of Seaforth, as she was known in north Liverpool, that symbolises the remembrance and the sacrifice of a promising poet called Hedd Wyn who did not roam far from his roots. The colliery in Abercynon and the military camp in Liverpool were the extent of his travels before the long and arduous journey to Pilkem Ridge. In her fourth verse, Megan's message is that the Black Chair of Birkenhead would be remembered for centuries to come. The pain and the praise of that day would be recalled. For her, Hedd Wyn passed away under the banner of freedom into the hands of Jesus, the gentle shepherd, victorious in the triumph of Calvary.

But when the war ended there was only a short break before Lloyd George began preparing for the 'khaki election' of 1918, with the Liberals under Lloyd George and the Tories forming a coalition government. The

Welsh wizard had a sweeping victory. The spirit of Lloyd George's victory, as the prime minister who won the war, percolated every layer of society.

Analysis of Welsh religious life in Liverpool

Around this time the process of analysing the failure of the chapels and churches during the war began, and included a trenchant essay by the Rev. William Francis Phillips. He was one of the most opinionated and anti-socialist dissenters during the decade of the First World War. However, in 1919 he wrote an essay for the Welsh pacifist periodical *Y Deyrnas* (The Kingdom) on the 'Failure of the Churches'. It is an important essay, but one that has largely been ignored. He speaks of the role of ministers in 'putting pressure on church members to enlist in the army' and he was absolutely right about that. He says:

> Many times, I felt that it was proof of unforgivable weakness in us, men of faith, that we left those men to suffer in gaol and suffer worse than that for using the right given them by the Military Service Law. This is one of the darkest chapters in the history of the war. And the behaviour of the churches was by no means pure.

He chastised the churches for failing to sympathise with labour rights, for being too negative in their attitudes, and for having turned the chapels into 'respectable clubs'. He saw that the chapels had a new opportunity at the end of the war as 'a new age was dawning'.

W F Phillips, who died a year later, had made a worthy attempt to analyse and change considerably his own attitude towards movements like the trade unions.

It is probable that few of the members of the chapel that supported him into the ministry read his essay, as the United Princes Park Choir, under the leadership of the full-time organist, G W Hughes, was having a big reception on the day it was published. The choir was full of talent: Edith Jones as accompanist, Mabel Roberts as solo soprano, contralto Gwen Taylor, tenor Gwilym Powell and bass E Walter Williams. Two of the same family, Alwena and Sioned Roberts, played the harp. There were eighty members in the choir but one must remember that the executive committee contained musicians from Welsh chapels throughout the Liverpool central area, like J R Jones, the precentor of Park Road Welsh Presbyterian Chapel; E T Barker, who was the organist of the Welsh Independent Chapel in Grove Street; Edith Jones, the accompanist from Webster Road Welsh Chapel, and the organist J P Taylor, who gave a lifetime's service to sacred music in Webster Road and Heathfield Road chapels. It is odd to note that Armon Jones, music teacher and precentor at Central Hall Methodist Church, was not included in the executive committee of the Princes Park United Choir.

Tragedy in Knowsley Road, Bootle

At the end of March 1919, Robert Roberts of 276 Knowsley Road went to the funeral of his father, Captain Edward Roberts, in Barmouth. When he arrived home that night, his house was full of gas and his forty-eight-year-old wife and nineteen-year-old daughter had lost their lives. They were members of Trinity Road Methodist Chapel. There was no explanation as to what had happened.

Remembering the poet Trefor

Another to be lost as the decade closed was John Jones (Trefor), 4 Briar Street, who died on 6 April 1919 at the age of seventy-two. He was a successful house painter in Liverpool for fifty years and played an important part in eisteddfodau as a poet and was always associated with the Liverpool Temperance Eisteddfod. He served as a teacher of *cynghanedd* in the Young Wales Hall, Parliament Street, and was a member of *Cymdeithas y Cylch Cyfrin* (Society of the Secret Circle), a private society of Welsh poets in Liverpool. Trisant, Treflyn, his brother Caros, Erfyl, Gwilym Mathafarn and other poets were all members of this private society too. Pedrog composed an *englyn* to Trefor, describing him as a quiet and gentle man who would always be remembered fondly.

Pryce Hughes, Allerton, and Robert John Roberts, Anfield

In the same month Pryce Hughes, a buyer with the Frisby Dyke company of Lord Street, died in Bryn Rhedydd, Garth Drive, Allerton, at the early age of forty. He was originally from Mostyn, Flintshire, and was known as an assistant preacher at the Mount Zion Welsh Methodist Circuit in Liverpool.

His wife was a sister of the Rev. W O Evans of Porthmadog, a well-known preacher in that denomination.

A family who had supported the war to the hilt among the Liverpool Welsh was that of Mr and Mrs Owen Roberts, 8 Alroy Road, Anfield. Each one of their five sons joined the armed forces and four served in the French trenches. Bob, one of the finest singers at Anfield Welsh Chapel, enlisted in 1914 and was made a lieutenant in 1918. He had four nightmarish years, was wounded in 1915 but rejoined the battle in the trenches in August 1918. He was injured and taken prisoner on 25 October 1918 and died three days later.

Chapter 19

The interwar years

I t was probably in 1920 that the golden age of the Liverpool Welsh reached its peak as far as the number of Welsh people living in the city was concerned. Life was wealthy – culturally, religiously and socially, throughout the city.

A society for people from Merionethshire

Several Welsh counties had societies that protected their history and traditions. Some men who were prominent in Liverpool life came from Merionethshire and were well known in the Merioneth Welsh Society of Liverpool. One of these was J C Roberts (1860–1941). He was born in Llanuwchllyn and, despite his disadvantaged childhood, succeeded amazingly and became a director of the Liverpool Rubber Company. In 1919 he, his wife, daughter and two sons moved into a fine house on the promenade in Southport, but this did not mean that he was retiring from Liverpool Welsh life. He supported the Welsh Society in Southport, and throughout this period (1920 to 1940) he was one of the most supportive of the wealthy Welsh. Another important person in the society was John Herbert Jones (1860–1943). He was given the task of turning *Y Brython* into a national paper by Hugh Evans, proprietor of the publishers Brython Press, and he succeeded. E Morgan Humphreys said of him: 'Some delighted in his style and others were maddened by it – but it was impossible not to read him.'

Although he lived most of his life in Birkenhead, his editorial office was in Stanley Road, Bootle, and the best of his writings were published in four volumes: *O'r Mwg i'r Mynydd* (From the Smoke to the Mountain) which came out in 1913, *Swp o Rug* (A Pile of Heather) in 1920, *Moelystota* in 1931, and *Gwin y Gorffennol* (Vintage Wine) in 1938. He retired as an editor in

1931 but continued to live on Merseyside until 1941, moving to live with his second daughter and her family in Penygroes, Dyffryn Nantlle, where he died on 23 March 1943.

The death of the Rev. David Powell

In 1920 the Liverpool Welsh Baptists lost a remarkable expositor of the Bible with the death of the Rev. David Powell, minister of Everton Village Welsh Baptist Chapel. He was unfailing in his duties as pastor of the Everton community for thirty-one years and was the editor of *Yr Heuwr* (The Sower) for many years. Everton Village Chapel placed a memorial to him on the chapel wall with this appropriate verse from the Book of Malachy (chapter 2, verse 6):

> The law of truth was in his mouth, and unrighteousness was not found in his lips: he walked with me in peace and uprightness, and he turned many from iniquity.

Helping organisations survive

The economic situation in Liverpool at the beginning of the 1920s was not at all easy and organisations and chapels had to organise all sorts of fundraising events to survive. The Young Wales society decided in December 1920 to hold a bazaar to raise enough money to clear its debts. E T John (1857–1931) was invited to open it – a man who had contributed greatly to the Welsh in Middlesborough, as he was the owner of a steelworks there and was Liberal MP for East Denbigh from 1910 to 1918. The Rev. W F Phillips says of him:

> E T John threw all his energy, for years, into debating Welsh rights and trying to improve the lot of the people. Everyone familiar with his public story knows that he carried out great and important work, but the dogs began to bark and would not be quieted until they had succeeded in blackening his name and driving him from his seat.

Consequently, he stood for the Labour Party in the Denbigh election in 1918, losing to Sir D S Davies, the National Liberal. But he was not embittered and was very influential as a decentraliser and president of Welsh societies and the Society for Peace and Reconciliation. He was warmly welcomed at the bazaar, together with the Prime Minister's daughter Megan Lloyd George.

The contribution of the poet and journalist Meuryn

The fundraising campaign was very successful and, in 1921, the society rejoiced when the journalist Robert John Rowlands (Meuryn, 1880–1967) won the Chair at the 1921 National Eisteddfod in Caernarfon for his fine poem *Min y Môr* (Beside the Sea). He had brought glory to the Liverpool Welsh two years earlier when he won the Chair at the 1919 National Eisteddfod for his ode *Ar y Traeth* (On the Beach). Meuryn came to Liverpool to work on the weekly *Y Cymro*, and was the Liverpool correspondent to Welsh newspapers when *Y Cymro* came to an end. It was in Liverpool, too, that his only volume of poetry, *Swynion Serch* (Love Charms), was published, in 1906. His decision to move back to Caernarfon was a major blow to literary life in Liverpool, as he was one of the founders of the Order of the Red Dragon.

The Red Dragon eisteddfodau

The aim of the organisation was to strengthen the Welsh language in the city, to bring poets and writers together, and to hold a grand eisteddfod attracting competitors from far away and inviting nationally renowned adjudicators. Among these during the 1920s were the musicians T Osborne Roberts, J E Jones of Llanbrynmair, the harpist Gwyngyll, and another composer, Dr D Vaughan Thomas. In the field of poetry, R Williams Parry was a regular visitor and, in the field of essays, short stories and dissertations, there were a variety of writers such as the outstanding short-story writer Kate Roberts, the dramatist Saunders Lewis, the versatile literary author E Tegla Davies and the essayist the Rev. Evan Roberts. J E Roberts (Ap Heli), a Liverpool poet, was in charge of the proceedings on stage. To add prestige to the eisteddfod, well-known names from the business world were invited to be presidents to deliver a few appropriate words and contribute towards the costs. One year the eisteddfod president was none other than William Lewis, head of the Pacific Steam Navigation Company.

The loss of two poets

In 1923 the world of the eisteddfod in Liverpool mourned two poets. The Rev. David Adams (Hawen, 1845–1923), a native of Talybont in Cardiganshire, was a well-known minister with the Welsh Independents in Grove Street. He became one of the exponents of liberal theology, something which he had learnt from research done at German universities. His treatise on the philosopher Hegel won first prize at the National Eisteddfod in Liverpool in 1884. He moved from Bethesda in north Wales to Liverpool in 1895 and spent twenty-eight years in the city, a highly influential man in the world of culture and faith. In 1922 he received a letter informing him that the University of Wales planned to give him the degree of Doctor of Divinity in one of its convocations, but he died on 10 July 1923 before receiving the degree he deserved for all his magnificent work.

Another poet who died in 1923 before achieving his potential was Dr Richard James Jones, aged just twenty-four, a minister's son and brother of the physician Dr Emyr Wyn Jones. He was educated at Liverpool University and went faithfully to Webster Road Welsh Chapel where he met the daughter of the builder J W Jones. In January 1922 he married Miss Gladys Jones, but their partnership was brief. He composed lyrical verses and skilful *englynion* and showed great promise as a poet. In his poem *Atgof* (Reminiscence), he speaks of his longing for his native land of Snowdonia and how, in the noise and thunder of the great city of Liverpool, he longs to see the River Gwyrfai and hear, in his dreams at night, the pure water washing over the foot of the hills. He hopes that, if his body is to be buried in a foreign land, and his ashes scattered by the winds to the four corners of the earth, his spirit will live on for ever in the ancient rocks of his home.

Farewell to a preacher-poet

In October that year also came news of the death of the Rev. John Cadvan Davies (Cadvan, 1846–1923), a prominent minister in the Wesleyan Methodist Church. He was well known in eisteddfod circles in Liverpool, both as a competitor and an adjudicator. He came to national attention when his epic poem, *Madog ab Owain Gwynedd*, took first prize at the National Eisteddfod of Wales in Liverpool in 1884. Four volumes of his work were published, and he gave good service to his denomination in Liverpool.

Leaders of the Red Dragon

During the 1920s, eisteddfodau inspired by the Red Dragon movement wanted to nurture new poets in the mould of Hawen and Cadvan, and aimed at encouraging Welsh people who would serve the Welsh nation, its language and its traditions. The eisteddfod was not its only activity. There was a preaching meeting on St David's Day and concerts were held regularly. The need to foster poets who could compose metrical poetry was recognised, and Dr Richard James Jones for example was one of many who went to classes to learn the rules and different versions of *cynghanedd*.

Welsh was the only language used by the movement and its eisteddfod. Red Dragon and Young Wales worked together in Upper Parliament Street. *Undeb y Ddraig Goch* (Union of the Red Dragon) was founded by ten prominent Liverpool Welsh patriots: Dr R T Williams, who was born in Ffestiniog; the bookseller J R Morris; his partner Rolant Wyn, the uncle of Hedd Wyn; the estate agent Cledwyn Hughes; banker Dan Thomas; and poets and playwrights William Morgan (Collwyn); W R Hughes; J E Roberts (Ap Heli); Meuryn and D R Jones. Each one was an unshakeable Welshman and the arrival of Saunders Lewis to lecture for them was greeted with gratitude.

A Welsh nucleus who nurtured a nation

In Liverpool, the movement awoke some of the most important and perceptive people to the vital role of language and the idea of nationhood. By 1922 Saunders Lewis had left Liverpool but a great deal of his influence remained and especially his famous lecture, *Egwyddorion Cenedlaetholdeb* (The Principles of Nationalism). This was well received by Young Wales societies in both Liverpool and London. One of those who enjoyed his lectures and essays was Isaac Griffiths, Thatto Heath, St Helens. It was he who wrote one of the most important letters in the early years of the Welsh Nationalist Party, indeed before its official birth in Pwllheli in August 1925. He had been so inspired by the St David's Day celebrations of the Cymmrodorion Society of

St Helens, on 7 March 1925, that he sent a letter in Welsh to *Y Brython* on 19 March:

Dear Sir

At the St David's Day celebrations of St Helens Cymmrodorion Society the suggestion of one of the Cymmrodorion 'that the time is ripe for establishing a National Party for Wales' was received enthusiastically. We feel that Welsh matters have been neglected, that the current political parties are too busy with their own particular policies and completely unconcerned by Welsh matters. What do readers of *Y Brython* have to say about this? What is the opinion of the nation's leaders?

Loss and success among the Liverpool Welsh

Eisteddfod y Golomen Wen (The White Dove Eisteddfod) was established in 1922 as a by-product of the 1917 Birkenhead Eisteddfod of the Black Chair, and was attracting a younger generation. One year they were fortunate to have the presence from London of the Rev. H Elvet Lewis (Elfed), later an Archdruid, to chair the poet who composed the best ode, as he was preaching at Great Mersey Street Chapel on the Saturday and Sunday evenings, 21 and 22 March 1925.

On that Sunday evening, the Rev. David Jones delivered a funeral sermon for the successful builder and JP, Richard Edward Jones, at Edge Lane Welsh Presbyterian Chapel.

An equally influential person was R Llewelyn Roberts, 20 Merton Road, Bootle, who died at the age of fifty-five in February 1925. He came from the outskirts of Caernarfon to Bootle to learn the ways of the timber trade with Lumley Lloyd. He was made a partner in the company in 1902 and was the principal partner after the death of his brother-in-law R R Lloyd. He was known in the borough as a great friend to the poor and he set up a fund for the unemployed. He married one of the young women brought up in Stanley Road Chapel, and his funeral was held at Anfield Cemetery on 4 February with the Rev. William Davies officiating.

During the same week the funeral took place of Robert Thomas of Cressington, aged seventy-four, in Allerton Cemetery. He had come to Liverpool as a young boy and was very successful, along with his brother William who was the founder of a shipping company. Robert Thomas gave a lifetime's service to the Calvinistic Methodist chapels at Crosshall Street and Garston. He was appointed an elder in Victoria Chapel, Crosshall Street, in 1887 and at Garston Church in 1896.

The talented W Moses Williams of Toxteth

The Liverpool Welsh rejoiced in their bright boys and girls. One of the most gifted was W Moses Williams, 26 Madelaine Street, Toxteth. He and his parents were members of Mount Zion Wesleyan Methodist Chapel and *Y Brython* headlined its account of him: 'Brilliant Moses of the Mount, that is, Mount Zion.' His parents had come from Flintshire and Williams was a product of Liverpool Welsh life. He was a student at Liverpool Institute (the academy for very many Welsh students) where he received prizes in four subjects: English language and literature, Latin and Greek. One of the first things he did at Oxford University was to join the foremost Welsh society there, the Dafydd ap Gwilym Society, which is still in existence.

Welsh students in the university eisteddfod

Another very talented Welsh student was Gwyneth Griffith of Wallasey, who won the Dr O T Williams and Robert Gee prizes and a first-class honours degree in medicine. One of the university students' highlights was the annual eisteddfod held in the Arts Theatre at the beginning of February. The competitions were open, and adjudicators came from across Merseyside. Oliver H Edwards, the full-time organist at Princes Road Chapel, Toxteth, was more than ready to be a music adjudicator, and J H Jones, editor of *Y Brython*, was in charge of the recitation competitions. The poets Pedrog and Moelwyn were there to assess the poets as the latter's son, Alun Moelwyn Hughes, was one of the eisteddfod secretaries. The other was Muriel Gruffydd. One of the well-off Welshmen of the city, the estate agent Arthur Venmore, was asked to be president as he was so generous towards every good cause. At the 1925 eisteddfod, the under-26 recitation was won by a young man from Anglesey, Michael Parry. In later years, as the Rev. Michael Parry of London, he became a compère at national eisteddfodau. His sister Elsie was educated at Edge Hill College and spent her life as a teacher and was one of the Edge Lane Chapel faithful, reaching the grand old age of 100.

The eisteddfodau of Liverpool

The evangelist Tom Nefyn Williams came to preach in Southport on 8 March 1925, and the organisers of the Bootle Welsh Society's Children's Eisteddfod took their opportunity and invited him to address the children in the Town Hall on the Saturday. Tom Nefyn did it in his own unique 'totally fresh and original' way, according to one reporter. The previous Saturday evening there was a St David's Day service at Liverpool Cathedral and, according to reports, it was an electrifying service with the cathedral packed to the rafters. Literally 'hundreds of Welsh folk were turned away' as there was no room.

During this period every chapel had its eisteddfod. There was a St David's Day Eisteddfod at Spellow Lane, where there were two chapels, one worshipping in English as part of the Presbyterian Church of Wales, and the other a Welsh Wesleyan Methodist Chapel. As neither building was big enough, the eisteddfod was held at Picton Hall in the city centre. The Trinity Road Welsh Independent Chapel in Bootle borrowed Bootle Town Hall for its annual eisteddfod. It was a loss to many Liverpool eisteddfodau when the Rev. Evan Roberts of Bootle left to minister to the Methodist church in Tregarth, near Bangor, one of its strongholds at the time. He was busy as a lecturer, writer and minister. He arranged weekly services in Walton Prison for Welsh speakers there. Another well-known Wesleyan Methodist minister, the Rev. J Maelor Hughes, a great friend of the preacher and gifted literary craftsman Tegla Davies, was moved to take care of Oakfield Chapel in Anfield. It was within Merseyside Welsh Methodism that the famous Baltimore, USA evangelist, the Rev. Dr David Hughes, was raised. There is frequent mention of his work at the large Abbot Chapel, Baltimore, with a membership of 1,500. In the 1920s the large Welsh Liverpool chapels of Princes Road and Stanley Road had rather fewer members than that, but still catered for more than 1,000 at least.

Preparing for the National Eisteddfod of Wales, 1929

During 1927 preparations began for the 1929 National Eisteddfod in Liverpool. The children's choir – with its different sections from north Liverpool, Bootle, Wallasey, south Liverpool and so on – began rehearsals. An invitation went out to the Welsh of all denominations, asking them to persuade parents and their children to join the choir. Ted Humphreys Jones, who was active in the Everton Welsh community all his life, remembered he and other children from Everton Village Welsh Baptist Chapel joining children from Douglas Road and Edge Lane (Calvinistic Methodists), Edge Lane (Baptists), Tabernacle (Welsh Independents), Belmont Road, Oakfield (Wesleyan Methodists) and meeting every Tuesday evening in the vestry of Edge Lane Presbyterian Chapel under conductor Henry Davies. The climax came on 5 August 1929 (the first day of the Eisteddfod in Sefton Park) with the Grand Children's Choir on the stage and all eyes on the conductor, Dr T Hopkin Evans.

Dr T Hopkin Evans was a busy musician and lived with his family near Edge Lane Welsh Presbyterian Chapel at Craig Nedd, 140 Edge Lane, Liverpool. He chose his house name because he came from Resolven in the Neath Valley. He came to Liverpool to conduct the Welsh Choral Union at the end of the First World War.

Pedrog was the Archdruid from 1928 to 1932 and the poet David Emrys James (Dewi Emrys, 1881–1952) won the Chair at the 1929 National Eisteddfod in Sefton Park for his excellent ode.

Lewis's store eisteddfod

One of the consequences of the National Eisteddfod coming to Liverpool was that more and more eisteddfodau were established. The large store, Lewis's in Renshaw Street, joined in the cultural renaissance. This eisteddfod became extremely popular for two generations and, though the Blitz on Liverpool in 1941 meant that it did not happen that year, it was held during the rest of the Second World War.

The organiser of both the concert and the three-day eisteddfod was W C Thomas, Ffordd Penrhos, Bangor, a man known in eisteddfod circles as Gwilym Bethel. It is understood that Lewis's employed him to arrange the eisteddfod and to prepare the list of subjects and winning compositions published each year by Hugh Evans and Sons Ltd, 9–11 Hackins Hey, Liverpool, and 350–360 Stanley Road, Bootle. The Welsh bookshop belonging to the Brython Press was in Hackins Hey and the offices, printshop and bookbinding were in Stanley Road. The eisteddfod slogan was seen on every item: 'The Red Dragon will rise again.' Competitors were expected to send their names and addresses to the organiser in Bangor beforehand, as every competitor was listed in the programme.

On the Thursday of the eisteddfod, there were youth competitions with some of the children's choirs early in the afternoon. The majority of the choirs came from Liverpool and Arfon, from towns like Caernarfon, Pen-y-groes, Dyffryn Nantlle and sometimes Pwllheli or Felinheli.

On the Friday there were the solo competitions and so forth, with huge crowds gathered by the middle of the afternoon. There were three sessions, the morning one from 9.30 a.m., the afternoon one at 1 p.m. and the last at 4 p.m. During the second session, at 3 p.m., the chairing of the bard ceremony would take place, according to the rituals of the Gorsedd of Bards of the National Eisteddfod.

The climax came on the Saturday, with this important eisteddfod starting at 9.15 a.m. Friday's winning soloists would compete against each other for the gold medal – likewise the winners of the recitation classes. In the afternoon there would be a feast of choral music.

The Cymric Male Voice Choir

Lewis's eisteddfod was in its heyday throughout the 1930s, and a wealth of other cultural activity stemmed from it. During that time the Cymric Male Voice Choir entertained and held concerts focusing on the forgotten and the disadvantaged. They would hold concerts at the Fazakerley Cottage Homes for orphaned children and then an evening concert at the Toxteth Workhouse. A short time later they made a second visit to Eventide Home in Yew Tree Road, an establishment which had been handed over to the Salvation Army by the generous Miss Fowler. Another outing was to Rainhill Mental Institution. The choir depended on a core of seven Welsh-speaking soloists: John James, Alun Garner (from Fitzclarence Street Chapel), Arfon Williams, A G Williams, Richard Williams, Tom Morris and Eric Pugh. Leslie Thomas was the accompanist and the choir was conducted by the fervent Baptist, J T Jones. The chairman was Mr Bootle Welsh, as he was lovingly called, the versatile R Vaughan Jones.

Leading role for drama

Drama was very important to the Liverpool Welsh. The arrival of the Rev. C Currie Hughes, as the new young minister of Peel Road Welsh Presbyterian Church in Seaforth, gave a boost to the Peel Road Dramatic Company. That company gave many memorable evening performances, including two on successive evenings in 1925 at the Gordon Institute. Currie Hughes had proved himself an excellent amateur actor in his role as one of the fiends of the sleeping bard, Ellis Wynne (1671–1734), in the Harlech Castle pageant in the summer of 1923.

The Woodchurch Road Chapel Drama Company in Birkenhead greatly enjoyed performing, and was always keen to appear in the schoolrooms of Liverpool chapels, with three of its principal actors at this time preparing for lifetime service in the Presbyterian ministry, namely the two brothers, Hugh Ll and Owain Tudur Hughes, and Maldwyn A Davies.

Commitment and energy for Welsh culture

There was energy and commitment in every aspect of Welsh chapel life. More than £1,000 was spent in 1924–25 to decorate Mount Zion Chapel in Princes Avenue. The fine organ was also restored. The chapel and all its rooms were painted and decorated by the company of Edward Jones, Bedford Street, Liverpool, a Welsh firm that carried out fine work on scores of chapels in Liverpool and district.

The *cymanfaoedd canu* (hymn-singing festivals) continued to attract large crowds and when the Presbyterian Church held their yearly session, they would hire the huge Sun Hall in Kensington. In 1925 the singing festival was due to be held on Monday evening, 23 March, and on the previous Sunday there were three rehearsals under the leadership of Professor David Evans (1874–1948) of University College, Cardiff. He was the composer of numerous tunes. The rehearsals were arranged for him on the Sunday morning at Stanley Road Chapel, at Douglas Road Chapel, Anfield, in the afternoon, and in the evening at Belvidere Road Chapel, Toxteth, before they all came together at Sun Hall on the Monday evening. Another man who frequented singing and preaching festivals in Liverpool was one of the great Welsh exile characters, John Hughes of Watford. He had family connections with Merseyside, namely the Roberts family of Olivia Street, Bootle. He had moved to London as a young man from Betws-y-Coed in 1871 and became a member of Walham Green Presbyterian Chapel in London. No traveller could miss him, with his flowing white beard to his waist!

Each denomination would hold its singing festivals. In the same year, the Liverpool and District Baptists staged one at Everton Village Chapel under the baton of the well-known Liverpool conductor J T Jones.

Plaid Cymru focuses on the exiles

Plaid Cymru wanted to establish a north-west England regional committee in 1933 and set up a branch in Liverpool. The president was Gwilym R Jones, editor of *Y Brython*, alongside the treasurer H Arthur Jones, who lived in Manchester, and R Gordon Williams, a young teacher in Ashton-in-Makerfield. On the executive committee there were keen Red Dragon members: J R Morris; William Morgan (Collwyn); the notable writer on science in Welsh, O E Roberts; as well as Mrs Llinos Jones (née Roberts), a native of Pen-y-groes; Miss Olwen Ellis, who was later on the staff of the Gee Press in Denbigh; J T Parry, a teacher in Chester and later in Menai Bridge; and Eilian Roberts and his wife. Roberts, an accountant and later a stockbroker, was one of the more colourful Liverpool Welsh characters and was distantly related to the Plaid Cymru leader Saunders Lewis. He and his wife had a second home in Llaneilian, Anglesey. In 1932 he was one of the founders of *Cylch y Pump ar Hugain* (The Circle of Twenty-Five) with the aim of:

> Deepening Welsh consciousness, nurturing language and discussing subjects of importance and interest to the nation, especially those to do with Welsh life on Merseyside.

The Circle of Twenty-Five

The wish to set up a society like this reflects the period. Unemployment kept the Welsh in their own communities. The incomers were now middle class, teachers mainly, rather than working-class people like Rolant Wyn and Gwilym Deudraeth. The 1930s was a period of crisis and Eilian Roberts and his friends realised that Liverpool Welsh life would have to depend more and more on the resources and talents of the Welsh who had put down their

Builders

Houses built by William (Klondyke) Jones in Orrell

Mona Street, Orrell

Another one of Klondyke Jones's streets

Bethel's new chapel in Heathfield Road

Ashton-in-Makerfield Chapel

Stained-glass window in memory
of Laura Jones

J W Jones & Sons' office
in Allerton

The gravestone of timber merchant
David Roberts, Hope Street, located
by the Anglican Cathedral

Well-known Welsh people in the City

The Rev. J Cadvan Davies

The Rev. David Adams (Hawen)

Pedrog, the preacher-poet

The Rev. D Hughson Jones, the leader of the Liverpool Welsh movement against the drowning of Tryweryn

Dr Owen Thomas

Dr H Gordon Roberts and supporters of his work at Shillong's hospital

The Rev. Peter Price, the minister at Great Mersey Street Chapel

The Archdruid Bryn Williams (who was raised in Patagonia)

Celebrating 150 years of the *Mimosa*

Carwyn Jones, First Minister of Wales

Dr Christine James, Archdruid of Wales

Lord Dafydd Wigley

Lord Mayor, Lady Mayoress, Dr Arthur Thomas, Ian Pollitt of Peel Holdings, Alicia Amalia Castro and D Ben Rees

Part of an enormous crowd at the Peel Holdings hall on the afternoon of Saturday, 30 May 2015

Children from the Chubut Valley singing near the memorial to the *Mimosa*

Mrs Elan Jones, Mossley Hill, formerly from Patagonia, addressing the crowd in the company of Dr Huw Edwards

1865   MIMOSA   2015

Cofnoda'r gofeb hon ymadawiad y llong hwylio 'Mimosa' o Lerpwl ar 28 Mai 1865, yn cludo 162 o Gymry (gan gofio hefyd y tri aeth allan o'u blaen). Glaniwyd ym Mhorth Madryn, Patagonia, ar 28 Gorffennaf 1865. Yno sefydlwyd gwladfa Gymreig sy'n bodoli hyd heddiw.

This plaque records the departure from Liverpool of the sailing ship 'Mimosa' on 28 May 1865, with 162 Welsh people (remembering also the three who went out before them). They landed at Port Madryn, Patagonia, on 28 July 1865 where they established a Welsh speaking settlement which survives to this day.

Cymdeithas Etifeddiaeth Cymry Glannau Mersi

Dadorchuddiwyd 30 Mai 2015 gan Mrs. Elan Jones

Merseyside Welsh Heritage Society

Unveiled 30 May 2015 by Mrs. Elan Jones

Plaque on the memorial in the Princes Dock, Liverpool

Dr Huw Edwards, London

Residents of Gaiman and the Chubut Valley at the ceremony in Liverpool

Children from Patagonia on the exact spot from where those brave souls sailed in 1865

The Work of John Gibson

John Gibson's statue of William Huskisson MP

John Gibson's grave in the Protestant cemetery in Rome

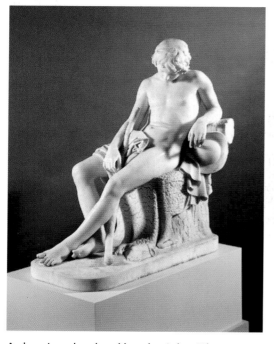

A sleeping shepherd boy by John Gibson

Benjamin Gibson's grave

Various Photographs

Ian Rush

Dr John Williams at the Gorsedd of Bards

Eddie Evans, composer of hymn tunes

John Davies, Chair of the Liverpool's
National Eisteddfod committee, 1884

Gwen Davies, the mother of George M Ll Davies, Glyn Davies and their brothers

Lena Jones, Centreville Road, Allerton

The Rev. Griffith Ellis, Bootle

Dr John Williams of Princes Road, Toxteth

Enid Hughes Jones (Broadgreen) and Ann Roberts (Childwall)

Gwynfor Evans greeted in Liverpool with the protesters from Capel Celyn on the Tryweryn issue

Courtesy of the National Library of Wales

D Ben Rees, Dafydd, Meinwen and Hefin Rees at Garth Drive, Liverpool

The Rev. and Mrs Coningsby Lloyd Williams, Anfield

Celebrating 40 years of *Yr Angor*

Yr Angor celebration sign

Norma and Roderick Owen, Dr Huw Edwards, Beryl and Dr John Williams

Gwerfyl Bain, Blodwen Roberts and Lilian Coulthard of the Liverpool Welsh Literary Society

Dr Huw Edwards and Dr D Ben Rees at the launch of the book, *Codi Angor*

Enjoying the feast at Woolton Golf Club, 20 July 2019

The Rev. Robert Parry, Y Glannau's Pastoral Assistant, entertaining at the dining table. Robert Parry became the minister of the Welsh Presbyterian chapels of Bethania, Waterloo, Seion, Birkenhead, Bethel, Heathfield Road, Liverpool, Willow Tree Road, Altrincham and Noddfa, West Didsbury, in April 2021.

John P Lyons,
Knowsley village,
and Dafydd Ll
Rees, London and
Liverpool

John G Williams,
Huw Edwards and
D Ben Rees

Members of
the Liverpool
Welsh Society /
Cymdeithas Cymry
Lerpwl

roots in the city. And there was always tension between the incomers and the second and third generation who had been born in Liverpool to Welsh parents. John Edward Jones (1913–98), who was Liverpool-born and later became a county court judge, often spoke about the conflict in his lectures. He said:

> That which should have united us – the Welsh language – was the obstacle.
> Neither party was comfortable using the first language of the other.

Jones noted how the chapels were operating by then. Liverpool children used a bilingual English-Welsh Bible, were only able to read the Welsh text with difficulty, not really understand it, and then were expected to discuss it with a fluent and eloquent teacher. J E Jones said:

> Certainly, there was an attempt, through Welsh classes, to improve things but with
> little success as, for the most part, the teacher would be unfamiliar with English. In
> a Welsh-speaking family it would be hard to succeed in making every child fluent.
> Usually, the first child would speak fluently, the second less well and, subsequently,
> the third and fourth prattling an adulterated language. Within the children's circle,
> things would be complicated by the fact that they were almost always speaking
> English to each other at the Band of Hope and, after growing up, would continue
> to do this even though they were able to speak the language well enough to chat
> and communicate. But they didn't.

After the 1914–18 war the new influx into Liverpool were mostly young people with some education, employed in banks, various offices as clerks, and taking on quite important roles in trade, finance, the law and education. Welsh people from both town and country enjoyed each other's company. In the world of sport many chapels, such as the brand new one in Heathfield Road which opened in 1927, set up tennis courts in Calderstones Park. One of the bastions of Young Wales, J R Jones, suggested forming a society to meet of an evening when they would be free for fuller and more thoughtful discussion. For the rest of the decade the routine was to meet 'every week during the winter months and once a month during the summer'. From the outset, numbers were limited to twenty-five men. No women were allowed, and this was a subject of intense discussion on more than one occasion.

Chapter 20

The Second World War and an Indian summer (1939–59)

T he Second World War was a terrible time for the people of Liverpool and brought challenges on every front. Active members of Young Wales, the Welsh societies and the chapels disappeared into the armed forces in their hundreds, and many a religious group was torn apart on the question of war and peace. The Liverpool Presbytery of the Welsh Presbyterian Church had a peace committee and that met at the beginning of March 1939. It was decided to identify the third Sunday of May as Peace Sunday, and that services that day would emphasise the need for peace. Also, every Sunday school was urged to focus on the situation and read a message from the Urdd to the children of the world. The two most prominent officers of *Cymdeithas Heddychwyr Cymru* (the Welsh Pacifist Society) had close links with the Liverpool Welsh. As noted, George M Ll Davies came from a notable Liverpool Welsh family. The secretary was none other than Gwynfor Evans, who had married a Liverpool Welsh woman, Rhiannon Thomas. She, her brother and her parents were members of the Liverpool branch of Plaid Cymru and of Chatham Street Welsh Presbyterian Church, and all confirmed pacifists. The family left Liverpool in 1937, though the son, Dewi Prys-Thomas, continued to lecture in architecture at the university for some time.

The attitude of the churches towards the war

The spokesmen for the Liverpool Welsh pacifists stirred up much debate, in particular this proposal to Fitzclarence Street Chapel on 5 April 1939:

We are making a personal appeal for freedom of conscience and the rights of the individual. We intend to oppose every attempt to make any war service obligatory under any circumstances.

The Rev. W Llewelyn Evans, minister of Edge Lane Welsh Chapel, redrafted the motion as follows:

We make a personal appeal for freedom of conscience and the rights of the individual. We also appeal to the government not to adopt compulsory military service.

This version was accepted before being sent to 10 Downing Street – but in vain. By the time Adolf Hitler and his armies had overrun Poland in September 1939, Liverpool knew it would be in the eye of the storm because of its importance as a strategic port to the British economy.

The death of Gwilym Deudraeth

During the period known as the phoney war, William Thomas Edwards (Gwilym Deudraeth, 1863–1940), one of the most prominent bards among the Liverpool Welsh, died on 20 March 1940 and was buried in Allerton Cemetery. He was an ordinary working man but, without doubt, a genius of *cynghanedd*, and he worked in the warehouse of Longmore Cotton Company alongside several cultured Welshmen like Collwyn, Ap Heli and John Roberts (Bootle), brother of the novelist Kate Roberts.

Fleeing the city

The authorities arranged for every school in Liverpool to leave the city for the safety of the Lake District and Wales, and that under the care of their teachers. One of the Welsh teachers who was sent from Bootle to Breconshire was Eirian Roberts. Her class from Christchurch Primary School, Bootle, travelled to the village of Beulah, near Llanwrtyd, and she maintained a close link with many of its inhabitants for the rest of her life.

Most of the Welsh chapels set up a soldier committee, to take care of young men and women from the church who were involved in military service. In Bootle and Waterloo they performed the same service as during the First World War, that is offering a warm welcome to the Welsh at the armed forces' camps and sailors at the port of Liverpool. In 1940 Waterloo Presbyterian Chapel established a good relationship with the Liverpool Welsh Battalion which had its camp in Blundellsands. John P Lyons mentions the many items received from generous and concerned members. He says:

> In the church there were received donations from individual members and from the general public such as blankets, socks, helmets, belts, cuffs, mufflers, gloves, shirts, bed jackets, chest protectors to be given to the soldiers. 42 waistcoats, 71 pair of socks, mittens, mufflers, handkerchiefs, 100 stamped post cards and pencils, overcoats, three shillings' worth of cough lozenges, shirts, woollen vests, pants, £5 worth of eucalyptus, 40 quarts of cough mixture, helmets, blankets and gloves.

The Blitz years, 1940–41

In reviewing the Blitz years from 1940–41, the Rev. D Tudor Jones, originally from Bwlch-llan, Cardiganshire, wrote:

> In 1940 and 1941 much came our way to dishearten us and let things slip from our hands. A number of our members left us for chapels and churches in Wales; we lost a whole host of our people who went to Wales for shelter; a number of church families were rendered homeless and without the means of survival; and we lived to mourn our lovely place of worship. These are harsh experiences to bear.

Among the Welsh who left Bootle for Wales was the family of John Evan and Maggie Roberts. Maggie Roberts described it vividly to her sister-in-law, the novelist Dr Kate Roberts, Denbigh, on 23 November 1940:

> It was an unforgettable night. The day was spent searching the ruins of a house in the nearby street for bodies. We were sure our end was at hand. The houses were plaster and soot and mud. The street lamps have been blacked out. Everyone is feeling unsettled and nobody wants to eat. Many houses were destroyed, the Welsh Independent Chapel has been completely ruined and every window in Stanley Road Chapel has been shattered. Thanks for your invitation to come and stay with you in Denbigh. I would greatly like to come but cannot think about leaving John and the children here.

Six nights later, on 29 November 1940, a German aircraft dropped a parachute mine which fell onto a junior instructional centre in Durning Road. In its cellar there were 300 men, women and children sheltering from the bombing. The building collapsed, killing scores of them immediately. Hot water and gas gushed out of the central heating pipes and filled the cellar and the blaze above made rescue almost impossible. Of the 166 people killed, a number were Welsh, and almost everyone who had been in the building was injured. Winston Churchill described the Durning Road tragedy as 'the single worst civilian incident of the war'.

A Welsh boy's experience

One of the children at nearby Clint Road School, which was also hit, was the Welshman Emrys Roberts. Years later he wrote a striking poem entitled 'Yn Saith Oed' (Seven Years of Age) describing his experience. Owen Elias Roberts, a man who twice won the prose medal at the National Eisteddfod, narrowly escaped the tragedy. He was walking home from the Welsh Club in Upper Parliament Street when a tram stopped in front of the school. He saw people seeking refuge in it from the bombing, but decided to set out for home. Half an hour later the German bombs fell.

At the mercy of the enemy

At the beginning of May 1941 Liverpool saw the worst of the bombing by the Germans. The port was defended by British warships, as Hitler sent his 'U-boat hunter-killer packs', as they were called, to destroy the merchant convoys. The Western Approaches Command Centre was in the cellar of Derby House, behind City Hall and known as the Citadel. In 100 rooms in the bowels of the earth, the Battle of the Atlantic was directed. Ships were defended by warships under the care of Captain Frederick John 'Johnnie' Walker (1896–1944).

The Germans dropped a string of bombs across Liverpool – no part of the city was spared. On 4 May a bomb fell on the 32 Micklefield Road home of one of the Heathfield Road Presbyterian Chapel leaders. David Griffiths was saved but his wife was killed. Griffiths found a new home at 32 Mapledale Road before moving back a few years later to Wales.

The destruction of Stanley Road Chapel

On the same day, the lovely Stanley Road Welsh Presbyterian Chapel in Bootle was demolished. The Rev. D Tudor Jones tried to alleviate the members' sadness, saying:

> The spire which pointed towards the heavens fell – despite that, the heavens are above our heads. The tuneful notes of the organ have been silenced but faith is turning the cacophony into the music of her victorious song. The white pulpit has been shattered but the holy Gospel which was preached from it is unstained. The beautiful windows have been shattered – the light has not been extinguished; the vision remains. Though the pews are pulverised, the throne of worship is unshaken.

They set about worshipping in the little schoolroom, giving thanks that the chapel caretaker, C O Evans, and his family had been saved. The memorial to the soldiers who had lost their lives in the 1914–18 war was also spared. And, on the Sunday morning of the destruction, E Meirion Evans (of the Brython Press), a leader in Stanley Road Chapel, saw an 'incomparable example of faith'. Mrs Benjamin Evans, the aunt of Professor David Alan Price Evans, walked three miles from her home in Waterloo to Bootle to participate in the morning service despite being more than eighty. By the time she reached Bootle she thought she was too late for the service, and instead went to sit in the park, waiting for the Sunday school to open, oblivious to the fact that her beloved chapel was in ruins. A memorial tablet to the first minister, the Rev. Griffith Ellis (1873–1912), was found intact amid the rubble.

The Bootle Welsh had a hard time of it since the docks were nearby, and many were injured and lost their homes. In 1939 there were 17,119 houses in Bootle. During the war 2,043 of them were destroyed, with 6,000 being severely damaged and about 8,000 sustaining less severe damage. After the war it cost £1,500,000 to repair them.

The destruction of Fitzclarence Street Welsh Chapel

Another fine chapel which was destroyed was the Fitzclarence Street Welsh Presbyterian Chapel in Everton. The moderator of the presbytery, the Rev. Aeron Davies, expressed his deep grief in two anguished sentences:

> Old Clarence Chapel. It is strange to think that it is now quiet on a Sunday. For many years it heard praise for the love of God but today (August 1942), more's the pity, it hears nothing – except that the rubble proclaims that man does not love man.

The minister, the Rev. H C Lewis, had died in April 1940. Enough money was received from the War Office to build a new chapel, and they also decided to transfer money to build a new church on a large housing estate in Sandfields, Aberavon, south Wales.

Another chapel which was almost entirely burnt to the ground was the Kensington Welsh Independent Chapel, where Pedrog was minister for decades. The interior was subsequently turned into a water reservoir for fire-fighters. On one occasion a boy from the nearby school was drowned when he fell while playing there. A policeman who tried to save him was also drowned.

Schooldays during the war

In an entertaining essay on *Dyddiau Ysgol Adeg y Rhyfel* (Schooldays during the War), J Trefor Williams described the experiences of evacuees who had returned or had not been evacuated. For the boys, the best lesson was practising fire-fighting in the schoolyard. The children were arranged in teams: one boy to carry buckets of water, another to dump the water on the flames. The best task of all was dowsing the flames. Schoolteachers in Liverpool city centre schools would also send boys around the terraced houses every afternoon to gather rubbish, as paper and metals were in such short supply.

Ministers do their bit

A large number of young people from the chapels joined the armed forces and the Rev. R Emrys Evans, a Presbyterian minister in Rock Ferry and West Kirby, decided to volunteer as a chaplain. Other ministers were unwilling to support the war. Among these were the Rev. Lewis Edwards and J Celyn Jones, Wesleyan ministers in Oakfield; W A Lewis of Tabernacle Chapel, Belmont Road; D J Bassett of Edge Lane Baptists; Llywelyn Jones of Bethlehem, Douglas Road, and his colleague, C Lloyd Williams. They were supported by laymen who were just as committed, such as O E Roberts of

Anfield Presbyterian Chapel; J C Hughes and Collwyn of Edge Lane Chapel; R J Pritchard of Douglas Road; Dilys Lloyd of Anfield Road; Beti Hughes of Everton Village, and Mr and Mrs Ben Davies of Oakfield Chapel.

Three centres were set up straightaway – Anfield, meeting in Newsham Park Chapel, Bootle in Stanley Road Chapel, and south Liverpool, using the Young Wales rooms in Upper Parliament Street. The Rev. Ifor Oswy Davies was active in the south, as was Pierce Roberts, an inspiring teacher, and J Morgan Parry, a Chatham Street elder and father of Morgan Parry who was a leading light in the anti-nuclear and environmental movements. An ambitious programme was arranged, and young people flocked to the exercise, handicraft, nursing and environmental classes, as well as to Welsh classes and topical lectures. In 1941 Heathfield Road Chapel persuaded the Rev. Dr R Glynne Lloyd to move from Ferndale in east Glamorgan to take care of the huge church near Penny Lane. Dr Lloyd began his ministry on the first Sunday of April 1942 and, within a month, had a baptism of fire as Liverpool was, quite literally, on fire. He expressed his appreciation of the calling in March 1942:

> I admire you as a church for your untiring devotion to the needs of the Christian cause in such terrible times. As the difficulties of the time have not caused you to let go, it will be a great privilege to work with you. I am confident that our church will be a home for Welsh people away from their own homes and in need of shelter, a firm defence against the temptations of the world and that it will lead you safely to the truth which is in Christ.

He joined a number of ministers who continued to work in Liverpool. The others in the southern district were the Revs Ifor Oswy Davies and W Llewelyn Evans. In 1939 Oswy Davies was called on to look after Belvidere Road Church and, in 1943, Chatham Street Church.

Among the Welsh Presbyterian ministers, four retired and moved back to Wales, namely the Rev. Robert Davies of Heathfield Road; J Ellis Jones of Huyton Quarry and Prescot; J D Evans of Garston, and Peron Hughes of St Helens to Anglesey, the last two having served well over forty years in Liverpool and district.

Still meeting for fellowship

Despite the devastation, troubles and grief, there were still signs of better days in the midst of the fiercest storms. The Young Wales club in Upper Parliament Street was an oasis for soldiers and sailors when they visited Liverpool. On 5 December 1942, the Home of the Welsh Forces was formally opened there by R Hopkin Morris, director of the BBC in Wales, along with the Lord Mayor of Liverpool, Sir Charles Jones, the chiefs of the armed forces, and Welsh civic leaders.

Preparing to welcome the soldiers home

In 1944 *Undeb Rhieni, Athrawon a Chyfeillion y Plant* (Union of Parents, Teachers and Friends of Children) was formed, and Urdd branches published a monthly periodical called *Y Glannau* (The Shores), since *Y Brython*, the Welsh weekly paper published in Bootle, had come to an end in 1939. In the same year the Welsh churches set about preparing to welcome their sons and daughters home from the war and established welcoming committees. The Rev. Ifor Oswy Davies struck an important note:

> The work of receiving our brothers and young sisters back to the churches after the war places a great responsibility on us. Their experiences and reactions will vary. Some will be more fervent and solid than we are, others may be unsure about the old anchors. We shall need great patience, vivid imagination and ceaseless sympathy. Only the love and gifts of the Good Shepherd will see us through.

The Rev. J D Williams Richards arrives

In the last year of the war, the Welsh Independents welcomed the Rev. J D Williams Richards from south Wales to Belmont Road Tabernacle Welsh Independent Chapel, and he stayed in the city for the rest of his life. He was elected as secretary of the Merseyside Free Church Federal Council and stayed in that post for many years. The Free Church Centre moved from Lord Street to Tarleton Street and opened a bookshop giving good space for Welsh books, papers and magazines. He cared for the shop until 1981.

The effects of the Second World War

The effect of the war on the Liverpool Welsh community was enormous. In 1938 membership of the Liverpool Presbytery numbered 6,945, with also another 1,042 children and 456 associates. At the end of the war Presbyterian membership had dwindled to 5,058 (a loss of nearly 2,000), 717 children and 157 associates.

Enormous changes were put in place after the Labour Party won the general election with a large majority on 5 July 1945, and Clement Attlee became Prime Minister in place of Winston Churchill. A Liverpool Welshman, Emrys Roberts, won the Merioneth seat for the Liberals with a small majority of 112. He kept the seat at the 1950 election but lost it to Labour in the 1951 election. Roberts was a member of the Circle of Twenty-Five and was steeped in the ideals of Young Wales. He expressed his thanks to the circle after his election victory:

> It is hardly necessary to say that there is no society of friends I prize more highly than the Circle of Twenty-Five … if I have the privilege of remaining an associate member, it will be a comfort to me that I will not lose that close contact.

A Welsh lunch club is formed

J R Jones of Menlove Avenue, Allerton, had suggested to the Circle of Twenty-Five before the war that they should set up a lunch club, where people could eat and listen to a talk on a topic of interest to Welsh folk. The war had put a stop to his idea, but it was resurrected in 1946. The first meeting was held on 20 February 1947 in Frances Café, Parker Street, with Alderman John Morris JP as speaker. He was one of the great Liverpool builders and a man who had refused the chance of standing as MP for his native Merioneth to focus on his business. The lunch club was very well received, and it was O E Roberts who organised it from start to finish alongside H Idris Williams (Allerton), R Norman Roberts (Wallasey) and John L Griffiths (Wavertree).

The National Health Service

The establishment of the NHS, the brilliant vision of the charismatic politician Aneurin Bevan, was welcomed by the Welsh. His idea was that every doctor and hospital would come under state regulation, but it met a lot of opposition from doctors and the British Medical Association. There was initial opposition among Welsh doctors in Liverpool, but there was a change in attitude as the NHS developed.

One of the surgeons who was most supportive was Welshman J Howell Hughes, and his autobiography, *A Surgeon's Journey*, published in 1990, is a revealing study of how medicine changed during his lifetime. For him, the NHS was the most important event in the history of medicine. He believed that Aneurin Bevan was a genius, and he had the privilege of meeting him in Cardiff early in 1948. Hughes had already seen the benefits of uniting Liverpool training hospitals during his early days as a doctor.

They were brought together as the United Liverpool Hospitals and the competition between individual hospitals for financial support ceased. Hughes saw the great value in nationalising hospitals, knowing that there would be an opportunity to increase wages, introduce new equipment and refurbish buildings. Hospitals were always suffering from neglect due to a lack of finance. The world of consultants and surgeons changed. In the years after the Second World War, J Howell Hughes's contribution was recognised throughout north Wales. He and David Annis shared responsibility for a surgical unit of 150 beds for twenty years at the Royal Infirmary in Pembroke Place.

Teachers moving to Liverpool

During the 1950s there was a brief Indian summer as far as Welsh activities were concerned, as many young teachers came to Liverpool, mainly from the training colleges in Bangor and Wrexham. One of the specialists in the city's department of education was Miss Laura Myfanwy Jones of Wavertree, and she would travel to the Bangor teachers' training colleges every year to persuade students to consider Liverpool as their destination. Gwilym M Jones of Edith Road, himself a deputy headteacher by then, would receive the names of new young teachers who wanted to stay with Welsh families. English families were also invited to take young teachers as lodgers, especially if they lived within easy reach of Welsh chapels and churches or societies.

Despite this, the Second World War had changed Welsh society in Liverpool for ever. But thanks to the young teachers, a plan was made for Welsh education. A public meeting was arranged in Hackins Hey Hall in 1950 and this led to the setting up of eight Welsh Merseyside schools. They were only Saturday morning schools and, though better than nothing, they did not change things dramatically among the Liverpool Welsh-born youngsters. The Indian summer came to an end. The Saturday morning Welsh schools disappeared one by one, and with them the hopes for the future of Welsh communities in Liverpool and Merseyside.

Losing talented leaders

During the 1950s a number of leaders who had held together Welsh life in the city were lost. In 1950 Gwynfryn Roberts of Calderstones, one of the city's teachers, died. He had been a teacher in London, Bristol, Cardiff and twice in Liverpool, where he became an active leader at Princes Road Chapel during the ministry of the Rev. H Harris Hughes and, after that, the Rev. Griffith Rees.

The city also lost William Morgan (Collwyn) and John Richard Jones of Menlove Avenue, an estate agent, who was a generous donor to good causes within Young Wales and the Urdd. He was a Liberal city councillor and one of the principal campaigners for a Welsh parliament.

Drowning of Capel Celyn

The influential J R Jones died before the Liverpool Welsh had to face the difficult issue of Tryweryn – a subject that was a tragedy for them. Cwm Tryweryn, between Bala and Trawsfynydd, was a Welsh-speaking community with the little village of Capel Celyn as its focal point. It had a primary school, a Presbyterian chapel, a post office, a number of houses and surrounding farms. The city of Liverpool had submerged a Welsh valley to meet the water needs of its inhabitants as long ago as 1894. At that time the chief engineer of Liverpool Corporation was a Welsh speaker, Joseph Parry (1843–1936). His links with the Corporation extended over fifty-seven years. He joined as an engineer in 1863, and when work began on Llanwddyn water works in 1881, he was also shouldering responsibility for Rivington water treatment works, another reservoir on which the city depended. Parry took overall charge for channelling the water supply from the rivers Conwy and Marchnant into Llanwddyn Reservoir. When he joined in 1863, 15.5 million gallons of water per day were sufficient for the needs of Liverpool but, when he was considering retiring in 1914, that had risen to 32.3 million. Though the drowning of Llanwddyn caused pain and distress, Parry and his colleagues managed the situation better than Liverpool Corporation under the insensitive leadership of Jack Braddock and Bessie Braddock MP, who were hostile and merciless. The Braddocks became an inextricable part of the tragic drowning of Cwm Tryweryn.

When the residents of this Merionethshire area heard about the threat from Liverpool, a Committee for the Defence of Capel Celyn was set up supported by a number of prominent Welshmen, such as the preacher Dr R Tudur Jones and Gwynfor Evans. The Liverpool Welsh set up a similar committee, with the architect Dewi-Prys Thomas (Gwynfor Evans's brother-in-law) as secretary, together with Mrs Anita Morgan (née Rowlands), a minister's daughter and deputy headmistress in Gateacre. This committee became a thorn in the side of the garrulous political couple who controlled the Labour Party on the council. It must be remembered that not all the Liverpool Welsh opposed the plan. As far as the editor of the monthly journal *Y Glannau* was concerned, the valley was not particularly attractive, and the land was pretty desolate. But that was the voice of the minority. Although farmers had expressed similar doubts in letters to politicians such as Goronwy Roberts, it was not a message heard by most Welsh people in the city.

The Tryweryn Welsh and their leaders, such as the historian Dafydd Roberts, Dr R Tudur Jones, based in Bangor, and Gwynfor Evans, president of Plaid Cymru, arrived at St George's Hall on 7 November 1956 in the hope of being able to address councillors. No invitation came. When Alderman Frank Cain, on behalf of the water committee, proposed that he was going to ignore them, Gwynfor Evans, who was in the visitors' gallery, rose to his feet to ask permission to urge the councillors and the Lord Mayor to accept the delegation. He was allowed to express his protest in a very difficult atmosphere. He spoke of the opposition to the plan among the inhabitants of Wales. Some of the councillors became annoyed; a few began to shout 'Go back to Wales'. Bessie Braddock was furious with the Plaid Cymru leader and parliamentary candidate for Merioneth, as was her husband John 'Jack' Braddock, leader of the council. The atmosphere deteriorated, ending shamefully with the police coming to usher the three nationalists from the council chamber. From the standpoint of Welsh nationalism, the protest had been effective enough, but for the two Braddocks, John and Bessie, it was all a waste of council time.

The protest gave a sliver of hope to the residents of Capel Celyn. It was decided that they would arrange a visit to the city on 21 November. They brought their slogans with them, the Welsh words shining out as they processed through the streets of Liverpool: 'Your homes are safe – why destroy ours? Please, Liverpool, be a great city not a big bully.'

This was an eleventh-hour attempt to try and stop the political leaders of Liverpool voting to drown their homes which, naturally, meant so much to them. The protest would never have taken place without the leadership of the defence committee secretary, Elizabeth Watkin Jones, the very able daughter of the cultured folk musician Watcyn of Meirion; the chairman Dafydd Roberts; the charismatic politician Gwynfor Evans, and Goronwy Roberts, the Labour MP for Caernarfon. Some doubted the effect the protest would have. One farmer's wife expressed her doubts to an English journalist:

> Do you think that this big council is going to listen to us, a few people from a Welsh village? We can't speak English fluently. We are Welsh through and through and our land and our language are Welsh.

In Liverpool the protesters were well supported by a large group of students, originally from Wales, who were studying at Liverpool University, as well as keen supporters from among the Liverpool Welsh. Gwynfor Evans, who was later to become the first Plaid Cymru MP following the Carmarthen by-election in 1966, led them with appropriate patriotic pride. When they reached City Hall, he asked for permission to address the council on behalf of the Committee for the Defence of Capel Celyn. At that moment Alderman John Braddock was in the act of presenting the case for drowning Cwm Tryweryn. With great surprise, he gave way to allow Gwynfor Evans a chance to say a brief word – only a fortnight after he had been ordered to leave the council chamber. It was an emotional moment. Both could hear Welsh hymns being sung with gusto outside the building, some of them written by hymn writers who had been ministers of religion in Liverpool. According to a journalist from the *Manchester Guardian* (a paper which took much more interest in Wales at that time than it does now):

> Mr Evans made such a brilliant plea for the presentation of the valley's economic and cultural life that the Council broke into spontaneous applause at the end.

Gwynfor Evans had achieved something of a feat, but now he had to listen to Braddock's case. The alderman argued that the case of Tryweryn was being exploited by Plaid Cymru for its own ends. It was, in his opinion, complete nonsense to argue that Liverpool was acting high-handedly. Throughout the whole process it had liaised with forty local authorities in Wales. Braddock's argument won the day, the councillors voted in favour of drowning the valley. But the vote was not unanimous. The result was ninety-five in favour, one against and three sitting on the fence. The councillor who voted against was one of the Liverpool Welsh leaders and a prominent member of the Conservative Party, Alderman David John Lewis, who stood as a parliamentary candidate in Kirkdale and who, in 1962, became Lord Mayor of Liverpool.

It took some years for the dam to be built and the whole project to be completed. The slogan *Cofiwch Dryweryn* (Remember Tryweryn) came to remind the Welsh world of the greedy nature of the city council and its lack of sensitivity. In his maiden speech as Lord Maelor in the House of Lords, on 19 October 1966 (another sad day in the history of Wales, namely the tragedy of Aberfan), T W Jones said of Liverpool's action:

> The Liverpool Corporation decided to construct a reservoir and, in order to do so, it was necessary to submerge a village including its church. It was a Methodist church. Had it been a church of the Church of Wales I doubt whether the reservoir would have been constructed.

Tryweryn is one of the reasons for the disillusionment of many Welsh people with the actions of Liverpool Corporation and its leaders. Liverpool has since apologised for its deed, as it has apologised for supporting the slave trade in the eighteenth century.

Chapter 21

Twist and shout (1959–76)

It was during this period that Liverpool became world famous as the cradle of British pop music. For generations Liverpool had welcomed choirs, singers, bands and lecturers. During the Victorian era the British were fond of singing. There was thrilling singing at the Kop in Anfield and around Goodison Park. The majority of Welsh homes gave pride of place to the piano, and in the 1960s four Scousers put Liverpool centre stage on the world's musical map. As one pop music historian put it:

> Playing an instrument in Liverpool you must tackle it as you must tackle life, with a deal of pugnacity, show it who the master is. A pianist need not be a great executant and can neglect niceties. But her audience expects her to approach the piano as a training heavyweight champ will approach his punch-bag.

Societies galore

At the beginning of this exciting period the Liverpool Welsh community boasted a number of societies, including *Cymdeithas y Brythoniaid* (Society of the Britons) which attracted prominent people as guest speakers, such as the poet-preacher, the Rev. William Morris of Caernarfon. The main purpose of a society such as the Cymric Choir, on the other hand, was to promote singing, and on Saturday evening, 7 February 1959, Bethlehem Presbyterian Chapel in Douglas Road was packed to the rafters to hear them under the leadership of D Leslie Thomas. The soloists were young people from Liverpool, like Miss Cynthia Stroud who lived near Penny Lane, and John Medwyn Jones who could be heard regularly on Sundays at Trinity Chapel, Toxteth, and, in the 1970s, at Heathfield Road Chapel. He continues to support choirs and community singing from his home in Colwyn Bay. The

Liverpool University Welsh Society was also very active at the beginning of the 1960s. Singing was important to them too, but not as much as whist drives. This society depended on the support of the University Graduates' Society and on prominent Welsh academic staff such as Professor D Seaborne Davies, head of the law department.

Strong support

Apart from the societies, there were still numerous chapels that stood up for Welsh and Christian values and opened their doors not only on Sundays but on evenings during the week as well. Douglas Road Presbyterian Chapel was proud to have a young minister to care for them in the person of the Rev. Griffith Tudor Owen. He was ordained in 1955 and started his pastoral duties in Ysbyty Ifan and Padog before moving in 1958 to Bethlehem Chapel in Douglas Road. He stayed in Anfield for sixteen years.

At Heathfield Road Chapel there was a young people's assembly led by Enid Williams and D E Williams. In 1959 the tradition of arranging a tea for young people after Sunday school was started so that they could attend the evening service.

The world of Welsh drama

During the Second World War an Urdd youth drama festival started up in Crane's Theatre over two nights. Edwin Williams, a drama specialist, paid tribute to the local companies and their actors. He came to the conclusion that 'this was another chance to confirm the opinion that there were talented men and women in drama among the Liverpool Welsh'. As far as he was concerned, what current Welsh amateur dramatics needed more than anything was competent producers:

> I would almost go so far as to say that this is the most significant requirement of amateur dramatics today. The raw materials – young actors – expect discipline and leadership.

The Urdd honours Iolo

The Liverpool Welshman Iolo Francis Roberts, who was brought up in Fitzclarence Street Chapel manse, was honoured as president of the

Urdd Eisteddfod in Dolgellau on Thursday, 9 June 1960. One reporter remarked:

> Although he is so well-known in Wales, to us in Liverpool he is best-known as the man who married Miss Menna Pritchard of Wallasey.

The teaching talent of O E Evans

The death in 1960 of O E Evans of Osterley Gardens was a great loss to the Liverpool Welsh. He hailed from Llanberis and was for a while at Clynnog Preparatory School, as he was considering training for the Presbyterian ministry. But he turned to the world of education and became one of Liverpool's most successful headteachers. Evered Avenue Secondary School became one of the leading schools in the city under his quiet and steady leadership. He supported Anfield Welsh Calvinistic Methodist Chapel but also made a huge contribution to one of the mission chapels on the outskirts of Liverpool in Runcorn.

At the same time, Miss Elsie Parry of Radstock Road, and Miss Katie Thomas of Connaught Road, retired – both teachers were active at Edge Lane Welsh Presbyterian Chapel. The contribution in this period of enthusiastic teachers gave a particular perspective to Welsh life in the city. Open-air activities and weekends at Colomendy, near Mold, were arranged under what was called the Merseyside Camp, owned by Liverpool education committee. Everyone over the age of fifteen was invited to spend three all-Welsh days there. In those days the programme included rambling, folk dancing, conversation, debates and entertainment evenings.

The contribution of the Rev. Llewelyn Jones

Another clergyman who, from 1930 when he first came to Liverpool until his death in 1961, emphasised the place of Welsh culture in the lives of exiled Welsh people was the Rev. Llewelyn Jones. He described his philosophy in an essay in *Y Glannau*:

> But I must stress that despite the excellent and important work done by the churches to keep the Welsh way of life alive, we must have our Welsh culture, our traditions, our tunes and music, our poetry and prose, our drama and our

eisteddfod and all our national traditions if we are to keep Welsh life at its best here. I would venture to say that there is no future for the Merseyside Welsh churches as Welsh churches if we do not nurture our national culture.

As far as he was concerned the spiritual aspect of things was not sufficient without the Welsh cultural aspect:

And to do that, it is not enough for them to frequent Welsh churches: they have to be steeped in the best Welsh traditions, they must have Welsh culture. This culture and these traditions are the background to Welsh life in the Welsh churches. What counts is that so many of the most active members of the churches are ready to give up so much of their precious leisure time to help with the work of the Urdd and the various other Welsh movements in our midst.

Indeed, Llewelyn Jones was chair of the general committee of the Urdd for years and supported the annual eisteddfod of the Merseyside branches. It was his idea, too, to set up a periodical for the Urdd branches, *Y Glannau*, and under his editorship it soon became a periodical for the Welsh of Liverpool and district. The Rev. R Emrys Evans, his successor as editor and as secretary of the Welsh Presbyterian Church Overseas Mission, said:

He won a warm place for himself in the hearts of our young people and it is hard to think of a minister who achieved so much in our era for the Welsh language and culture in this area.

He worked tirelessly at the beginning of the Second World War to avoid seeing young Liverpool Welsh enrolling as cadets in the armed forces. He persuaded many of them to enrol in the Urdd.

One who experienced the horror of the bombing of Liverpool was the young poet Rhydwen Williams, who worked for a year with the Quaker ambulance team. As he said in his autobiography, *Gorwelion* (Horizons, 1984):

Houses which were houses last night. Lights combing the sky. The ugly, guilty moon which shows the city to the enemy, caught and condemned under the lights. I walk around like a man lost. I am lost! Bricks and bodies piling up – a refuge bombed. I see a foot in a shoe. A head – where was the body?

Soon after the death of the Rev. Llewelyn Jones, the influential George Williams, one of the city's headteachers, died. According to Gwilym M Jones he was in the same tradition:

> He was an artistic man. He could mould words with craft, he ran his fingers lightly over the black and white keys of the piano and he painted fluidly and colourfully in oils. He often worried about the future of Wales, her religion, her language, her young people and he was conscious of his responsibility to contemporary society in the Merseyside area. He worked and toiled constantly in his Welsh Presbyterian church in Edge Lane, with the Saturday morning Welsh school, with community hymn singing, he nurtured every Welsh movement and, in everything, he was enthusiastic and thorough.

Born and brought up with the Beatles

The Welsh Nonconformist chapels were a nursery for future teachers, as the institution always valued education and took great pride in the educational success of the younger generation. In 1961 three young people from Heathfield Road Chapel, who were studying to be teachers, were congratulated on reaching their goal. One was Barbara Thomas, who was in the same class as John Lennon at Dovedale Primary School; David Meirion Jones, who knew the Beatles well, and Robin Hughes. These had all been born and brought up in Liverpool.

Carl Jung

By this time, the quotation of the famous Swiss theologian and psychiatrist, Carl Jung, was known to everyone, everywhere. He called Liverpool 'the pool of life':

> I had a dream. I found myself in a dirty, sooty city. It was night and winter; and dark and raining. I was in Liverpool. The various quarters of the city were arranged radially around the square. In the centre was a round pool; in the middle of it, a small island. While everything around it was obscured by rain, fog smoke and dimly-lit darkness, the little island blazed with sunlight. On it stood a single tree, a magnolia in a shower of reddish blossoms. It was as though the tree stood in the sunlight and were, at the same time, the source of light. Everything was extremely unpleasant; black and opaque – fast as I felt then. But I had a

vision of unearthly beauty … and that's why I was able to love it all. Liverpool is the 'pool of life'.

Not everyone takes the words of the famous psychoanalyst seriously – the man who fell in love with Liverpool, though I never heard of him visiting the port. Yet, there is a message in his words, that Liverpool casts its spell over those who come to live within its domain. This happened to so many of us – Roderick and Norma Owen, Humphrey Wyn Jones and Louie Jones, Dafydd and Nan Hughes Parry, Richard and Pat Williams. Each of them was enchanted by the city and its landscape, by its culture, its people and the opportunities to live full lives as Welsh people within the city.

As someone who was raised in Allerton, where many of the Welsh have lived since Welsh builders brought the suburb into being, Paul McCartney said:

> Liverpool has its own identity. It's even got its own accent within about a ten-mile radius. Once you go outside that ten miles it's 'deep Lancashire lad'. I think you do feel that apartness, growing up there.

The Welsh Lunch Club

By the 1960s the Liverpool Welsh Lunch Club was still meeting in the Kardomah Café in Bold Street at one o'clock on the third Thursday of the month. Women were not invited as speakers but there were exceptions, such as Mrs Enid Wyn Jones, a stalwart of the YWCA and the Free Churches of the city. Others included T Elwyn Griffiths, a librarian and founder of the Union of Wales and the World, a movement for the Welsh diaspora, and Wallis Evans of Bangor, a specialist in the field of education.

Llanowain and The Beatles

The Beatles were becoming famous worldwide, and the Liverpool Welsh poet O Trefor Roberts (Llanowain) ventured to make them the subject of two *englynion* which were simultaneously supportive and cynical. He was the first Liverpool Welsh poet to write about the phenomenon. He describes their long hairstyle and unique garb which is attractive to young girls and draws attention to their memorable choice of name, yet also praises their music.

Television makes its mark

In 1965 the Liverpool Welsh Drama Society wound up. In the 1930s it had made an exceptional contribution to Liverpool Welsh life, and indeed that of the whole of Wales with the high standard of its actors. The company won a competition at the National Eisteddfod three times in succession under the direction of Morris Jones, then of Kensington. By 1965 there were only five trustees remaining – Morus Roberts, Heulwen Lewis and her brother Emrys, Aneirin Hughes and Morris Jones. It was decided to share the money in the funds between Young Wales and the Garthewin Players and Merseyside Urdd branches.

Campaign for a Welsh school

By the mid–1960s it was clear that there was a lot of coming and going among young Welsh people. Many of them were gaining experience as teachers and, usually after about five years, they would be looking for teaching posts in north Wales. Gwyndaf and Hafwen Roberts moved to Bangor because of his work with the civil service. Both were keen leaders of Urdd meetings in north Liverpool, and made a huge contribution to the movement's activities in the city.

Some of Wales's leading lights in the 1960s were surprised that there was no Welsh school in Liverpool. The Welsh were well represented in the world of education, and the 1947 Education Act gave parents the right to educate their children as they wished. Alderman Bill Sefton, the Labour Party leader on the city council after Jack Braddock, announced that Liverpool was willing to make up for its behaviour regarding the drowning of the Tryweryn Valley. The actor Meredith Edwards saw this as a chance for compensation, and argued the case for a Welsh-language nursery and primary school. A meeting was called in 1971 which Edwards addressed, along with T Gwyn Jones, headteacher of Bodalaw Primary School, Colwyn Bay; Aled Lloyd Davies, headteacher of Maes Garmon School in Mold; and Mrs Mari Blainey of Llanfairfechan, former head of London Welsh School. It was decided to hold another meeting in Waterloo schoolhouse on 10 September under the chairmanship of the Rev. R Maurice Williams, another who was enthusiastic about the plan.

Meredith Edwards knew the problem well from within his own family, and he was one of three people who came together in London with the idea of setting up a Welsh-language school. By 1966 there was already a Welsh class of thirty Welsh speakers between the ages of five and seven at one school in London, and another school met in the vestry of Willesden Green Welsh Chapel for children up to eleven. This was his appeal:

> Go to it now in Liverpool to set up a Saturday morning and weekday nursery school. Collect the names of children who will be ready for the Welsh School. Take the list to the education authority. Ask the churches and chapels to help you – and ask for a Welsh School. It means a fair bit of work – perseverance and determination – but think about the prize! Generation after generation of Welsh speakers growing up again on Merseyside.

There was an immediate objection from the writer and teacher, Gwilym M Jones. He and the Rev. D Hughes Parry were of the opinion that the answer was to form a number of small groups of parents with children under five, which could play in Welsh together for two hours each week. A public meeting was arranged under the auspices of the Liverpool and District Sunday School Union. The Rev. Dafydd Hughes Parry argued that Welsh Sunday schools on Merseyside depended on efforts like this to safeguard the language. There was a unanimous decision to set up two playgroups at once, one for the north end of Liverpool and the other for the south. Two young mothers were chosen to be responsible for them: Mrs M Bryn Jones of Aughton Park, near Ormskirk in the north, and Nan Hughes Parry of Woolton, in the south.

A meeting with the education director was held on 21 June 1972, resulting in a promise of a peripatetic teacher for Welsh classes. Liverpool Corporation and its education department were prepared to be generous, but it proved impossible to find the twelve names necessary to start a class. However, the effort was not in vain as the debate paved the way for enabling young Welsh people to take O and A levels in Welsh.

Attracting the young to Penny Lane

By the end of the 1960s Urdd branches had become centralised in Liverpool city centre at the Catholic church in Seel Street and, *Urdd y Bobl Ieuanc* (League

THE WELSH IN LIVERPOOL

of Young People), a movement within the Welsh Presbyterian denomination, wanted to do the same. The leaders of Heathfield Road Chapel, under their new minister, opposed the move, and it was arranged for the young people to meet in the chapel schoolhouse. These meetings became the most important activities for young Welsh people at the time. The society grew from half a dozen to more than seventy members who would come to the service and then the meeting, all within fifty yards of Penny Lane.

Uniting four chapels in south Liverpool

During the 1970s there were countless committee meetings between the leaders of four chapels, namely Heathfield Road, Edge Lane, Trinity Church and Garston. In a vote on 8 June 1975, of the 149 votes cast, 97 (65 per cent) were keen to see unification, with 52 (35 per cent) against. It was felt that this was enough foundation to unify three churches – Heathfield Road, Edge Lane and Trinity – under the name Bethel.

Both Bethel and the Welsh Centre overlook the famous Penny Lane – a street named, rather unfortunately, after a slave owner. But, because of the Beatles' connection to it, no-one wants to change it.

Chapter 22

The Welsh of Bootle

Bootle is named in the Domesday Book and, by the Victorian era, it was surrounded by a number of other settlements: Kirkdale and Sandhills to the south, Walton to the east and, to the north, Litherland, Seaforth, Waterloo, Crosby and Blundellsands, where there were very many Welsh families.

Rich Liverpool families head for Bootle

Business people such as Sir John Gladstone were looking for somewhere quieter and more attractive to live. Bootle and Bootle Bay became a seaside destination for rich people to restore their energies. Houses and mansions were built with surrounding orchards. What brought Bootle to the attention of Liverpool councillors was 'the lively streams of water' which could be used for the benefit of residents. In 1797 the Bootle Waterworks Co. was formed with an Anglesey Welshman having the main responsibility for the reservoir. Robert Jerman, who lived in Waterworks Street, Bootle, was an influential man and hailed originally from Llangristiolus on Anglesey. The company took care of Liverpool's needs for almost a century, from 1797 to 1895, but after that, Liverpool was responsible for a reservoir in Lancashire and then Llanwddyn Reservoir in Montgomeryshire.

Bootle develops into a borough

Bootle grew over the years. In 1859 the Canada Dock was opened and was immortalised in one of the most famous verses written by William Thomas Edwards (Gwilym Deudraeth) when the Duke of Windsor visited in the 1930s.

More docks were built and the timber trade expanded significantly. In

1831 the population was 1,133 but, by 1861, it was 10,000. In July that year there was a census of the Welsh who were living in north Liverpool (Bootle, Seaforth, Waterloo and Crosby). It was noted that there were 211 adults and 81 children, making a total of 292.

The young scholar Griffith Ellis arrives

The Calvinistic Methodist chapel at Miller's Bridge, Bootle, succeeded in attracting a highly-gifted young man, Griffith Ellis of Corris, a promising student at Balliol College, Oxford. The chapel leaders were planning to build a fine new chapel in Stanley Road. Ellis married Mary, the daughter of John Williams of Moss Bank, and became part of one of the most important Calvinistic Methodist families in Liverpool.

Griffith Ellis (1844–1913) was an enthusiastic intellectual. The new chapel schoolhouse opened in Stanley Road and he was the first to preach in the chapel in December 1876. He was responsible for opening a mission room in Clyde Street in 1879. From there it moved to St John's Road and then in 1900 to York Hall near Bank Hall railway station.

When Griffith Ellis left Oxford in 1873, there were 284 members of the Welsh Calvinistic chapel, and by 1900 Stanley Road Chapel had 480 members. Other Calvinistic Methodist chapels were built by the mother church, Stanley Road. Walton Park came into existence in 1878, Peel Road, Seaforth, in 1883 and Waterloo Chapel in 1879. However, in 1901 Griffith Ellis and the Bootle Presbyterians were weary of the schism in Chatham Street Chapel and the behaviour of the minister, William Owen Jones. He had married the daughter of a Stanley Road Chapel elder and the effects of the rift were felt throughout the Welsh community in Bootle. Eighty-two members left to build a new chapel in nearby Merton Road. One of the most unconventional figures in Welsh Nonconformity was called to minister there – David Emrys James (1881–1952), much better known by his bardic name, Dewi Emrys. He came to Merton Road from Carmarthen Presbyterian College, but he only had a short stay. Within two years he moved to Dowlais on the outskirts of Merthyr and, by 1917, he had left the ministry altogether.

There was another gifted minister in the area, namely the Rev. Peter Williams, better known by his bardic name of Pedr Hir. He was called to minister to the Welsh Baptists in Bootle in April 1897, and began his ministry on the first Sunday of August. One Sunday he preached in the old Welsh Baptist chapel in Brasenose Street and soon afterwards it was decided to build a new chapel. The new place of worship in Balliol Road was completed by Easter 1898. It took twenty years to pay off the debt of more than £2,000. It is a shame to think that the whole of his ministry in Bootle was overshadowed by this debt. He died on 24 March 1922. Pedr Hir was a pioneer in the world of drama; he published two scriptural dramas in 1903 and 1907, one of them on Moses, but his most significant, in 1915, was about Owain Glyndŵr. Like Griffith Ellis, Pedr Hir was possessed by the spirit of the Revival and it was in an attempt to help the young people in his care, many with a poor command of the Welsh language, that he published his textbook, *Key and Guide to the Welsh Language*.

Bootle's chapels at the beginning of the twentieth century had talented people like Hugh Evans of the Brython Press, and the historian of the Puritan movement, Dr Tom Richards, to name only two. Richards was a Cardigan man but spent his apprenticeship as a scholar and teacher in Bootle Boys' Middle School. When he decided to move to Maesteg, *Y Brython* noted:

> It is a bitter shame; as he was so supportive of everything Welsh in Bootle and Liverpool. He was a bastion of the Young Wales society in Bootle for years; he was the most eloquent, fieriest speaker and the one most difficult to grapple with; and there was no-one more learned or with a better grasp on the topics of the day – especially history and politics. He often lectured to Merseyside literary societies on such matters; and he will leave a great gap, especially in Balliol Road Baptist Church where he was such a hard worker.

On 15 December 1911 there was a lively meeting in Balliol Road Welsh Baptist schoolroom to wish Tom Richards well on his move to the Llyfni Valley. There were humorous speeches from his minister Pedr Hir and from Hugh Roberts, and bardic greetings by Trefor and Madryn. The latter, Robert Parry, composed a skilful *englyn* to him, suggesting that Maesteg had a greater need of Tom than Bootle – and he did have a point. After all, Bootle Corporation was much more supportive to the teaching of Welsh than the district councils of Llyfni, as well as Ogwr and Ogmore.

It was even more of a loss that the Rev. Griffith Ellis was giving up the ministry of Stanley Road after serving it faithfully for thirty-eight years. He died not long after, on 14 July 1913, when he was sixty-nine. He had a dignified funeral, with the chapel full to bursting point and there was a procession from Stanley Road to Anfield Cemetery, some two-and-a-half miles away. He was laid to rest near his hero, Dr Owen Thomas, the minister of Princes Road Chapel.

The Rev. Owen Lloyd Jones disappears

His successor, the Rev. Owen Lloyd Jones, of Brynsiencyn, Anglesey, a scholar with glowing academic credentials, was welcomed on 20 February 1912. But soon the First World War broke out and 228 young members decided to join the armed forces. This pained him deeply and, on 15 March 1917, after he had been the church leader for five years, he suddenly left his flock after preparing an address for the 1916 annual report of the church. He said nothing more to his wife than that he was going to hand over the report to the chapel secretary. He shook hands with one of his elders – and he was never seen again. Gossip, among both English and Welsh in Bootle, suggested he had sought refuge in Ireland. Others thought he caught a ship from Liverpool to the Far East. But it is sad that his family never knew what had happened, but Owen Lloyd Jones remains a mysterious part of the story of the Welsh in Bootle.

Welsh builders see their chance

As in Liverpool itself, the Welsh in Bootle saw their opportunity in the building trade. One who stands out is William Jones of Merton Road, Bootle. He was from Llannerchymedd on Anglesey. He came to Liverpool in 1860 and very soon had set up his building company in the suburbs of Everton and Toxteth where there were many Welsh people in the trade. He saw that he had a better opportunity in Bootle. He bought Bootle Hall, as it was called, pulled it down and built streets of houses on the land. Then he built Marsh Lane and established a whole village called Orrell. He gave a host of Welsh names to the streets around the Welsh Independent Church in Marsh Lane – his company built Aber Street, Anglesey Street, Bangor

Street, Bala Street, Conway Street, Denbigh Street, Flint Street, Holywell Street and Rhyl Street.

One terraced street contained seventy-six houses, and in all he built more than 600 houses. He also decided to install electricity in each house. There were three types of houses in the Orrell settlement. Firstly, he built terraced houses containing four rooms and asked a rent of five shillings per week from those fortunate tenants. Secondly, there were five-roomed terraced houses which he rented out at seven shillings. Thirdly, houses with more than six rooms attracted a rent of eight shillings. To light the houses with the electricity that he and his sons produced, two eight-candlepower lights were installed in the four-room houses, three in the five-room ones and four in the biggest. Tenants were expected to pay threepence for two lights and sixpence for three. He also put a lamp post on the corner of each road, at his own cost. William Jones ensured that there was a lamp every hundred yards to save people from walking in total darkness. The house lights would go on each evening as it was getting dark, staying on until midnight, while the street lamps would continue until daybreak. In the winter the houses would be lit from 5 p.m. until dawn. This progressive and ambitious venture cost William Jones and Co. £3,000 but, during the First World War, all the street lights had to be extinguished. One of the community buildings that took advantage of electric light was Springfield Road Chapel where people worshipped in English, although it belonged to the Welsh Presbyterian Church – one of the 'English causes', as Emrys ap Iwan called them. It was in this chapel that the socialist minister Cyril Summers, later mayor of Newport, was brought up.

William Jones was known in the building world as Klondyke Jones, as he was building houses in Bootle at the same time as gold was discovered in the River Klondyke in Canada in 1896. William Jones had himself discovered a vein of gold, as it were, in Bootle, on the piece of land called Orrell. The land, about 370 acres, belonged to Lord Sefton. It was a pretty desolate site and something of a wilderness when William Jones got hold of it and created streets of terraced houses. The task was not at all easy. Bricks were in short supply, but this did not hold him back. He built a kiln to make his own in a huge building between Hawthorne Road and the canal. The furnace worked day and night until the outbreak of the First World War.

William Jones served on Bootle Town Council for forty years as a hard-working councillor and then as an alderman and JP. In 1886 he was the first Welshman to be mayor of Bootle, and insisted on holding the civic service at Stanley Road Chapel.

He became the member for Knowsley ward in 1879 and remained on Bootle Council until his death in 1918. Welsh was recognised in the council's activities throughout the years. In 1902 he was elected an elder at Stanley Road Chapel.

His son, Owen Kendrick Jones (1870–1943), followed in his father's footsteps. He was elected to the council in 1895 and became mayor in 1904, an alderman in 1905 and, in 1907, a JP. He was on the council for thirty years. He too was elected an elder at Stanley Road in 1919, but did not accept the office to the great disappointment of the members.

Another William Jones

There was another builder of the same name in Bootle, William Jones of Balliol Road. He was from Brynsiencyn and he built the first Welsh chapel in Bootle, at Miller's Bridge. He was an elder there in 1879 and his brother, David Jones of Cremlyn Street, was in business with him. Both were very influential. William died in 1911 and David Jones in 1925. William was a very cultured man and his grave can be seen in Anfield Cemetery. The builder and poet Gwilym Mathafarn wrote an *englyn* in his memory, stating he was a good and gentle man who loved peace and whose legacy would live on among his admirers. This is literally true. So many of the Bootle streets are a memorial to him.

Mission Hall at Monfa Road, Orrell

Welsh speakers who were members of Peel Road Welsh Presbyterian Chapel in Seaforth took their opportunity in 1900 to build a Welsh Mission Hall in Monfa Road, Orrell, and then another in 1916 on the corner of Stanley Street and Hawthorne Street. This became a Welsh meeting place and the first caretakers were Mr and Mrs W J Williams, parents of the late Mrs Bet Williams of Stanley Road, and grandparents of Mrs Pam McNamara of Litherland, and the Rev. David Williams of Crosby. The Mission Hall became a place of learning and culture. On a Tuesday evening, young people would practise for the Bootle Children's Eisteddfod. Maggie Edwards would be the accompanist and one of the keen leaders was Gwen Williams of Arvon Street who, in 1930, was elected as an elder at Peel Road Chapel. There was a weekly prayer meeting and Sister Kate Evans came from her home in Kensington to teach the children the essentials of their faith. One of those children was Bet Williams's husband, Evan Williams. He became a teacher at Orrell School and later headteacher of Gray Street School. The Mission Hall continued until 1960.

Importance of York Hall

Another important mission centre was the York Hall schoolroom. This was on the outskirts of Bootle and bordering Kirkdale or, as that suburb was called by the Welsh, Llangwm. At the end of the century, in 1899, the Liverpool Presbytery was asked by a number of the Welsh community for permission to build York Hall. The matter was discussed by the chapel committee and refused. The minister and elders of Stanley Road decided to build the hall at their own cost. But, in the meantime, one of the Bootle builders, Peter Lloyd Jones (a member of Stanley Road Chapel) offered to take responsibility for building the hall. He would cover the whole cost on condition that the tenants of the hall paid rent for the first five years. However, rent was paid for years until the closure of the building at the beginning of the Second World War.

It was a very successful centre, full of activities and enterprise, with many faithful and committed teachers. During the First World War concerts were held for Welsh soldiers from Litherland camp. One of those who was in the hall on at least two occasions was the shepherd and poet from Yr Ysgwrn, Trawsfynydd, Ellis Humphrey Evans (Hedd Wyn, 1887–1917). There were concerts on these Saturday evenings, and children were welcomed to the meetings which were held on weekdays and on Sunday afternoon. At the end of 1925, 125 young people over fifteen attended, and 104 children under fifteen, making a sizeable total of 229.

A medical practitioner and an elder

Another prominent person among the Bootle Welsh was Dr R E Roberts. He was born in Bangor and was a teacher before becoming a well known and successful doctor. He was elected to Bootle Town Council and took the initiative in matters concerning education, schools and the place of Welsh in the town's schools. In 1902 he was elected an elder at Peel Road Chapel.

The conversion of John Hughes of Seaforth

In the same year John Hughes of Tennyson Street, and later Elm Drive, was also elected an elder. He came to Bootle from Llangefni and one of his best friends was William Jones (1857–1915), Liberal MP for Arfon from 1895 until 1915. Hughes had a religious experience as he walked Pacific Road one evening: 'A light from heaven shone around him', he said. He became a reader and took on a number of responsibilities. His premature death at the age of fifty-six was a loss to the Welsh community in Seaforth.

Founder of the Brython Press

It is important, too, to remember the contribution of the Brython Press and that of its founder Hugh Evans (1854–1934). He came to Bootle from the Uwchaled area of Denbighshire in 1855, and worked for a year building the Calvinistic Methodist Chapel in Stanley Road, and then making clocks for seven years in J R Jones's company of Vauxhall Works, Liverpool. He set up a printing press in 1897 and that was the beginning of publishing on a large scale.

The Second World War and its destruction of Welsh life

The Welsh newspaper *Y Brython* wound up in 1939 and it was in that year that Welsh life in Bootle was thrown into disarray. The Second World War brought heartbreak to the whole area. Many Welsh families were dispersed and driven to seek shelter and refuge in Wales. The homes of many of them were destroyed in 1941 and others suffered dreadfully. Welsh religious meeting centres were also destroyed – Merton Road, Marsh Lane and Stanley Road chapels, all in Bootle, were struck by enemy bombs.

Although Bootle enjoyed a fillip when Stanley Road Chapel was reopened in 1956 after being bombed, the writing was on the wall. A new chapel was built for the Welsh Independents in Hawthorne Road. After Balliol Road Chapel closed, the rest of the congregation joined up with Salem in Hawthorne Road.

A high percentage of the Bootle Welsh moved back to Wales between 1950 and 2000. There was also a shortage of ministers in all the Welsh chapels there, after the Rev. William Jones retired from Stanley Road Chapel and the Rev. Cyril John retired from the Baptist chapel in the 1970s. The Bootle Welsh were very well served by the Rev. J Price Davies, the leader of the Welsh Independents. He was the compère at the annual Widnes Welsh Eisteddfod. Within the Calvinistic Methodists, we should acknowledge the contribution between the wars of the Rev. William Davies in Bootle. He was originally from Ffaldybrenin in Carmarthenshire but moved to Bootle from Bethania Presbyterian Chapel in Aberdare, and he stayed for twenty years. He was appointed as one of three delegates to go out to the mission field in north-east India from 1935 to 1936. He visited Shillong, Cherra and Sylhet but suffered terribly with his health afterwards, and died in 1938.

The Welsh chapels managed to attract followers until the 1970s and, after that, there were great changes, with one chapel after another closing or amalgamating, until there was only one Welsh chapel remaining in Bootle. Thanks to the efforts of the leaders of Stanley Road Chapel, namely John P Lyons, T Selwyn Williams and Dewi Garmon Roberts, it was possible to unite with Waterloo Welsh Chapel in 1993. The new centre in Crosby Road was called Bethania, and it still survives as a centre for Welsh people today.

The sad story of the Bootle Welsh is summarised in a poem by O Trevor Roberts (Llanowain), a devout member of Trinity Road Wesleyan Methodist Chapel, Bootle. The subject of the poem is *Dringo* (Climbing), and it tells the whole story in the form of a rather beautiful parable. He uses the symbolism of a brother and sister helping one another at various stages in their life – as children, then in their mature years, and finally during old age with its besetting frustration and problems.

Chapter 23

Is it sometimes worth becoming an exile? (1976–88)

Merseyside Eisteddfod

An unusually interesting event in the history of the Liverpool Welsh was the establishment, in 1976, of the Merseyside Eisteddfod, a partnership between Liverpool University's Welsh students and the Liverpool Welsh. The young man who shouldered most of the responsibility was Hywel Morris, a native of the Cerrigydrudion area of Denbighshire and a medical student. There were various literature-loving Welsh still in Liverpool, such as the poet-preacher, the Rev. R Maurice Williams (of Waterloo) and O Trevor Roberts (Llanowain), and keen supporters of the eisteddfod such as William Jones, Harry Williams, Hugh John Jones, Dr D Ben Rees, Dr Pat Williams and Nan Hughes Parry. All the committee meetings were held at the university and the eisteddfod itself in the Students' Union. Members of the university staff were more than ready to give a hand, among them William James Dutton, a librarian who was learning Welsh.

The eisteddfod came to an end when the first generation of students moved away from Liverpool, and also because of the Toxteth riots in 1981.

The Toxteth Riots, July 1981

The riots in Toxteth came in the wake of long-standing tensions between the police and the black community. The Rialto in Parliament Street, which was designed by Welshman David John Lewis, was completely burned down. A new Rialto was built, and D J Lewis's iconic building was lost.

A new newspaper

An important event during this period was the launch in 1979 of the community newspaper, *Yr Angor*, after *Y Bont* had come to an end the previous year when the editor, the Rev. R Maurice Williams, decided to retire and move with his wife Enid to Llanrwst in the Conwy Valley. When celebrating the centenary of Waterloo Chapel in 1979, R Maurice Williams wrote a summary of its history in a little booklet. He said:

> I have seen a great change in church life in this church of Waterloo and all
> Merseyside churches and, indeed, in the nature of Welsh society in general from
> 1952 onwards. Sometimes I wonder how the church has lasted so long despite so
> many obstacles, and especially when I see English churches, with many members
> until comparatively recently, now fighting for their existence.

The leaders of *Y Bont* believed it was impossible to carry on without the Rev. R Maurice Williams, who had been the editor for nineteen years. The deputy editor at the time was Gwilym Meredydd Jones and he did not want the responsibility. They also had help from T M Owens of Aigburth, who was treasurer as well as being one of the treasurers of Bethel Chapel after the unification.

At the first meeting of *Yr Angor*, D Ben Rees became editor, an office he has held ever since. T Meilyr Owens agreed to be treasurer, the Rev. Ieuan A Jenkins was secretary, and Mr Rolly Pritchard of Broadgreen was manager and distributor. A Wesleyan Methodist minister, the Rev. B Ifor Williams, suggested the name – a very appropriate one for a famous port such as Liverpool.

The chair of the executive committee of *Y Bont*, Judge John Edward Jones, gave his backing to the new community paper and some years later wrote in his entertaining book, *Anturiaeth a Menter Cymry Lerpwl* (The Adventure and Effectiveness of the Liverpool Welsh, 1987):

> It is a point of connection for the Merseyside Welsh and many of those who have
> moved back to Wales to give generously to it. It is a quality paper, filling a big
> gap especially as the Welsh are so scattered. *Yr Angor* was extremely significant
> as a means of informing people about meetings and concerts, and there was an

opportunity to write obituaries for the men and women who had been very important in Liverpool Welsh life.

Supporting Welsh learners

During this period the rector of Liverpool Polytechnic was persuaded to make arrangements for people who wanted to sit A level Welsh. Welsh classes were held under the auspices of University of Liverpool extra-mural department, Liverpool Corporation education department and the Workers' Educational Association. There was no-one more supportive among the learners than Glyn Rees Hughes of Walton, and Eric Thomas of West Derby.

The loss of Welsh leaders

Welsh society lost a number of prominent people during the 1980s, none more so than Canon Hywel Islwyn Davies (1909–81) of Aigburth. He was a first-class theologian who had been a lecturer at St David's University College, Lampeter, then a professor at Ife University in Nigeria, a vicar in Llanelli and dean of Bangor Cathedral. He decided to retire to Liverpool as his wife Glenys had close links with the city and was a great friend of Miss Nansi Pugh, and Mrs Ruth Davies who lived in Alma Road, Aigburth. They too had retired from London to Liverpool because of their strong connections to the place. Miss Pugh was a daughter of the Rev. E Cynolwyn Pugh, who was a minister in Birkenhead before moving to minister in Chicago. He won the prose medal at the Ebbw Vale National Eisteddfod in 1957 for his autobiography *Ei Ffanfer Ei Hun*, which was published the following year by Gomer Press. His daughter translated the book into English as *His Own Fanfare*, which was published by Modern Welsh Publications.

Mrs Davies was a daughter of the Rev. and Mrs J Oldfield Davies and, towards the end of his life, her father was minister at Grove Street Welsh Independent Chapel. Liverpool Welsh life was enriched by the arrival of these two families and Canon Islwyn Davies was happy to conduct services at Welsh chapels in Liverpool on a Sunday.

The sudden death, on 22 January 1982, of Mrs Lena Jones of Allerton, the wife of Hugh John Jones and mother to Alun Vaughan Jones, was a great loss. Lena endeared herself to generations of Welsh people, and her upbringing in Llanbedrog on the Lleyn peninsula influenced her throughout her life.

Llanowain composed an *englyn* about her death, honouring her lifetime's service as a nurse, particularly at Sefton General Hospital.

During the same year a former Lord Mayor, Alderman David John Lewis (1893–1982), died after making a long contribution to political and public life in Liverpool. The Welsh community also lost Emrys Anwyl Jones – Emrys NFS as he was called, because of his links to the fire brigade. He came from Nanmor and Beddgelert in Snowdonia and never lost his pronounced Welsh accent despite living in Liverpool for so many years. There was no-one better at selling tickets for the Welsh concerts arranged by the Liverpool Welsh Society.

A volume on the history of the Welsh

In 1984 the first bilingual volume of the history of the Liverpool Welsh for some years was published under the title *Cymry Lerpwl a'u Crefydd – The Liverpool Welsh and their Faith*. This was a joint venture between Dr R Merfyn Jones, who had recently been appointed director of extra-mural studies at the University of Liverpool, and D Ben Rees. The book was launched at a successful gathering with the Liverpool Welsh Choral Union under conductor Edmund Walters from Pembrokeshire. During his period as conductor of the choir, there was a close relationship between the Liverpool Welsh community and the Liverpool Welsh Choral Union.

Establishing a council for Welsh chapels and churches

During the 1980s there was an attempt to bring the Nonconformist religious Welsh centres closer together. The Council of Liverpool and District Welsh Churches was formed in 1985, known usually as CECLAC. This meant that the chapels of Bethel in Heathfield Road, Garston Welsh, Central Hall Welsh, Edge Lane Baptist, Earlsfield Road Baptist, Wavertree, and Tabernacle Welsh Independent, Woolton Road, Allerton, worked together.

Establishing the Welsh chaplaincy

Liverpool continued to be an important medical centre for people from north Wales and that is why the Merseyside Welsh Chaplaincy was established. There was an enormous need for a chaplain, as I was the only full-time Welsh

Nonconformist minister in Liverpool in 1984, and calls for chaplaincy were endless. Requests from Wales for D Ben Rees to visit Welsh patients in the hospitals of Liverpool never stopped. Some relief came at the end of 1985 when the Rev. R E Hughes of Nefyn was in charge of two north Liverpool chapels, Waterloo and Stanley Road, as well as Salem in Birkenhead, and Rake Lane in Wallasey.

The plan to have a chaplain was discussed at the local district meeting and thoroughly investigated by the courts of the Connexion, then by the Presbyterian Church of Wales Mission Board. In the end John Sam Jones from Barmouth was appointed to the post. He started on his work as chaplain to patients from Wales, to Welsh students and to Welsh prisoners. He remained in the post for two years.

After he left it was decided to enlarge the partnership to include other denominations: the Welsh Independents, the Baptists, the Episcopal Church, the Methodist Church and the Welsh Presbyterians. For three months Dafydd Ll Rees served on graduating from Oxford University, and then Ms Rachel Gooding, a theological graduate from Stalybridge who had learned Welsh fluently when she was a student at the Welsh Independents' College in Aberystwyth. She was followed by Eleri Edwards, who had been a missionary in Madagascar. After her ordination she accepted an invitation from the Manchester Welsh. She was succeeded by the Rev. Nan Wyn Powell-Davies of Mold for a further period before the chaplaincy was brought to an end. The experiment had been important.

Chapter 24

The story of Everton and Liverpool football clubs

Every Saturday from August to May we see thousands of people flocking to Anfield football ground or Goodison Park to watch Liverpool or Everton. Supporters come in all weathers from all over Liverpool, from Merseyside, from north and mid Wales.

Footballing's chapel roots

Both clubs had their roots in the Methodist chapel of St Domingo. One of the early founders was Joseph Wade, who was born in Halifax in 1815 and moved to Liverpool from Yorkshire. He set up a company in the suburb of Everton, one of the Welsh strongholds. He was one of the main supporters of the new St Domingo Chapel which was built in 1868.

A butcher's role in Everton's story

Another family which supported both the Methodist religion and Everton club was the Cuff family. Like Joseph Wade, Henry Cuff was a trustee of St Domingo Chapel. He came from Middlesex, and in Liverpool he met a Welsh woman called Mary who came from Rhiwlas near Bangor. The two were married and he opened a pork butcher's shop. By 1881 he was able to employ two assistants in his shop at 34 Spellow Lane, which was within a stone's throw of Goodison Park. Henry and Mary had eight children, four boys and four girls. Like his father, the second son William Cuff, who was born on 19 August 1868, combined faithfulness both to the Methodist Church and Everton Football Club and became a very influential figure in it.

Football's answer to strong drink

Another name which should not be forgotten is that of the Rev. Benjamin Swift Chambers who became the pastor of the chapel in July 1877. He felt that the best way to overcome the temptation of drink was to introduce young people to football. He also supported cricket, and was instrumental in establishing the St Domingo cricket team. A year later he persuaded the cricket team to consider playing football in winter. So that the name was memorable, he suggested they should call themselves St Domingo Football Club.

Building a presence in Stanley Park

These young people had a good field to play both games, namely Stanley Park, although they had no goalposts and nobody was able to create a proper football field. At the outset it was a matter of playing among themselves, but things were to change when Will Cuff, though only ten years old, came along to watch his older friends from the chapel having so much fun on a Saturday afternoon. It was not just children from St Domingo Chapel who were in Stanley Park. There was a team of Welsh children from the surrounding chapels and also from the United Church, St Benedict's Church and St Peter's. This was a phenomenon of Liverpool life in the 1880s – there were football clubs for young people throughout the city.

By 1885 there were at least 112 clubs playing regularly in Liverpool, and at least twenty-five linked to churches. This raised a problem. To create a successful team it was necessary to look outside the chapel and welcome players from other organisations. A public meeting was called to discuss the situation and it was decided the only answer was to change the name – to Everton, the area in which they lived.

Under its new name the club was dynamic, winning 6–0 against one of its opponents, St Peter's. By 1880 four of the team were Welsh. This was the team that was accepted into the Lancashire Football League for the 1880–81 season. Everton managed to win fifteen games out of seventeen, drew one but lost 8–1 to Great Lever in the Cup final.

John Houlding

Before the beginning of the 1881–82 season, the club elected its first chairman, John Houlding, who lived in a grand house overlooking Stanley Park. Like many of the Welsh in the area, he had climbed the ladder from messenger boy to owner of a successful drinks business, Houlding's Sparkling Ales.

Within three years, Houlding's team had made its mark and a crowd of some 2,000 would come to support it. But the support did not create any capital or income for the club, as nobody had bothered to lay proper foundations. Houlding set about changing things, asking William Cruitt, a rich merchant, for the right to rent land near his home in Priory Road. The request was granted, and they set about creating a playing field, building a changing room and a small stand for the 1884–85 season. It was a memorable season, as Everton won its first trophy, the Liverpool Cup, winning by one goal against Earlestown. Everton was a dangerous team and exceedingly successful. But there were problems. William Cruitt couldn't tolerate the behaviour of the supporters shouting and singing throughout the afternoon. Everton was asked to look for a new home.

Anfield

Once again John Houlding stepped into the breach. He saw that his friend Joseph Orrell owned a field near Anfield Road which would be ideal. A good deal was struck and Anfield football ground was born. It was possible to change kit for the game in the Sandon Hotel, on the corner of Oakfield Road and Houlding Street, which was quite close to the ground. The first game played at the Anfield ground was on 27 September 1884 against Earlestown, with Everton winning easily 5–0. Twenty-three games were played at Anfield and Everton managed to win fourteen, with two games drawn and seven lost. The situation away from home was similar, with nine wins and four defeats.

When the Football Association came into existence in 1888 to organise the English professional teams, Everton was admitted without any trouble. By the 1890–91 season Everton was crowned champions. One of the important members of the Everton team committee was the accountant George Mahon. He had two interests outside his family and his work, namely St Domingo

Chapel and Everton Football Club. He was delighted when the Rev. Ben Chambers joined the chapel as minister in 1890.

However, one thing bothered Mahon, as it did Ben Chambers, and that was Houlding's autocratic behaviour. He managed to make himself unpopular with various key personnel on the committee. He expected a good return on his loan and set about raising the rent in line with the increase in income. Alcohol abstainers disapproved of his behaviour in continuing to expect the players to use the Sandon Hotel. An extraordinary annual meeting was held at the Collegiate School in Shaw Street on 23 January 1892, and more than 500 members of the club came together to listen to Mahon's interpretation of the situation, refusing the chair's recommendations, and calling for the club to have the courage to leave Anfield. Mahon spoke so effectively that only eighteen people voted against him. Houlding was furious and annoyed with Mahon. And on 1 March another blow fell, when John Houlding was removed as chairman.

Houlding sees his opportunity

His enthusiasm did not lessen however, and having got rid of Everton, he ventured to reform the club and call it the Everton Football Club and Athletic Ground Co. Ltd. Mahon and his supporters appealed to the Football Association council for guidance. The issue was discussed, and it was decided that Houlding did not have the right to use the name of Everton. It was a victory which pleased Mahon and his supporters. The next step Houlding took was to choose a new name, and so, in May 1892, another football club came into existence, namely Liverpool Association Football Club.

Goodison Park

In the meantime Mahon was busy searching for another ground, and in January 1892 came across a good piece of land called Mere Green, near Goodison Road in Walton. According to the Everton Club historians, the piece of land with the enchanting name Mere Green was no more than a barren wilderness. The accountant saw his chance, made an agreement about the lease, and raised money to transform the desolate land into an acceptable football ground. The club was turned into a limited company and the medical practitioner Dr James Baxter, one of Mahon's good friends, gave a substantial loan.

By the beginning of the 1892–93 season there was an acceptable ground at hand. The stadium was built and the whole complex was called Goodison Park. There was a colourful opening ceremony, with Lord Kinnaird privileged to do the honours. He was the ideal choice: a famous player, chairman of the Football Association for a long period, and a Christian by conviction. A crowd of 10,000 attended the ceremony, and a concert and fireworks display were staged.

At Stanley Park in Anfield, Liverpool football team had made a good start and, to the surprise of many, there was not one single English player in the team. Every one of the players had been born in Scotland. The club's application to join the Football League was turned down, and it was asked to prove its worth in the Lancashire League.

The freemasons' influence on football

John Houlding was determined to have a club that was free of any Roman Catholic Church influence. So Unionist Protestants and freemasons were in charge, together with Conservatives. Of the forty-six who set up the Liverpool club, seventeen were freemasons and that was the story up until the First World War. Fifteen out of the twenty-three Liverpool club directors were freemasons.

Support grows for both teams

In its first year about 5,000 people came to Anfield, but at Goodison there were more than twice that number, reaching 13,230. It was obvious that loyalty to Everton was on the increase. But there were two other teams which were also ambitious: Bootle Football Club and Liverpool Caledonian. The latter mainly depended on the support of the Scottish, and by the middle of the 1890s both of these teams were in trouble. It's worth noting that Anfield and Everton were middle-class areas. Everton failed to win in the 1893 FA Cup at Fallowfield, Manchester, against Wolverhampton. The Liverpool press criticised the railway companies for raising exorbitant fares for supporters to travel to Manchester, and the Football Association for its poor arrangements. About 60,000 watched the game.

Contribution of George Mahon

At Everton, George Mahon did important work as club chairman from 1892 to 1895. During that time the club finished second on four occasions, and won the Cup in 1906, beating Newcastle United 1–0 at Crystal Palace before a crowd of 76,000. Mahon died at the age of fifty-five and was buried in Anfield Cemetery in 1908, a week after the death of his son Herbert at twenty-five.

The versatile Leigh Richmond Roose

One of the earliest Welshmen associated with the Everton team is Leigh Richmond Roose. He was born in Holt, near Wrexham, on 27 November 1877, the son of the Rev. R H Roose, a Presbyterian minister. Leigh was educated at Holt Academy and University College of Wales, Aberystwyth. There he became well known as a goalkeeper, and in February 1900 he was invited to play for Wales against Ireland. He played for his country twenty-four times and looked forward particularly to the games against the other home nations. He played for Sunderland, Stoke and Glasgow Rangers. His vocation was as a doctor, and he became a favourite of the Welsh supporters at Goodison Park. He volunteered to join the armed forces in 1914 and died at the age of thirty-eight towards the end of the Battle of the Somme. One of the most able players of the early twentieth century was lost.

Charles Parry

In 1889 the name of Charlie Frederick Parry appears in the Everton team. He was born in the village of Llansilin on the Welsh-English border, a few miles from Oswestry. During a six-year period he played eighty-six times for Everton and wore his country Wales's shirt thirteen times. But there was a wild element to Charlie's character, and from time to time he would drink too much to the great disappointment of George Mahon and other directors. On one occasion he was banned for two weeks without pay for being drunk on the football field. He later became involved with teams such as Newtown and Aberystwyth for a while, and Everton was kind to him when he was hard up.

The clever footballer from Connah's Quay

In 1936 Everton paid Wrexham £3,000 for Thomas George Jones, or TG as he was fondly known to supporters. He came from Connah's Quay on Deeside and was an excellent, dependable midfielder. He played 178 times for Everton from 1936 to 1950 and won a First Division winners' medal in his second full season for the club in 1938–39. He served as a physical instructor in the RAF during the war and returned to Everton in 1946. AS Roma offered £15,000 for him but the Everton directors preferred to sell Tommy Lawson to Chelsea and Joe Mercer to Arsenal rather than let TG wear AS Roma's jersey.

He captained the club in 1949 but left in 1950 to become player-manager of Pwllheli, where he stayed for six years. From there he went to Bangor and later to Rhyl. He was fully at home in the Wales team and remained active on Deeside and in north Wales until his death in 2004.

He was counted as one of the giants by some of the best players in the game, like Stanley Matthews, Tommy Lawton and Joe Mercer (two of his best friends) and even Dixie Dean. Indeed, he was honoured in 2000 – the first of the eleven Everton players from over the years to be chosen as Millennium Giants.

Feeling the pressure

Another talented player who moved from Wrexham to Everton was David Smallman. He played only twenty-one games for Everton and said more than once that the experience of moving from Wrexham to Everton was indescribable. The standard was so much higher and there was the expectation that he and others like him should adapt at once.

Dai from the Valley

During the 1970s the arrival of William David Davies, or Dai Davies as he was known, was very much appreciated by the Liverpool Welsh. The goalkeeper, who was born in Glanaman in the Aman Valley, came to Everton in December 1970. He was as talented on the rugby field as the football field and had joined Swansea Town FC the previous year. His father had been very involved with football: hence the striking title of his autobiography, *Half as*

Good as My Father, which was published in Welsh in 1984 with an English version two years later.

He was Welsh both in language and by conviction and steeped in the intricacies of the language. And out of all the Welsh who played for the Everton and Liverpool teams, he was the one who made the greatest effort to link up and socialise with the Welsh in the city. That is why his being honoured by acceptance into the Gorsedd of Bards at the National Eisteddfod in Cardiff in 1978 was so well deserved. He was the first professional footballer to be honoured in this way, and was known by the name Dai o'r Cwm (Dai from the Valley). He made eighty-two appearances for Everton and won fifty-two caps for Wales. In 1977 he moved back to Wales – to Wrexham. He and a friend owned two bookshops called *Y Sisiwrn* (The Scissors) in Wrexham and Mold; he was also in charge of a health centre in Llangollen and, after his playing days were over, became well known as a football commentator on S4C.

Leaving the nest in Mancot to become captain of Everton

One of Dai Davies's close contemporaries was Kevin Radcliffe, who was born in Mancot, Flintshire. He joined Everton as an apprentice in 1977 and made his first appearance in 1980. He played 359 games between 1980 and 1992 and won fifty-eight caps for Wales. He was made captain when he was only twenty-three, and under his leadership Everton lifted the FA Cup in 1984, the Football League championship in 1984–85, again in 1986–87, and won the European Cup Winners' Cup in 1984–85.

Neville Southall, a giant in goal

Another player counted among Everton's greats in the 1980s was Neville Southall who joined the club from Bury in 1981. Everton paid £150,000 for him but he was soon on loan to the Port Vale team until Jim Arnold gave him a place in the first team. By 1983 he was the first-choice goalkeeper for Everton and kept that position for the next fourteen years. He became one of Britain's finest goalkeepers and played for Wales ninety-two times. In 1985 he was chosen Footballer of the Year and in 1996 was awarded the MBE for his services to sport.

Welsh players at Everton

Barry Horne had a successful spell with Everton from 1992 to 1996. His most important goal was at the end of the 1993–94 season against Wimbledon, with Everton in danger of being relegated. Horne scored an amazing goal from thirty yards to equalise before Everton went on to win 3–2.

Mark Anthony Hughes did not have the same success at Everton, although he was a very important player. In March 2000 he joined as a defender and played nine games during his first season and the same number during his second season before being transferred to Blackburn Rovers.

Gary Speed's time with Everton was a short one between 1996 and 1998. He played in fifty-eight games and managed to get the ball into the net sixteen times. As a boy he lived in Mancot, on the same street as Kevin Ratcliffe, another of the Everton stars, and supported the team while he was at Hawarden High School. He had a number of memorable games at Goodison Park, in particular when Everton beat Southampton 7–1, with Speed scoring the only hat-trick of his career. When Howard Kendall became manager, Speed was made captain but sadly the two did not get on. Speed played his last game on 18 January 1998 against Chelsea. His time as the Wales manager was a happy one, and his sudden and unexpected death was a great shock to the football world and the Deeside community.

Another Welshman who shone at Everton was Simon Davies, who was born in Haverfordwest but brought up in the village of Solva, near St Davids. He showed talent at school, and when he was fifteen was invited to join Peterborough. He joined Everton in 2005 for a fee of four million pounds. He had a poor season at Goodison during 2005–06 and, not surprisingly, left for Fulham in January 2007. He had a better season there and indeed was voted Player of the Year at Fulham during 2007–08. He returned to play at his childhood club in Pembrokeshire in 2013. Altogether, he played fifty-eight times for Wales.

The Wales international Ashley Williams is among the most recent who have had a fine career with the club.

Welsh players at Liverpool

Everton has been home to many more Welsh footballers than Liverpool – but Ben Woodburn and Harry Wilson are two youngsters with a bright future ahead of them. In recent years Joe Allen has been a fine representative of the Pembrokeshire Welsh. Brendan Rodgers, when he was Liverpool manager, once described him as 'the Welsh Xavi'. Another unforgettable name is Cyril Sidlow. He was born in Colwyn Bay, and Liverpool paid £4,000 for him in 1946 – a record fee at the time. He played 165 times for Liverpool between 1946 amd 1952.

Another great, John Toshack, moved to Liverpool from Cardiff for £110,000. He played his first game against Coventry on 14 November 1970. During his time with Liverpool, between 1970 and 1978, the team won the UEFA Cup in 1972–73 and the League Championship in 1972–73 and 1973–74.

However, during the 1980s and 1990s a new hero was born. Ian Rush came on loan to Liverpool in 1986 before signing in 1988. He moved to Leeds in 1996.

Dean Saunders played for Liverpool for one season. He joined from Derby for the 1991–92 season, costing nearly three million pounds, and scored twenty-five goals in sixty-one matches. Joey Jones also had a short spell with Liverpool and played seventy-two times between 1975 and 1978.

Fellow feeling

Both clubs engendered incredible loyalty among their followers and when tragedy struck, at Heysel and Hillsborough, both clubs felt for each other. It is only a small contingent who refuse to acknowledge how talented both teams are and how incredibly successful they have been over many decades. And likewise, over the years, the ups and downs of the Everton and Liverpool teams have played an important part in the lives of the Liverpool Welsh.

Chapter 25

Keeping up the good work (1989–2000)

A new charity, Hope into Action

After finishing school, Hefin Rees wished to perform humanitarian work and stayed in the home of Pastor Ephraim M Mathuri, an evangelist from Nairobi, during his time in Kokarkocho. On returning to Liverpool, the Nairobi Appeal project was set up and was well supported. Bethel Welsh Chapel in Heathfield Road collected £2,103.51, and £1,100 was raised through other organisations, making a total of £3,203.51. A school for underprivileged slum children was built and a charity called Hope into Action was formed with the responsibility of funding the school, paying teachers and feeding the children. Members of the Liverpool Welsh community were the officers – Gareth James of Aintree, as treasurer, and on the executive committee were Humphrey Wyn Jones, Hefin Rees and his brother Dafydd, Meinwen Rees and D Ben Rees.

When the Northern Association of the Welsh Presbyterian Church visited Bethel Chapel, a public meeting was held and a memorable speech on behalf of the charity was given by Gareth James. Pastor Ephraim M Mathuri visited Allerton for a week and addressed meetings at Bethel, Birkenhead and Hoylake, as well as local schools to speak about the charity's work. As the project was located so far away, the main problem was communication and supervising the work. After a while a message was received from the headteacher informing the charity that it had been conned by those who had received the funds and, much to the sorrow of the charity, it was necessary to end the relationship.

Tribute to Hefin Hughes

In 1990 the Liverpool Welsh community was shocked by the death of Hefin Hughes (1925–90) who had moved from Liverpool back to his home patch in Blaenau Ffestiniog. He was a committed member of the Welsh Society in Liverpool and in every aspect of Welsh life. The poet Selwyn Griffith, of Penisarwaun (later Archdruid of the National Eisteddfod), was inspired to compose a moving verse in his memory.

Maintaining a centre for the Welsh

On 7 February 1993 a meeting was held to instate D Ben Rees as minister of Bethania Church, Crosby Road South, Waterloo. Bethania was formed by the unification of Waterloo chapel and Stanley Road, Bootle. This was an important step in maintaining a centre for the Welsh in north Liverpool. The Independents' chapel in Hawthorn Road had closed and some of the faithful moved to Bethania. The eisteddfod was resurrected in 1993, with Rachel Gooding, Dr Glyn Roberts of Aigburth, and Cenric Clement Evans shouldering the administrative responsibility of staging the event.

The loss of Laura Jones and Dorothy Thomas

With the death of Laura Myfanwy Jones of Allerton, Liverpool lost its oldest Welsh woman. She was born in the town in 1890 and could remember meeting David Lloyd George at Bryncir station, where her maternal grandmother lived, and where she spent holidays as a child.

She enjoyed a notable career as a teacher, headteacher and as a schools' inspector for Liverpool Corporation. She was one of five children, none of whom married. In her last days four fellow Welsh women were a great comfort to her, namely Marged Jones of Birkenhead (widow of the Rev. Idwal Jones), Rachel Gooding, Elan Jones and Meinwen Rees.

Another of the Liverpool Welsh who died at the beginning of the 1990s was Dorothy Thomas of Allerton Road, daughter of the builder T W Thomas. Dorothy and her sister Eunice were fluent Welsh speakers, although neither had ever lived in Wales.

Toxteth Rotary Club

The Welsh contributed to Liverpool society in a number of ways, and many were members of the Rotary. Toxteth's Rotary Club boasted the largest number of Welsh speakers and in 1990 a carol concert was arranged at Bethel Chapel. Local schools took part in the evening and the first concert was held on Wednesday, 12 December 1990. The concert was an amazing success and was held every year for the next seven years. The organist was Margaret Anwyl Williams. D Ben Rees would introduce the carols, while John Thornton or the Rev. Bob Metcalfe, the Archdeacon of Liverpool, would compère and entertain the children. E Goronwy Owen and W Meirion Evans arranged for all proceeds to be donated to the Rotary Club's international work. There was a good relationship between the communities of Allerton, Mossley Hill, Wavertree, Childwall, Woolton, Toxteth and the Welsh chapel near Penny Lane. This was an important activity – local, civic, national, as Welsh people and religious members of the Church in England and a Nonconformist chapel mixed together.

Keeping up the tradition

The community continued to be enthusiastic over support for the Welsh language and the Liverpool and District Eisteddfod. It was all a labour of love. In the 1990s, under the patronage of the Presbyterian Church, an annual singing festival and Sunday schools' festival were held. Carols were sung around the houses of south Liverpool and Bethel choir, under R Ifor Griffith, who was in charge of Welsh songs of praise services as well as contributing to Liverpool Welsh Choral for more than half a century.

Chronicling the Welsh presence

By the middle of the 1990s it was felt that there was a need to record the history of the Liverpool Welsh, and two volumes were published by Modern Welsh Publications, *The Welsh of Merseyside*, along with a version in Welsh – both are now out of print.

An important event for the Liverpool Welsh in 1998 was the opportunity to welcome buses of Welsh people, on Saturdays and Sundays, to see the interesting sites connected with the Welsh in the city. There are plenty of buildings to be seen – from Albert Dock to Princes Road Church and the beautiful building of Chatham Street Chapel to Sefton Park where the National Eisteddfod of 1929 was held. Not to mention Penny Lane, Allerton and south Liverpool.

Buses came from Anglesey, the Conwy Valley and Clwyd, and from the Chester Welsh and Wrexham and district. These visits grew over the year, giving pleasure to hundreds and hundreds of Welsh people. It was an important development at the end of the twentieth century. When the writer Hafina Clwyd, from Ruthin, visited on one of the bus trips, she wrote an article for the *Western Mail* about the pioneering Welsh who contributed to the growth and wealth of Liverpool. What surprised her was the city's beauty:

> I had not realised how beautiful it is with its Georgian terraces – including the famous Rodney Street – and its extensive parks. And the trees were at their best after the rain.

It is worth noting, too, the words of Robert Lloyd (Llwyd o'r Bryn), from Edeyrnion, after one of his frequent lecture visits to the city:

> Yes, there are workers once more on Merseyside… we still believe here in the north that the Liverpool Welsh are our blood brothers.

That was the feeling and the attitude as the twentieth century closed.

Methodist Church on the move

An important development in the 1990s was the decision of the Welsh Methodist Church to leave Renshaw Street and set up home in Bethel Chapel, Heathfield Road. The leaders were John Williams of Wavertree, and Euryn Roberts of Childwall. John Williams died only a short time later but Euryn Roberts served for a longer time until he and his wife Morfudd married and moved to Abergele.

Facing the Millennium

A Millennium Committee for the Welsh of Liverpool and District was formed and provided a substantial impetus as the new century dawned. The year

2000 began with a united service at Bebington Methodist Church. As part of the Millennium celebrations a book entitled *The Welsh of Merseyside in the Twentieth Century* was published, along with a Welsh version.

Chapter 26

The Liverpool Welsh in the twenty-first century

To many of the ardent Liverpool Welsh, the communities where they live are an extension of the Welsh nation; nowadays mainly in Allerton, Childwall, Woolton, Aigburth, Anfield, Waterloo and Crosby.

Establishing the Merseyside Welsh Heritage Society

The Merseyside Welsh Heritage Society was established by Hugh Begley from Birkenhead, a Welsh learner who became a gifted and successful teacher of Welsh learners, and D Ben Rees. Because of illness Hugh Begley had to give up as secretary after five years and was followed by Dr Arthur Thomas, a Liverpool University lecturer before his retirement. Rachel Gooding was the society's treasurer and, like Hugh, had learnt the language fluently. Dr Pat Williams, Beryl Williams, Nan Hughes Parry, Elin Bryn Boyd and Brian Thomas served as trustees, and for a while were helped by Nerys Brookes, Carys Williams and Rhiannon Liddell. They were responsible for many festivals and exciting and important events including honouring Saunders Lewis, the only Welsh-language writer to be nominated for the Nobel Prize in Literature, in 1970.

The first action of the Merseyside Welsh Heritage Society, in February 2001, was to place a plaque on 6 Wilton Street, Liscard, the Wallasey house where Saunders Lewis was brought up. Bishop Daniel John Mullins, who had ministered to him in his final days, attended as well as the poet and dramatist's daughter Mair Jones, who also unveiled the plaque.

The society has honoured a host of Liverpool Welsh – Gwilym Hiraethog,

J Glyn Davies, Gwilym Deudraeth – Welsh communities like Bootle, builders and publishers, musical directors of the Liverpool Welsh Choral Union and the world-famous sculptor John Gibson. The committee that prepared the City of Liverpool's bid to be the 2008 European City of Culture was wise enough to ensure that the Welsh Heritage Society and the Liverpool Welsh Choral Union were part of the preparations.

Support from Welsh organisations

Another task was persuading establishments and organisations from Wales to consider holding some of their activities in Liverpool. The Cymmrodorion Society agreed to celebrate the bicentenary of the birth of Gwilym Hiraethog, with a presentation by Professor Aled Gruffydd Jones of Aberystwyth at Hope University in 2002. The National Library of Wales arranged two lectures in 2008 – in Welsh by Hywel Teifi Edwards at Bethel Chapel, and in English by Trevor Fishlock at Hope University. Welsh doctors came to hold two one-day schools. The first was taken by D Ben Rees, with Dr John G Williams, a Liverpool doctor, taking the second.

The Fellowship of the Lord's Day in Wales held its annual congress on the theme of 'Faith and Culture', finishing with a fine hymn-singing festival led by one of the Liverpool musicians, R Ifor Griffith.

Welsh Week

The Welsh media have always been supportive. A Welsh Week was organised for 1–8 March 2008. There was an excellent lecture by Dr Robin Gwyndaf of the St Fagans Museum of Welsh Life outside Cardiff, and two highly-talented artists brought up in Liverpool, the harpist Robin Huw Bowen and Ellis Roberts of BBC News, joined the St David's Day celebrations. A poetry evening was organised with Professor Gwyn Thomas of Bangor, and Deryn Rees Jones of Liverpool, participating. There were concerts in the company of Aled Jones, Bryn Terfel, and Llŷr Williams on the piano in St Nicholas Church.

Seventeen events were staged during the European Capital of Culture year, with the Welsh Society and the Heritage Society at the forefront. It was a proud achievement considering that there was only one event organised by the Scottish community. A Gwynedd-Liverpool exhibition was held at Bangor Art Gallery during September and October, an excellent way of cementing the relationship between the Liverpool Welsh and those still in the old country.

Two books were published in partnership with Trelawnyd Male Choir, *Labour of Love in Liverpool*, along with a version in Welsh.

The *Mimosa* Festival

The *Mimosa* Festival was held from 29 May to 1 June 2015, the third time for it to be held. The first was in 1965 when 1,500 Welsh went for a three-hour River Mersey cruise aboard the *Royal Daffodil* to commemorate the departure of the *Mimosa* from Liverpool for Patagonia in 1865. In 2005, the executive committee of the Merseyside Welsh Heritage Society set about commissioning a fine model of the *Mimosa* by a specialist in Poole at a cost of £2,500. The Liverpool Culture Company gave some financial help and the ship model can now be seen at the Liverpool Maritime Museum, Pier Head. Large numbers of people have seen the model *Mimosa* ship in the last decade. It was unveiled by Elan Jones, Mossley Hill, the great-granddaughter of Edwin Cynric Roberts, one of the two founders of Y Wladfa Gymreig in Patagonia and it was she, too, who unveiled the memorial to commemorate the pioneers situated near Princes Dock at another festival on 30 May 2015.

On Friday evening, 30 May, at the Quaker Meeting House under the chairmanship of Roderick Owen (chair of the city's Welsh Society) there were talks by D Ben Rees on the background to the *Mimosa*'s journey; by Mrs Susan Wilkinson, Toronto, Canada, on the ship itself; by Dr Arthur Thomas on Liverpool docks and economic life, and by Wayne Jones, Llandeilo, on the history of the original picture of the *Mimosa*.

On the Saturday morning there was a performance by four members of Theatr Clwyd Youth Company. The festival lecture was delivered by the Elvey MacDonald from Argentina. A question and answer session was chaired by Lord Dafydd Wigley. D Ben Rees was one of the panel, along with Marli Pugh, Irma Roberts and Wendell Davies. By the afternoon a large crowd had arrived at the Peel Holdings headquarters where the ceremony, speeches, singing and presentation took place under the leadership of Dr Huw Edwards, a great friend of the Liverpool Welsh. Everyone who spoke on the stage was invited by the Lord Mayor of Liverpool to enjoy a welcome at the City Hall parlour and have tea with him and the Lady Mayoress. These included Carwyn Jones, the First Minister of Wales; Dr Christine James, the Archdruid; and Alicia Amalia Castro, the Argentinian ambassador. It was lovely to see the Liverpool Corporation giving a parcel to every one of the children of Hendre Welsh School, Trelew, Patagonia, to commemorate their contribution to the festival.

That night there was a concert at Elm Hall Drive English Methodist Church with the Edeyrnion Ladies' Choir, under the baton of Manon Easter Ellis, the daughter of the Rev. Easter Ellis, one of the gifted ministers who served the Liverpool Welsh. The soloists were concert favourite Trebor Edwards, Betws Gwerfil Goch, together with the opera singer Siôn Goronwy, Talybont, near Bala. The honoured guest was Emeritus Professor Huw Rees, the chair of Liverpool Welsh Choral Union.

The Sunday was a day of praise, worship, prayer and consecration. The service was taken by D Ben Rees at Bluecoat Chapel, along with guest preacher, the Rev. Robert W Jones, of Wrexham, and Canon Tegid Roberts, Llanrug, who had been a minister in Patagonia. Children from Hendre School, Trelew, took part and a donation of £809 was presented to the school.

In the afternoon a *cymanfa ganu* was held, the like of which Liverpool had not seen since the 1970s, with 300 singers under the baton of R Ifor Griffith and Margaret Anwyl Williams at the organ. David Mawdsley presided over the event and the blessing was given by the Rev. Eirian Lewis of Mynachlog Ddu.

Over the whole weekend it is estimated that about 2,000 had attended the festival. Forty-four of them came from Patagonia itself, such as Marli Pugh, Irma Roberts, Wendell Davies and Luned Vychan Roberts de Gonzalez.

Thus, in the middle of the second decade of the twenty-first century, the Welsh presence in Liverpool is far from extinguished. It continues to be relevant and, from year to year, there continue to be different activities. The Welsh Presbyterians of Merseyside, Altrincham and Manchester have formed a pastorate in 2021 and extended an invitation to Robert Parry to be the new minister in the month of April. He had been a deputy to Dr Rees from 2019 to 2021. The Welsh language is not as common as it used to be, but it is still to be heard every week, and the Welsh heritage is not forgotten. But care must be taken to ensure generations to come know about the achievements of the Welsh in Liverpool and Merseyside over the past centuries. We have a rich history to be proud of, recorded in Welsh and, in the last thirty years, in English. As Professor D J Bowen put it: 'The only thing that endures is what someone has written down.'

Short biographies of selected personalities deserving more extensive details

John Davies (1766–1829)

A native of Tremeirchion in Denbighshire, John Davies had no formal education. A farmhand from the age of seven, he married in 1790 and the couple decided to move to Liverpool five years later.

He saw his life change completely due to being a member of Pall Mall Welsh Chapel and was one of the main supporters of the move to establish a centre in Jamaica Street for the Calvinistic Methodists, and later Bedford Street Chapel.

He took charge of the flock in Bedford Street and influenced a number of young men like John Roberts (Minimus) who was an accomplished hymnwriter. He represented Liverpool in the *Sasiwn* (Association of Welsh Presbyterians) in the north, as he knew so many of the missionaries who arrived constantly from Wales. He died on 19 October 1829 and is buried in St Michael's Cemetery.

The Rev. John Breese (1789–1842)

Born in Llanbrynmair in September 1789, John Breese was raised by an uncle and aunt. He began preaching at the age of twenty-four under the instruction of the Rev. John Roberts, Hen Gapel. He went to school in Shrewsbury and later to Llanfyllin Institute. In 1817 he was called to the Welsh Independents' church in Edmund Street, Liverpool. He married Margaret, the daughter of

David Williams of Saethon, Lleyn, and they had a son, Edward Breese (1835–81) who became a successful solicitor in Porthmadog. He was the man who gave David Lloyd George an opening in his office to follow his profession.

After arriving in Liverpool, Breese supervised the building of the Old Tabernacle, as it was called, on the corner of Great Crosshall Street. The foundation stone was laid in April 1817 and speeches were given by the Rev. Williams, Y Wern, and John Elias. The building cost £2,700 and was opened on 12 October 1877. His old minister came to give a sermon on the duties of the young minister, and eight other ministers were present to install him in the role. He worked exceptionally hard in Liverpool for seventeen years, and would walk to and from Manchester to serve the Welsh Independents there. He accepted a call to look after Heol Awst Church in Carmarthen in 1835, but the strain of the work he had undertaken in Liverpool was beginning to tell and he did not enjoy good health in his latter years. He died in August 1842 at the age of fifty-three and was buried in Heol Awst Cemetery.

David Davies (1797–1861)

Born in Clocaenog, Vale of Clwyd, David Davies was among the most prominent of the Liverpool Welsh in his day. He received very little education and worked on farms before moving to work in Dolgellau with his uncle, the well-known Calvinistic Methodist, Gabriel Davies, Bala, in 1820. He made a name for himself in the financial world in Liverpool and supported the Methodist cause to the utmost. He was an elder at Mulberry Street Chapel and students knew there was always a warm welcome for them at his beautiful house in Mount Gardens.

He was elected a trustee of the Society for Foreign Missions and was generous to the first missionary, Thomas Jones (1810–49). He was treasurer of the Liverpool Welsh branch of the Bible Society.

The Rev. Thomas Pierce (1801–57)

Born in Denbigh on 24 May 1801, Thomas was the son of William and Eleanor Pierce. As a young man he moved to Manchester but missed Swan Lane Chapel in Denbigh so much that he soon returned. In 1831 he was called to the Welsh Independent Chapel in Greenland Street, Liverpool, and was installed on 24 December 1832. One of his great admirers was the Rev. William Rees (Gwilym Hiraethog), who composed a fine *englyn* in his honour, and the two were firm friends in Liverpool from 1843 to 1857.

The Rev. Josiah Thomas (1830–1905)

The son of Owen and Mary Thomas, Josiah was born in Bangor on 7 August 1830. He was the brother of two gifted theologians and men of letters – Dr Owen Thomas (1812–91), minister at Princes Road, Liverpool, for more than twenty years, and William Thomas, leader of the temperance movement in Liverpool for decades. Like his brother Owen, he went to Bala College and Edinburgh University, where he graduated in 1857. After serving as a minister in Jerusalem, Bethesda, he ran a school in Bangor from 1862 to 1866, but he was then appointed as successor to John Roberts (Minimus). He moved to Liverpool a year after his brother Owen moved from London to Netherfield Road. The Mission Society, which had been relatively unremarkable up until then, grew into a significant institution under his leadership. He was on good terms with the directors of the executive committee and won the wholehearted trust of most of the missionaries in north-east India. It was a great disappointment when he resigned in June 1900 because of ill health. Because of his wide experience as general secretary of the Mission Society for over thirty-four years, and his familiarity with every aspect of its work, he was invited to be a consultant secretary. He was highly respected, and he was chairman of the Northern Association in 1896. He and his wife moved to Webster Road Chapel in December 1903 where he remained a member until his death on 21 May 1905.

N M Jones (Cymro Gwyllt, 'Wild Welshman', 1832–94)

Born in Neath Abbey, Glamorgan, on 9 December 1832, N M Jones moved as a baby with his parents to Aberdare before emigrating to the United States. He had his early education there but, as a youngster of fourteen, he decided to venture across the Atlantic to Liverpool. He managed to borrow enough capital to buy some commercial premises in Union Street, where emigrants were able to stay and receive advice from him. His centre became a meeting place for scores of young Welsh people on their way to New York.

He married Llinos Cynwyd, a prominent Welsh singer, and they had a son, Llewelyn. His moniker, 'Wild Welshman', became familiar throughout Wales and especially to readers of *Y Gwladgarwr* (The Patriot), since he contributed extensively to its columns. He died on 12 September 1894 and was buried in Anfield Cemetery.

The Rev. John Jones (1835–91)

John Jones came from Llanefydd and was heavily influenced by the multi-talented minister, the Rev. Robert Ellis. He moved to Liverpool in 1849 and worked as a tailor. He enjoyed the fellowship on offer at Liverpool's Welsh Baptist chapels and he was given the opportunity to practise his skills as a speaker and preacher at Athol Street Chapel. He moved to Liverpool from Bangor and was accepted into the Baptist College in Pontypool in 1859. He was mature enough to be ordained within a year, and was put to work in Glyn Ceiriog in August 1860. From there he moved to Talybont, Cardiganshire, in 1866. He moved, for the last time, to Blaenllechau in the Rhondda Fach in 1876.

Elizabeth Jones (1836–61)

Elizabeth Jones was an unusually religious girl. At the age of seven she was able to recite the 176 verses of Psalm 119 from memory. She moved to Liverpool after hearing that her hero, the Rev. Henry Rees, was a minister there and made her home at 59 York Terrace. She died in her prime in 1861 at the age of only twenty-five. She left behind her a child and a husband, and her body was taken all the way from Liverpool to her old home and to Llansadwrn Cemetery on Anglesey.

The Rev. William Williams (1836–98)

A native of Rhymney, William Williams was inspired to become a preacher and was accepted into Haverfordwest Baptist College in 1861. Three years later he accepted the call to Bethel Chapel, Abernant, in the Cynon Valley, and from there to Soar Chapel, Ebbw Vale, and Abercarn, Monmouthshire. He was called to Bousfield Street Chapel in Walton, Liverpool, in 1876.

In Liverpool he did his greatest work. The new chapel in Bousfield Street had opened five months previously and cost £2,500 to build.

After fourteen years he accepted the call to New Tredegar where he remained for six years before retiring because of ill health. He died on 23 January 1898 at the age of sixty-two and his remains were brought back to Liverpool.

The Rev. David Howells (1841–90)

David Howells was born in a farmhouse called Cwrt-y-gledden, near Pontyberem in the Gwendraeth Valley, on 21 August 1841. He lost his mother at the age of only two and, when he was seven, his father also died. He and his brother were looked after by his maternal grandfather, Jeremiah Griffiths, of Horeb, Llanelli. At the age of fourteen he went to live with an uncle in Maesteg. He began preaching at the age of nineteen and was admitted to Pontypool Institute in 1862 where he made good use of his opportunity. In 1866 he accepted the call to the Welsh Baptists in Mount Vernon Street, Liverpool. He was their first minister, but the congregation was looking for a more convenient piece of land to build a new chapel. They saw a possibility in Hall Lane and Howells enlisted nine helpers from Mount Vernon Street onto the building committee. The builder was a Welshman from Cerrigydrudion, William Jones, Catherine Street and Upper Duke Street, Liverpool. The work was completed in November 1868 at a cost of £2,400, although the minister had said it would be done for £1,000. Howells was a man of commitment who was never idle, and he raised substantial amounts of money. But the debt proved too much and broke his spirit. He moved to the countryside of Breconshire – away from the hurt of Hall Lane. In April 1870 he moved to Glasbury and Penyrheol for a more relaxed life. He died on 6 February 1890.

Edward M Evans (Morfryn, 1848–1915)

A slate worker brought up in Tŷ'n yr Ardd, Penrhyndeudraeth, Edward M Evans moved from Merionethshire to Liverpool in 1875 and spent forty years there, working for the same company for thirty-six of them. For twenty-five years he and his wife kept Crosshall Street chapel-house in the days of the fervent Calvinist, David Williams. Under his bardic name of Morfryn, he played a large part in Liverpool's eisteddfod life as a talented poet, writer and musician.

He died in March 1915 at the home of his daughter and son-in-law, R J Ellis, 62 Holt Road, Edge Lane, and the funeral at Anfield Cemetery was officiated by the Revs John Hughes Morris and J O Williams (Pedrog).

Richard Edward Jones (1849–1925)

The son of Edward Jones of Caergwrli, Llantrisant, Anglesey, R E Jones was educated in Llantrisant and at a private school in Amlwch and was trained as a furniture maker. He moved to Liverpool and worked for a Welsh builder before striking out on his own. He was exceptionally fortunate in his craftsmen and built in Bootle initially, before venturing to Anfield and Old Swan, concentrating on the neighbourhood of Kensington. There he literally built hundreds and hundreds of houses between Hall Lane and Jubilee Drive and Coleridge Street and Sheil Road. J R Jones ventured that 'few Liverpool builders, Welsh or English, built more houses than he, or were more successful'.

He took an interest in public life on Anglesey and in Liverpool. He was elected to Anglesey County Council in 1904, became an alderman in 1912, a JP in 1906 and high sheriff in 1908. He was active in the Liverpool Presbytery of the Welsh Presbyterian Church and was one of the founders of Holt Road Chapel, and later moved to Edge Lane. He became one of the first elders at Holt Road Chapel in 1886 and was their chairman in 1901. His eldest son, Joseph Edward Jones, was his business partner and followed in his father's footsteps. Joseph Jones made his home in Baroda, Crompton Lane, and was elected an elder in 1923. He was prominent in the missionary movement and director of a number of building societies.

The Rev. John Hughes (1850–1932)

Born in May 1850 to Dafydd and Elizabeth Hughes, John moved with his family to Cwmafan near Port Talbot and was brought up with his brothers, three of whom served as ministers in the Anglican Church, namely the Revs Lewis Hughes of Rhossili, Gower; Williams Hughes of Colton, Salisbury, and James J Hughes of Minetown, Hereford.

He graduated with an MA from Glasgow University and was ordained in 1877. Then he went to Machynlleth and later Fitzclarence Street, Liverpool, where he was known as an author, poet and preacher. He was also a prolific writer in Welsh and English and his works include *Ysgol Jacob* (Jacob's Ladder, 1897) and *Marwolaeth y Saint* (Death of the Saints, 1905). He was a well-known poet and his verse is to be found in Welsh and English in *Songs in the Night* (1885), *Tristora* (1896) and *Dan y Gwlith* (Under the Dew, 1911).

At the end of his ministry he moved to Glamorgan and died in Bridgend on 24 July 1932.

John Williams (Maldwyn, 1851–1933)

The journalistic pen name of Maldwyn came from his home county of Montgomeryshire where he was born on 15 March 1851. He was privately educated, and at the age of eleven was sent to Liverpool Institute. He had intended to follow a career in the law and played with the idea for some years. He managed to get a job as a clerk in a law firm but soon decided to go it alone as a journalist. For years he earned a living writing about the strong Welsh community in the city for the *Liverpool Daily Post* and other papers. He had a weekly column in the *Liverpool Echo* under the pen name Maldwyn. His articles and his column were highly regarded and reflected Welsh society at its best.

Griffith Owen (1852–1919)

Griffith Owen was regarded as one of the most likeable characters among the Welsh of Bootle and Orrell. He was very well known in both Welsh and English circles and brought up two sons who were a credit to him; namely Hugh Owen, who was connected to Douglas Road Chapel, and the captivating tenor Griff Owen, who was a regular performer at concerts throughout Liverpool.

George Jenkins (1859–1946)

A native of Cilgerran in Pembrokeshire, George Jenkins moved to Liverpool in 1879 at the age of twenty, but emigrated eight years later to the United States and remained there for six years, living in Kansas City, Denver and

Colorado. He returned to Liverpool in 1893 and played a leading role at Webster Road Chapel and was elected an elder there in 1919.

He was proud of his work in adult Sunday school classes. He died at the age of eighty-seven on 18 April 1946.

John Hughes (1863–1936)

Born in Llanrhuddlad, Anglesey, in 1863, John Hughes came to Liverpool as a youngster and lived in Wavertree. He and his wife, Mary Ann (née Williams), originally from Llanystumdwy, moved to Ramilies Road in March 1897 but remained active at Webster Road Chapel. By 1899 he was one of four financial assessors and a joint secretary with J W Jones. He built his own home, Moneivion, in Green Lane, in 1906. He was elected an elder in 1900 and by 1903 he was treasurer of the denominational gatherings. In the same year he resigned as an elder but continued to be a member and contributed generously when it was decided to build a new chapel in Heathfield Road.

He became an important builder, not only in Liverpool but also in Birkenhead, Wallasey, Newton-le-Willows, Birmingham and London. He was responsible for building Polo Estate in Childwall, Kenton Estate in London, and Shirley Estate in Birmingham. He was considered a top expert in his field and his advice was sought by the government's housing minister, Sir Kingsley Wood. He enjoyed sport – golf, billiards, and especially croquet, in which he won a host of prizes and was invited to play for England against Australia.

Isaac Roberts (Ap Carrog, 1864–1929)

Originally from Llyndyfrdwy, where he was born in 1864, Isaac Roberts moved with his parents to the village of Carrog when he was twelve. Later in life he adopted the bardic name Ap Carrog. He came to Liverpool to work in the building industry, and in November 1909 he and his wife were living at 16 Mayville Road, Allerton.

He was a member of the Junior Reform and Young Wales clubs in Upper Parliament Street where he was very active. He and his brother, J O Roberts, Upper Parliament Street, worked in the building industry and were members of Princes Road Chapel. Isaac ventured out on his own as well as working for other Welsh builders. He built homes in Wavertree, Anfield, Kensington and Childwall.

John William Jones (1868–1945)

Born in Cae Hafod, Cyffylliog, Conwy Valley, in 1868, J W Jones came to Liverpool as a carpenter with the firm of David Roberts in 1886. Nine years later he married Sarah Catherine Owens from Llanrhaeadr-ym-Mochnant. He was very active at Webster Road Chapel and, when he and his wife were living in 50 Webb Street in 1897, he was made treasurer of the chapel's temperance committee. That was the first of a number of important posts he held. By 1910 the family were living in Hiraethog, Garth Drive, and the following year he was made an elder.

He was a great help during the building of a new chapel in Heathfield Road from 1925 to 1927, and generous as well. If it were not for him and his family, and the family of John Jones of Mayfield, the chapel would not have been built on the same scale. He contributed the considerable sum of £4,300 to the building fund every year until 1937. In 1933 he was elected chairman of the Liverpool Presbytery and he sat on a host of committees as well as the executive committee of the Foreign Missions' Society in Liverpool. In 1938 he translated an English pageant by James Broadbent & Sons of Leeds into Welsh, under the title *Adeiladu'r Eglwys* (Building the Church). The intention of the pageant was to inform both children and adults of the requirements of the church, at home as in India – courage, care and service. He and his wife raised five children – four boys and a girl – and the sons were all directors of his building firm.

The Rev. Thomas Davies (1870–1912)

Born in Clocaenog, Vale of Clwyd, Thomas was the son of Thomas Davies, Bryngwyn, and his wife. He moved to Liverpool at the age of fifteen and was employed at the well-known grocery store Irwin's. His talented minister at Stanley Road Chapel, Bootle, the Rev. Griffith Ellis, saw him as having the makings of a preacher. He had deeply-held views on social issues and became a leading socialist among the Liverpool Welsh. He served as a missionary for a while under the patronage of his church and concentrated his efforts on the mission centre and Sunday school in Bankhall.

To further his education he attended the preparatory school in Bala where he was a spokesman for socialism among the students and it was he, along with others, who established the Fabian Society there. He attended the University of Wales in Bangor and became an admirer of the socialist T Hudson Williams who taught Classics. He graduated with a BA and went to Mansfield College, Oxford. Before completing his course there, he was recommended by the Liverpool Foreign Missions' Society for missionary work in India, but the doctors who examined him decided he should not go to north-east India and, with the help of his professors at Oxford, he was sent on a six-month trip to Australia.

He stayed there and married his sweetheart from his Liverpool days, Miss Beryl Lloyd. He was called to Bowral Presbyterian Church in New South Wales. Because of his poor health he had to leave the church and he and his wife moved to Wentworth Falls where he died on 23 July 1912.

Robert Owen Jones (1871–1923)

A native of Dolrhyd, Dolgellau, R O Jones was one of five children born to Maria and John Jones. After being educated locally and working on the land, he saw his opportunity to move to Liverpool in 1899 where he was employed by the tea company Chaloner and Ridgway. He believed he could earn more by setting up his own business, so he opened a chandlery and ironmonger's shop. Poor health hampered his prospects of a successful business and he died on 17 May 1923.

Dr Thomas Hopkin Evans (1879–1940)

The musician was born in Resolven, near Neath, in 1879, but left school at twelve to work as a collier. He immersed himself in music from an early age, and by 1900 seized on the chance of work as a chapel organist. He formed Resolven Mixed Choir which won first prize at the 1905 National Eisteddfod. In 1909 he moved to Neath as organist of the Presbyterian Church (English section) in London Road and became conductor of the town's mixed choir. In 1919 he moved to Liverpool as the paid director of Liverpool Welsh Choral Union where he remained for the rest of his life.

He was conductor of the Birkenhead National Eisteddfod Choir in 1917, Neath (1918), Liverpool (1929), Wrexham (1933) and Denbigh (1939). He was an adjudicator at the National Eisteddfod for a quarter of a century. He lectured often and was in great demand as a leader of hymn-singing festivals. He was also a prolific composer of tunes such as 'Penmachno', 'Tregeiriog', 'Gorof' and 'Arosfa'.

He was awarded a doctorate from Oxford University towards the end of his life in 1940. His final concert was *Elijah* on 16 March 1940, and a week later he died suddenly at his brother's home in Neath.

Thomas Jones (1879–1937)

Born in 1879 at Pistyll Gwyn farm, Llanfair Dyffryn Clwyd, Thomas Jones was educated at the local school. He worked as a farm labourer but he did not like the work and wanted to be a carpenter. At the age of sixteen he came to Liverpool and was employed by J W Jones, who had just formed a company. At the age of twenty-one he emigrated to South Africa and, in 1900, married a Welsh girl from Anglesey in Cape Town. Because of his health, the two returned to Liverpool and he worked in the building industry in Mossley Hill, Calderstones, Childwall and Allerton. He lived in Newlands, Queen's Drive, and was active at Heathfield Road Chapel. For a period he was treasurer of the chapel's temperance society, with David Griffiths of Micklefield Road as chairman, and Doris Thomas of Allerton Road as secretary.

He was one of the earliest builders to put every inch of space in a house to practical use, and introduced purpose-built shelving, built-in cupboards and wardrobes as an integral part of rooms.

John Lloyd (1880–1966)

Born in 1880 at Tŷ Mawr chapel-house near Rhydlydan, Merionethshire, John Lloyd came to Liverpool at the age of sixteen from Cwm Penanner. He lodged with his aunt and attached himself immediately to Webster Road Church while the Rev. William Owen was minister there. He was employed in building and became a builder of note. His expertise was a great help to the church on many occasions. He was a loyal and committed member of Webster Road, and later at Heathfield Road.

His particular contribution was teaching adults at Sunday school and he was considered to be outstandingly successful at it. He was elected an elder in 1939 and he gave unwavering support to the church's spiritual gatherings and prayer meetings to which he contributed in his own unique way.

His wife hailed from Y Felinheli and she died on 1 April 1960. He left his home in 11 Towers Road and lived with his daughter Mrs Dilys Jones in Hilltop Road, and with his son Arthur in Dulas Road. He died on 26 March 1966 at the age of eighty-six.

Dr Gwilym Owen (1880–1940)

A native of Denbigh, Gwilym Owen was born on 19 July 1880. He and his sister Mary came to Liverpool when their parents moved to 11 Rossett Avenue in 1896. He was active at Webster Road Chapel in 1899, while still a student at Liverpool University, and became an officer in the young people's religious movement and the Sunday school in 1900 at the age of only twenty. He graduated from Liverpool University in 1901 with flying colours, and won a Royal Commission for the 1851 exhibition scholarship which enabled him to attend Christ College, Cambridge, to undertake research at Cavendish Laboratory under Sir J J Thomson. In 1905, at the end of his time at Cambridge, he was appointed a physics lecturer at Liverpool University where he remained until 1913, and lived with his parents at 11 Greenbank Road. When he was made an elder in 1911, the unusual situation arose of having a father as minister and a son as elder at the same chapel.

He was appointed to the Chair of physics at Auckland University, New Zealand, in 1913, and in 1919 he accepted a similar post at Aberystwyth University. He was vice-principal in 1932 and played a prominent role in college life until his health broke down in 1936.

As a writer he was a pioneer in presenting science through the medium of Welsh. His polished work can still be appreciated – *Athroniaeth Pethau Cyffredin* (Philosophy of Ordinary Things, 1907); *Rhyfeddodau'r Cread* (Wonders of Creation, 1933), and *Y Mawr a'r Bach* (The Large and the Small,

1936). He died on 9 November 1940 and was buried with his mother in Toxteth Cemetery.

Robert John Rowlands (Meuryn, 1880–1967)

Born in Abergwyngregyn to William and Mary Rowlands, Robert John Rowlands was unfortunate to suffer an accident that left him lame at the age of three. After a brief spell working in a shop in Llanfairfechan, he moved to Y Cymro's offices under Isaac Foulkes. Apart from a short time in Porthmadog, he spent more than quarter of a century as a reporter on Y Darian and Yr Herald Cymraeg where he was later in charge of the Liverpool edition.

He was one of the founders of Undeb y Ddraig Goch. He published his only collection of verse, Swynion Serch (Love Charms) in 1906, although he composed englynion to his friends. He won eisteddfod chairs while in Liverpool, and in 1921 he won the Chair of the Caernarfon National Eisteddfod for an ode.

In November 1921 he became editor of Yr Herald Cymraeg and Papur Pawb in Caernarfon, and when the company which owned the Herald and the Y Genedl Gymreig company merged in April 1937, along with other titles from those companies, Meuryn remained editor of them until he retired in March 1959. He also became a children's writer and his books include Chwedlau'r Meini (Tales of the Stones, 1946) and Dirgelwch Plas y Coed (The Mystery of Plas y Coed, 1948).

Henry Humphrey Jones (1881–1971)

A native of Maenan, near Llanrwst, Henry Humphrey Jones was the son of William Maurice and Elisabeth Jones. He moved to Liverpool on 20 December 1897. His brother William was an elder at Bethlehem Chapel, Douglas Road, and his brother Robert of Hamilton Road was a carpenter and elder at Fitzclarence Street Chapel. A third brother, the Rev. David Morris Jones (1887–1957), was a chaplain in the First World War and officiated at Hedd Wyn's funeral. He also taught at Aberystwyth Theological College from 1934 to 1957.

Humphrey Jones was a chemist and worked at Clay & Abraham in Bold

Street before becoming principal of the Liverpool School of Pharmacy in Blackburn Place from 1908 until he retired in 1950.

He was president of the Liverpool Welsh Choral Union from 1934 to 1971 and prominent in the Free Church movement. With its help, he published his autobiography, *My Yesteryears: from Farm to Pharmacy* (Aughton, 1971). He was chairman of the Eastern Association of the Welsh Presbyterians in 1954, and an elder in the denomination's English chapel. He stood for the Liberal Party in the city council's Granby ward in 1934 but did not win. He was High Sheriff of Caernarfonshire in 1951, and in 1961 accepted an honorary MA from Liverpool University. On his eightieth birthday in 1961 Liverpool's Lord Mayor said of him:

> I am not sure whether it is true to say that Mr Humphrey Jones is a Liverpool Welshman or a Welsh Liverpudlian, but whatever he is, he has made his mark on the city.

He spent his last years with his daughter and family in Aughton where he died in 1971.

John Richard Jones (1881–1955)

Born in 1881, John Richard Jones was the son of John Jones, the builder, and Catherine Parry, both natives of Anglesey and living in Barrington Road.

He was immersed in the life of Webster Road Chapel and was invited to become accounts' auditor in 1902, one of many important posts he held. He was secretary of the literary association while his father was treasurer.

He worked on behalf of the Liberal Party and was chairman of the Wavertree division, and gave much of his time to the Free Church movement and was treasurer of the Merseyside section.

He contributed extensively to the work of the church in time, talents and money, especially during the building of Heathfield Road Chapel from 1925 to 1927. He was elected an elder in 1931, the only time for that community to have a father and son serving as church elders.

He served many Welsh causes and associations. He was High Sheriff of Anglesey (1940–41) and treasurer of the Parliament for Wales Campaign. He self-published the useful volume, *The Welsh Builder on Merseyside*, in 1946.

He married Mary, a member of Webster Road Chapel, in 1912. He died at Cintra, Menlove Avenue, Liverpool, on 28 January 1955 and was buried in Allerton Cemetery.

Isaac Bleddyn Edwards (1889–1943)

Born in Liverpool in 1899 to a family belonging to Webster Road Chapel, Isaac Bleddyn Edwards was the younger son of John Edwards, originally from Anglesey, and his wife Ann, from Abersoch. Their elder son was Richard John Edwards and then there were Margaret Ellen and Olwen, all of whose names are recorded in the children's section of the chapel in 1899.

Isaac married Margaret (née Ashton) of Trefeglwys, who came to Liverpool in 1910 to serve with Miss Elizabeth Jones of Staylittle, who kept house for Alderman Harrison Jones, an elder in Princes Road Church, and stayed for fourteen years. Isaac and Margaret had six children, a son, John; one set of twins, Elizabeth and Margaret; another set, Glenys and Emrys, and a daughter, Meinwen Ann, who died from whooping cough at the age of eighteen months. When the Second World War broke out, like so many other Liverpool Welsh, the family was scattered to parts of north Wales, and Mrs Edwards moved back to Llawr-y-Glyn, Montgomeryshire. Isaac Bleddyn remained in Liverpool, living at 19 Ferndale Road. On 26 May 1942, on his way home to Liverpool from Llawr-y-Glyn, he had a bike accident and died of his injuries. His minister, the Rev. Dr R Glynne Lloyd, said of him:

> Although raised in Liverpool, he stuck to the language and traditions of his forefathers. He and his family attended services regularly and he did everything he could to further the Great Cause.

In 1943 his son, John Ashton Edwards, was struck by palsy and left seriously disabled, but he overcame his difficulties and became a lecturer.

William Davies (1861–1927)

Counted among the pioneers of the Calvinistic Methodists in the suburb of Wavertree, William Davies and his wife became members of Webster Road Chapel in 1891. He led the singing and helped John Jones of Barrington Road (later Mayfield) in the children's meetings. He was a member of the library committee in 1896 and a deputy inspector of the Sunday school in 1898. Not surprisingly, he was elected an elder in 1900.

By 1928 he had moved to Preswylfa, 8 Heydale Road, Allerton, where he died on 30 December 1934.

Owen Hughes (1860–1947)

Owen Hughes was one of the leading community workers around Webster Road and Heathfield Road. In 1894 he was made joint secretary of the church with Edward Owen of 365 Smithdown Road. He also served as a deputy Sunday school inspector and was elected an elder in 1894.

He died on 21 February 1947. In a tribute to his long, unstinting labour, the Rev. Dr R Glynne Lloyd said of him:

> As a church we are indebted to him for his thorough and untiring work over such a long period. He is remembered as a wise leader, a competent teacher in Sunday school, a diligent visitor to the sick, and as one who performed an enormous amount of work for the church behind the scenes. He was outstandingly faithful in his attendance at all the meetings and a fitting friend to young people.

Robert John Roberts (1897–1918)

The second son of Mr and Mrs Owen Roberts of 8 Alroy Road, Anfield, Robert John Roberts was educated at local schools and at the Calvinistic Methodist Chapel in Anfield. He was one of five brothers, all of whom joined the armed forces during the First World War. Four of them fought in the trenches in France. Robert joined the army in 1914 and was made lieutenant in 1918. He was injured in France in 1915 and was in hospital for a long time. He returned to the trenches in August 1918 and was injured again on 25 October 1918 and imprisoned by the Germans. He died three days later.

The Rev. William Davies

Born in Rhydycymerau, William Davies began preaching as a young man in east Glamorgan. He attended the University of Wales in Cardiff, studying for a degree in Welsh and Greek and later an MA. His first church was Bethania, Aberdare, where he got to know the short-story writer Kate Roberts who was a teacher in the town. She said of him:

William Davies was a countryman and cultured farmers could enjoy themselves in his company. He had a host of stories and an inimitable laugh, he laughed from the bottom of his heart.

In 1918 he moved to Stanley Road Chapel, Bootle, and saw it reach its highpoint in 1920 with 943 members. He cleared the chapel's debt by 1928, and was extremely active with the Foreign Missions' Society. He was a leader of the Liverpool Welsh Ministers, a popular and successful group in his day. He was equally in his element at Bootle children's eisteddfod. During a visit to the mission field in India, he was struck by a throat virus that robbed him of his ability to preach. He remained there from October 1935 to March 1936. He died of the disease at 58 Trinity Road, Bootle, on 22 July 1938.

The Rev. W Llewelyn Evans (1897–1958)

A native of Bala, W Llewelyn Evans was educated locally and served in France during the First World War. On leaving the armed forces he made the most of his chance to study at University College of North Wales, Bangor, and Jesus College, Oxford. He was ordained in 1928 and accepted a call to Seilo Presbyterian Chapel in Caernarfon, before moving in 1937 to the Welsh Presbyterian Chapel in Edge Lane, and it was in Liverpool that he achieved his life's greatest work.

At the end of his time in Edge Lane, he supported a suggestion by the elders that the membership should be weeded, especially the members on paper who did not keep up their 'church duties'. Twenty-five were deleted and the membership of Edge Lane Chapel fell from 504 in 1949 to 463 in 1950. In the same year W Llywelyn Evans accepted the call to minister to some of the smaller churches in the Vale of Clwyd. He served them for three years before retiring in 1950 to his home in Abergele. He was taken seriously ill and died in 1958. He was one of the most important leaders among the Liverpool Presbyterians in the 1930s and 1940s.

Dr Goronwy Evan Thomas (1907–84)

A member at Heathfield Road Chapel from his arrival in Liverpool in the 1930s, Dr Goronwy Evan Thomas was one of Liverpool's most noted orthopaedic doctors. A native of Cyffylliog, he was educated at the village school, Denbigh County School and Liverpool University.

The Rev. Iorwerth Cyril John (1913–81)

Born on 6 December 1913 in Greenhill, Bancffosfelen, Gwendraeth Valley, Iorwerth Cyril John left school to work in a grocer's shop before being called to the ministry. He was trained at Myrddin School and Carmarthen Presbyterian College and ordained in 1945. His first church was Seion, Cwmgors, and in 1949 he succeeded the Rev. D J Bassett as minister at the Welsh Baptists chapel in Edge Lane. In 1954 he was invited to Earlsfield Road Welsh Chapel in Wavertree. Because of a lack of ministers, he took charge of the famous Balliol Road Chapel in Bootle in 1968, and in 1971 he took responsibility for two other chapels, Woodlands, Birkenhead, and Liscard Road, Wallasey. By then he was the minister of five chapels, as well as Free Church chaplain at the Royal Infirmary in Pembroke Place.

Howell Vaughan Jones (1913–79)

Born in 1913, Howell Vaughan Jones was the youngest son of J W and Sarah C Jones (née Owens) of Hiraethog, Allerton, and like his brothers was a director in his father's building firm. He married Gwen Tegla Davies and the couple settled down in Garth, Reservoir Road, Woolton. In 1960 he was elected an elder at Heathfield Road Chapel. He was appointed chapel treasurer and served in that role for fourteen years.

Judge John Edward Jones (1914–98)

The son of Elizabeth Jones (née Roberts), of Pensarn, Anglesey, and Thomas Robert Jones of Mold, John Edward Jones was born on 23 December 1914 in Mulliner Street, Wavertree, within 200 yards of Webster Road Chapel. He was educated at Sefton Park Council School, which has now disappeared, and later at Liverpool Institute High School. He earned his two degrees, BCom (1942) and LLB (1945) externally from the University of London. He worked in the insurance industry for twelve years and was a conscientious objector during the Second World War. In 1946 he was accepted as a barrister, and from 1966 to 1969 he worked as vice-chairman of Lancashire Quarter Sessions and vice-chairman of the Workmen's Compensation (Supplementation) and Pneumoconiosis and Business Benefit Boards (1968–69) when he was promoted to county court judge and then circuit judge.

He was elected an elder at Heathfield Road Chapel in 1947. He was prominent among the Liverpool Welsh as vice-president and president of the Liverpool Welsh Choral Union and a fellow of the Merseyside Eisteddfod. He was president of Liverpool Presbytery on two occasions, in 1971 and 1977. He was a stalwart of the magazine *Y Bont* as its chairman, and to the community paper *Yr Angor* as its chapel correspondent. He was proud of his connection to the freemasons and his work as a governor of Aigburth Vale Comprehensive School, also his work with the Red Cross and *Cylch y Pump ar Hugain*. He died in Lourdes Hospital on 28 June 1998.

John Alun Hughes (?–1990)

Born in Llanfrothen, and one of eight children, John Alun Hughes worked as a slate miner in Blaenau Ffestiniog after leaving school. He was obliged to move away to look for work after a time in the armed forces and then around Wrexham. He came to Liverpool to stay with his sister Ceridwen Jones and her family in Trent Avenue, Roby. He spent the rest of his days in Liverpool and worked for English Electric for many years. He met Elen Williams at Newsham Park Presbyterian Chapel, where her parents kept the chapel-house, and they married and set up home at 44 Romer Road where they brought up three daughters.

He was very involved in the life of Edge Lane Welsh Chapel and was a keen member of the literary association. He attended Sunday evening services there and meetings of the literary association, and was very useful to the executive committee of the community paper *Yr Angor*, which he distributed over many years. He died on 4 December 1990 in Heath Hospital, Cardiff, where one of his daughters lived, and his body was brought back to Liverpool.

Elizabeth (Betty) Hughes (1916–97)

In Amlwch, Mr and Mrs Hugh Hughes and their family were stalwarts of the Welsh Baptists' cause. Early in 1920 they moved with their daughters, Betty and Nellie, to Liverpool. A few months later they had the opportunity to live at Everton Village Baptists' chapel-house where she became known as Betty Tŷ Capel. She worked for S Reece & Sons in Hawke Street, and later for the company of Vernon in the city.

She was a supporter of the Welsh-speaking community, particularly when a branch of the Urdd was formed in Anfield. She joined Balliol Road Chapel in Bootle, and was later elected a deacon. When Balliol Road Chapel closed, she moved to the Welsh Independents at Salem, Bootle, where she served equally diligently – and when Salem closed, she moved to Tabernacle Chapel, Woolton Road.

Goronwy Davies (1898–1975)

Born in the Clawddnewydd area, Goronwy Davies was heavily influenced by his father who had been inspired during the religious Revival of 1904–05. His upbringing at Sunday school and chapel provided firm foundations for his detailed knowledge of the scriptures.

He came to Liverpool in the early 1920s and spent his first years in the city in the building trade and was responsible for the upkeep of the chapel and manse. He was elected an elder at Heathfield Road Chapel in 1955 and served in a number of capacities both within and outside the church and was prominent in the activities of Liverpool Presbytery. As president of the ministry's organising committee he travelled much to look after the needs of members belonging to his area, which stretched from Blackburn to Runcorn.

Griffith Robert Jones (1901–1979)

A native of the Lleyn peninsula, Griffith R Jones and his wife were initially members of Heathfield Road Chapel where he was made an elder in 1953 and was the elders' secretary from 1956 to 1970. He was also secretary of the Presbyterian South Liverpool district for a while.

His prayers at church meetings were memorable, as were his preparations in broaching a subject for discussion, and his leadership as a teacher in the Sunday school for adults. He was assisted by his first wife, Gladys Ellen Jones, Madryn, 29 Allangate Road, who died on 19 December 1945.

On 11 April 1949 he remarried, to Jennie Thomas, 21 Stand Park Road, Childwall.

Gwilym Meredydd Jones (1920–92)

Born in Glanrafon, Edeyrnion, Merionethshire, in 1920, Gwilym Meredydd Jones was educated at Bala Grammar School and the Normal College, Bangor. He served as a soldier during the Second World War and moved to Liverpool at the end of the war to teach. In 1948 he married Gwerfyl Morris, daughter of a well-known family at Douglas Road Presbyterian Chapel, and they had two sons, Gwyn and Hugh.

He joined Anfield Road Chapel where he was made an elder in 1953, and was very active in the Merseyside Sunday School Union, the Urdd and Welsh cultural life in the city. When Anfield Road Chapel closed in 1974, he joined Bethel Church in Heathfield Road, and soon took on the responsibility of publications' secretary from 1981 to 1984. He was himself an accomplished lay preacher who was in great demand, and a polished lecturer. He was an influential headteacher in Liverpool and won a host of eisteddfod prizes during the 1970s. His volume of short stories won the prose medal at Swansea's National Eisteddfod in 1982 and was published under the title, *Ochr Arall y Geiniog* (The Other Side of the Coin).

Mary Blodwen Owen (1919–1985)

Mary Blodwen Owen was born in Arnold Street, Toxteth, a stone's throw from Princes Road Church. After graduating with a BA from Liverpool University, she was a schoolteacher and ended her professional career at Holt Comprehensive School. She maintained her interest in teaching after her retirement, and was a stalwart of the Association of Teachers. Her main contribution was to her chapel, Trinity Church, in Princes Road, where she was made an elder, and then after 1976 at Bethel, Heathfield Road.

Henry Williams (1879–1945)

From Llanallgo on Anglesey, Henry Williams made his way to Liverpool where he became a skilled builder. He and another builder, J W Jones, were elected elders in 1911 at Webster Road Chapel. In the 1920s he was one of the secretaries of Heathfield Road Church and lived at 13 Grovedale Road, Allerton. He was president of the Liverpool Presbytery in 1937, along with the Rev. R Emrys Evans BA, Birkenhead.

Edward Goronwy Owen (1920–2015)

On 19 July 2015 the Presbyterian Church lost one of the most committed elders on Merseyside, with the death of Edward Goronwy Owen. He was an elder for sixty-three years and relished every aspect of his duties. His parents, the Rev. W R Owen and Margaret (née Davies), also had a daughter, Eirwen, who married an Anglican priest, author, historian and theologian, David Price. Goronwy was born in Trefeglwys but his father moved in 1922 to accept a call at Weston Rhyn. Goronwy built up a successful business as a pharmacist, with five shops across the city from Bootle to Dingle. He was connected to three chapels – Trinity Church, Toxteth, Garston and Bethel, Heathfield Road. He was made an elder at Garston in 1952 and at Bethel in 1977.

He was a wise leader in several organisations including the Liverpool Presbytery, the North-East India Wales Trust, the Rotary, the Merseyside Chaplaincy and the community paper, *Yr Angor*, where he was chairman for over two decades.

Henry Richard Williams (1932–87)

Born in Rhewl, Vale of Clwyd, Henry Richard Williams was the son of Robert Herbert Williams, of Rhewl, and Mary (née Jones), from Harlech. He was educated at Rhewl Primary School, Grove Park Boys' Grammar School, Wrexham, and Liverpool University. He married Patricia Hughes from Bwlch-gwyn, near Wrexham, who was a staunch supporter of Welsh life and her church.

Richard was a valuable asset on the maintenance committee, and a strong supporter of establishing a club for young people at Heathfield Presbyterian Church of Wales. He was exceptionally talented in a number of areas, especially in organ music, and could turn his hand to repairing harps, as well as being a lecturer in his own speciality of dentistry.

Publications by the author, D Ben Rees, which are connected to the Liverpool Welsh

- D Ben Rees, *Cymry Adnabyddus 1951–1972* (Liverpool/Pontypridd, 1978).
- D Ben Rees, *Haneswyr yr Hen Gorff* (Liverpool/Llanddewi Brefi, 1981).
- D Ben Rees, *Pregethwr y Bobl: Bywyd a Gwaith Dr Owen Thomas* (Liverpool, 1979).
- D Ben Rees, *The Life and Work of Owen Thomas, 1812–1891* (Lewiston/Queenston/Lampeter, 1991).
- D Ben Rees & R Merfyn Jones, *The Liverpool Welsh and their Religion: Two Centuries of Welsh Calvinistic Methodism* (Liverpool, 1984).
- D Ben Rees, *Local and Parliamentary Politics of Liverpool from 1800 to 1911* (1999).
- D Ben Rees, *Dathlu Grawnsypiau Canaan a Detholiad* (Liverpool, 1995).
- D Ben Rees, *The Welsh of Merseyside, Vol 1* (Liverpool/Llanddewi Brefi, 1997).
- D Ben Rees, *The Welsh of Merseyside, Vol 2* (Liverpool, 2001).
- D Ben Rees, *Vehicles of Grace and Hope: Welsh Missionaries in India 1800–1970* (Liverpool, 2002).
- D Ben Rees (ed.), *Ffydd a Gwreiddiau John Saunders Lewis* (Liverpool, 2002).

- D Ben Rees, *The Polymath: Rev. William Rees ('Gwilym Hiraethog', 1802–1883) of Liverpool* (Liverpool, 2002).

- D Ben Rees, *Cwmni Deg Dawnus* (Essays on Sir Alfred Lewis Jones and Dr Emyr Wyn Jones; Liverpool, 2003).

- D Ben Rees (ed.), *The Call and Contribution of Dr Robert Arthur Hughes, OBE, FRCS (1910–1996) and Some of his Predecessors in North-east India, Vol 1* (Liverpool, 2004).

- D Ben Rees, *Alpha and Omega: Welsh Presbyterian Witness in Laird Street, Birkenhead 1906–2006* (Liverpool, 2006).

- D Ben Rees, *Labour of Love in Liverpool: The History of the Welsh Congregation in the Chapels of Smithdown Lane, Webster Road, Ramilies Road, Heathfield Road and Bethel, Liverpool* (Liverpool, 2008).

- D Ben Rees, *The Welsh Missionary Witness in Ellesmere Port (1907–2007)* (Liverpool, 2012).

- John Gwynfor Jones (ed.), *Dyddiau o Lawen Chwedl: Hanner Can Mlwyddiant Cyhoeddiadau Modern Cymreig 1963–2013; ynghyd ag Ysgrifau ar Gyhoeddi yn Lerpwl a Chymru* (Liverpool, 2014), includes two articles by D Ben Rees on Liverpool, '*Cofio Cyfraniad Isaac Foulkes ('Llyfrbryf'; 1834–1904)*' and '*Cylchgronau a Newyddiaduron Cymraeg a Gweisg Lerpwl (1795–2013)*'.

- D Ben Rees, *Di-Ben-Draw: Hunangofiant D Ben Rees* (Talybont, 2015), including the author's time in Liverpool from 1968 to 2015.

- D Ben Rees, *Josiah Hughes (1804–1840): The Reluctant Welsh Calvinistic Methodist Missionary of Malacca* (Liverpool, 2016).

- D Ben Rees, *The Healer of Shillong: Rev. Dr Hugh Gordon Roberts and the Welsh Mission Hospital* (Liverpool, 2016).

- D Ben Rees (ed.), *Programme of The Black Chair Centenary 1917–2017, 9–10 September 2017 in Birkenhead* (Liverpool, 2017).

- D Ben Rees (ed.), *The Family of David Roberts* (Liverpool, 2018).

- D Ben Rees (ed.), *Hedd Wyn Festival* (Talybont, 2018).

- D Ben Rees, *A Life Unlimited: An Autobiography of D Ben Rees from Llanddewi Brefi to Liverpool* (London, 2018).

- D Ben Rees, *Hanes Rhyfeddol Cymry Lerpwl* (Talybont, 2019)

- D Ben Rees (ed.), *Codi Angor yn Lerpwl, Penbedw a Manceinion* (Liverpool, 2019).

Liverpool Welshmen and their bardic names

Collwyn – William Morgan (1882–1952).

Corfanydd – Robert Herbert Williams (1805–76), Basnett Street.

Dewi o Ddyfed – Rev. David James (1803–71), Kirkdale. An Anglican priest.

Dic Aberdaron – Richard Robert Jones (1780–1843). A vagabond.

Emrys – Rev. William Ambrose (1813–1873).

Gwilym Hiraethog – Rev. William Rees (1802–1883), Grove Street.

Gwynedd – Thomas Jones has been laid to rest in St John's Gardens.

Gwilym Deudraeth – William Thomas Edwards (1863–1940).

Hawen – Rev. David Adams (1845–1923), Grove Street.

Hughes Cadfan or Cadfan Gwynedd – Hugh Hughes (1824–1898).

Ieuan Gwyllt – John Roberts (1822–1877), St Anne's Street.

Llanowain – O Trevor Roberts, Bootle.

Llyfrbryf – Isaac Foulkes (1836–1904), outstanding publisher.

Meuryn – Robert John Rowlands (1880–1967), journalist and a poet of distinction.

Minimus – Rev. John Roberts (1808–1880), Liverpool and Edinburgh.

Pedr Fardd – Peter Jones (1775–1845), Pall Mall.

Pedr Hir – Rev. Peter Williams (1847–1922), Bootle.

Pedrog – Rev. John Owen Williams (1853–1932), Islington.

Pencerdd Gwynedd – John Henry Roberts (1848–1924), Chatham Street.

Appendix 4

Generous supporters
of this volume

Capel Bethel Literary Association, Heathfield Road, Liverpool.

Merseyside Welsh Heritage Society.

St David's Trust, Liverpool.

North-east India–Wales Trust.

Gobaith mewn Gweithrediad/ Generating Hope in Action, Allerton, Liverpool.

Liverpool branch of the University of Wales Guild of Graduates.

Professor D Ben Rees and Mrs Meinwen Rees, Allerton, Liverpool.

Mr and Mrs Arwel Williams, Roby.

In memory of Mrs Elizabeth Winifred Morris, from her son, the Rev. John G Morris, Llanddaniel, Anglesey.

Dr Lewis Evans and Sian Evans, Cardiff.

Dr Rhys R Davies, Liverpool.

RSJ Financial Planning, Liverpool.

Elin and Jim Boyd, Aughton.

Dr Huw Edwards and family, London.

Mike Chitty, Gateacre, Liverpool.

Liverpool Welsh Society to the author and organiser of the Fund, Dr Ben Rees, for his lecture to them as a society on 15 March 2020 at the Welsh Centre

Campbell Insurance Services, Allerton, Liverpool.

Ultra Security Systems, Old Swan, Liverpool.

Gwyn and Basia Evans, London.

The Rex Makin Trust, Liverpool.

Joe Clithero and his family, Kensington.

Canon Rev. D Owain Bell, Kempsey, Worcester.

Dafydd Ll Rees, West Hampstead, London.

Hefin Ednyfed Rees QC and Dr Bethan Rees, Harpenden, Hertfordshire.

Jennifer Cunningham, Blundellsands, Liverpool.

Menna Edwards, Blundellsands, Liverpool.

Elizabeth and Mal Owen, Halewood.

Elwyn S Jones, Nant Peris, near Llanberis, Gwynedd.

Carys Cooper, Wirral: 'Er Cof am fy Nhad, Gwilym Esmor Jones a'i ewythr, John Herbert Jones'.

Alun Vaughan and Helen M Jones, Childwall, Liverpool.

In Memory of Trystan John Turton (1938–2019) by Rosamonde Turton and family.

Sian Spink, Newton-le-Willows.

Tomos Llywelyn Rees, Harpenden, Hertfordshire.

Joshua Caradog Rees, Harpenden , Hertfordshire.

Dr W Ken Davies, Croesyceiliog, Cwmbrân, Gwent.

Mrs N A Jones, Llanwrin, near Machynlleth.

W Meirion Evans and Mrs Eirlys Evans, Allerton, Liverpool.

Hywel Wyn Roberts and Margaret Roberts, Caernarfon, Gwynedd.

Anon.

Susan, Helen and Mark Lyons, son and daughters of John P Lyons and the late Mrs Marian Lyons, Knowley Village.

Rev. Robert Parry, Coe-llai/Leeswood, Flintshire.

Clifford and Myfanwy Owen, Llanfairfechan (late of Ellesmere Port).

Mrs Angela Lansley, Liverpool.

N Harrison, Morton Diaries Ltd, Maghull.

Eurfyn and Sian Arwel Davies, Llandegfan, Anglesey.

Trevor H Jones, Bala (late of Liverpool).

Alun Owen, Burscough, near Ormskirk.

Henry Pearson, Heswall, Wirral.

Yr Hybarch Archabad y Tad Deiniol, Wales Orthodox Mission, Blaenau Ffestiniog.

Mair Jones, Childwall, Liverpool.

Tegwyn Jones, Nottingham.

Mike Farnworth, Allerton, Liverpool.

Eryl W Jones, Woolton, Liverpool.

Dr Seimon Brooks, Borth-y-Gest, Porthmadog, Gwynedd.

Ted Clement-Evans, Aigburth, Liverpool.

Mrs Beryl M Jones, Welwyn Garden City, Hertfordshire.

David Fletcher, Kingsley, Frodsham.

Dewi Hughes, Llanbadarn Fawr, Aberystwyth, Ceredigion.

Anon., Liverpool.

Bob Farnham, Hoylake, Wirral.

Jane Lloyd Hughes, Llandudno.

Kitty Bronwen Jones, Rock Ferry, Birkenhead.

John and K E Norton, Woolton, Liverpool.

D Glynn Marsden, Formby, Liverpool.

Cymdeithas Cymry Lerpwl (Liverpool Welsh Society).

Brian and Hilda Thomas, Mossley Hall, Liverpool, in memory of their beloved
    son, Alwyn.

Dr Bleddyn Owen Hughes, Prifysgol Aberystwyth, Ceredigion.

David and Penny Mawdsley, Bodfari, near Denbigh.

John Wynne Jones, West Cross, Swansea.

Mair Rees Jones, Claughton, Wirral.

Er cof am Nain, sef Mrs Elizabeth Winifred Morris, gynt o 45 Borrowdale
    Road a Llanddaniel Fab, Sir Fôn, oddi wrth Rhys G Morris a Llŷr G
    Morris.

Mrs Margaret Anwyl Williams, Allerton, Liverpool.

D Ben Rees, Meinwen Rees, Dafydd and Hefin Rees, Directors of Modern
    Welsh Publications, Allerton, Liverpool.

Glossary

A glossary of Welsh-language words and titles that appear in the book:

Yr Angor – community paper 'The Anchor' which began in 1979 and is still published. Dr D Ben Rees has been the editor since 1979.

Yr Amserau – 'The Times', the earliest weekly newspaper published in 1843 in Liverpool.

Baner ac Amserau Cymru – 'The Banner and Times of Wales', a newspaper that first appeared in 1839.

Y Beirniad – 'The Critic', a publication edited by John Morris-Jones, Llanfair PG, printed by Brython Press and published by the Welsh societies of the University of Wales in the second decade of the twentieth century.

Blaenor – Elder in a Presbyterian Church.

Y Bont – 'The Bridge', a journal that appeared on Merseyside from 1959 until 1979 when the editor, the Rev. R Maurice Williams, retired to Llanrwst.

Y Brython – 'The Briton', newspaper published in Liverpool from 1906 until 1939.

Cynghanedd – A system of consonance or alliteration in a line of strict metre poetry.

Cymanfa ganu – Singing festival in which half a dozen or more chapels come together under a visiting conductor.

Y Cymro – 'The Welshman', a weekly newspaper published in Liverpool from 1890 till 1909, and since the 1930s in Oswestry.

Cywydd – A poem in strict metre consisting of rhyming couplets, one rhyme accented and the other unaccented. Each line has seven syllables and contains *cynghanedd* (see above).

Cariad – Love or darling.

Cymdeithasfa – Assocation, as it is called by the Presbyterian Church of Wales. The denomination is divided into three, North Wales Association, South Wales Association, and Association in the East for the English-speaking chapels.

Cymru am Byth – Wales for Ever.

Cymru Fydd – The Wales of the Future, Young Wales, a political grouping within the Welsh Liberal Party that T E Ellis, David Lloyd George, Herbert Lewis and others championed in the early 1890s.

Diacon – Deacon, leaders in Welsh Baptist and Welsh Independent chapels.

Y Drysorfa – 'The Treasury', a monthly journal published by the Presbyterian Church of Wales, no longer in existence.

Y Dysgedydd – 'The Educator', a journal published by the Welsh Independents, no longer in existence.

Eisteddfod – Welsh cultural gathering.

Eglwys Rydd y Cymry – Welsh Free Church based on Merseyside with a small cause in the town of Caernarfon and led by the Rev. W O Jones.

Englyn (pl. *englynion*) – a quatrain in strict metre involving a set number of syllables and a rigid pattern of alliteration.

Y Goleuad – 'The Illuminator', the publication of the Welsh Calvinistic Methodists or the Presbyterian Church of Wales. First published in 1868, still appearing in Covid-19 times as a digital as well as in paper form. Amalgamated in 2021.

Y Glannau – 'The Shores', a publication.

Glannau Merswy – Merseyside.

Gwasg y Brython – Brython Press.

Y Gymanfa Gyffredinol – General Assembly.

Hanes – Story, history.

Hiraeth – Nostalgia, longing.

Lerpwl – Liverpool.

Llynlleifiad – A name devised by Peter Jones (Pedr Fardd) of Liverpool around 1800.

Y Tyst Cymraeg – 'The Welsh Witness', a publication.

Y Tyst a'r Dydd – 'The Witness and the Day', a publication.

Pantycelyn – the homestead of William Williams (1717–1791), the great eighteenth–century hymnwriter. He was often referred to in articles and speech as just Pantycelyn or Y Pêr Ganiedydd.

Tyddyn – Smallholding.

Y Wawr – 'The Dawn', a publication.

Y Werin – 'The People', a publication.

Y Wladfa – Homeland, Patagonia.

Y Ddraig Goch – The Red Dragon (national emblem of Wales) and in the 1860s a paper which only appeared for a few issues in favour of Patagonia in Liverpool.

Index

Also from Y Lolfa:

Gasmasks and Garston
A Liverpool Childhood (1937–1953)

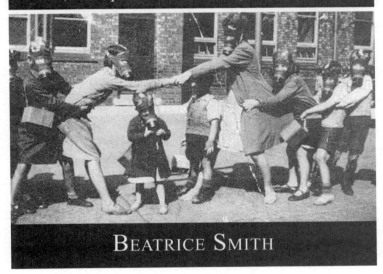

BEATRICE SMITH

£9.99

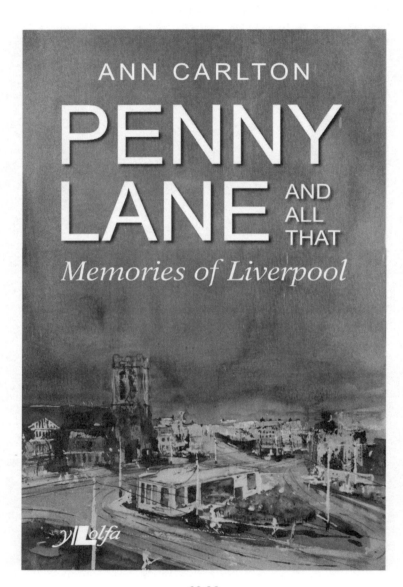

ANN CARLTON

PENNY LANE AND ALL THAT

Memories of Liverpool

yLolfa

£9.99

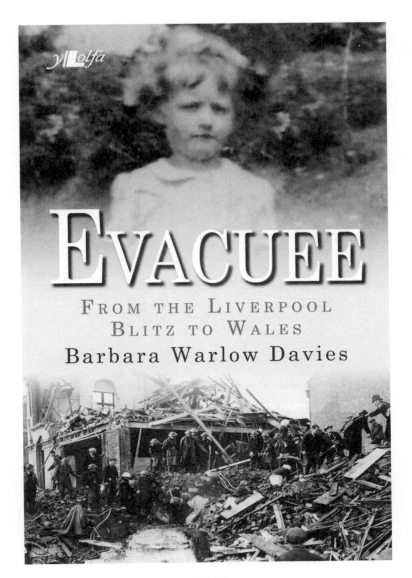

EVACUEE

FROM THE LIVERPOOL
BLITZ TO WALES

Barbara Warlow Davies

£7.99